MW00776365

Hybrids Super Soldiers & the Coming Genetic Apocalypse Vol.1

FIRST PRINTING

Billy Crone

Cover Design:
CHRIS TAYLOR

To Robert Johnson.

If ever there was an example
of a Super Soldier for Christ,
it is you.

Your tireless dedication to details,
your willingness to work long and hard hours,
your tenacity to never say no and always find a way,
has made serving our Lord together a blessing.

Thank you for not only being
a faithful friend and fellow servant,
but a joy to minister with.

I love you.

Contents

Preface

The journey began several years ago when I was preaching at a conference in Gettysburg, Pennsylvania. On the plane ride out there, I was reading an article on "epigenetics" and the various means of which scientists today can alter the human genome. Now fast forward to one particular evening there after I gave one of my messages, a group of us trekked across the street to a local restaurant for a bite to eat. It was there I just so happened to sit directly across a large rectangular table to a young woman who I then asked the proverbial question, "So what is it you do?" She then proceeded to tell me that she was finishing up here doctoral thesis. I then inquired, "And what is that on." Amazingly she replied, "Epigenetics." Not only is that not a word that most people have never even heard of, let alone even have in their vocabulary, I recognized this as a "divine appointment" from the Lord. Thus, for the next hour and a half we basically ignored our food and the company around us and rapped back and forth on this new emerging technology. I had heard stories of various genetic modifications being done to plants and animals for many years, but here was firsthand scientific evidence of someone in the actual genetic field that humans had not escaped these laboratory experiments as well. Needless to say, I was blown away and my mind was racing, chomping at the bit to discover more.

What you will read in these pages is an exhaustive multiple year study on probably one of the freakiest and most unfortunate topics ever contemplated. All sources are meticulously documented for obvious reasons. You can hear the skeptic say even now, "Surely, this is just another in a long line of wacky conspiracy theories and end times embellishments by greedy authors who are just trying to sell a book. Oh, how I wish that was all there was to it. Rather, these shocking genetic alterations are not only taking place all over the world as we speak, but even those who are doing so admit, "If we keep this up, will there be any true humans left?" Also, you will discover that while this might be new news to you, it's not to God. He actually prophesied in the Bible that all this wicked behavior would be a sign that you're living in the Last Days.

That Jesus Crist is getting ready to come back to this planet again and put a stop to it.

One last piece of advice; when you are through reading this book, will you please READ YOUR BIBLE? I mean that in the nicest possible way. Enjoy, and I'm looking forward to seeing you someday!

Billy Crone
Las Vegas, Nevada
2020

Chapter One

The Sign of Hybrids

Well, I want to start off by personally thanking you for having the courage to begin this journey entitled, "Hybrid, Super Soldiers & the Coming Genetic Apocalypse." As you can tell, right out of the gates, by the title itself, this is quite the eclectic topic, isn't it? In fact, some of you might be tempted to think, "Okay, you've really lost it this time. Why in the world are you doing a study on such a wild and crazy subject matter? Did you get knocked in the head or something?"

Well, folks believe it or not, all head injuries aside, what you are about to see, is not only coming, and in some cases is already here, but it has everything to do with a major mega sign that we are living in the Last Days and that time for humanity is simply running out. In fact, let me give you a little teaser of where we're headed and show you how none of what you are about to encounter in this study is embellished or guilty of hyper sensationalism.

The following piece is an actual scientific paper from, "The Institute for Ethics and Emerging Technologies," and they clearly and openly share what kind of genetically modified world they are getting ready to create for you and I, whether we like it or not, or want it or not. And of course, they try to tell us how wonderful it will be.

"You enter the wellness center and tell the receptionist avatar that you're here for an annual restoration, and though your real age is 110, you would like to be restored to the age of a 20-something. A nurse then injects billions of genome-specific 'bots non-invasively through the skin; you're now set for another year.

The above scenario may sound like something out of a sci-fi tale, but experts predict nanorobotics will one day turn this fantasy into reality. Nanotech pioneer Robert Freitas believes that as the technology matures, every adult's appearance could be restored once a year to a biological age chosen by the individual.

In fact, Freitas has designed 'bots smaller than red blood cells that can travel through the human body destroying harmful pathogens and repairing faulty DNA. The tiny machines would be constructed of carbon atoms and powered by utilizing glucose or natural sugars and oxygen from the body.

Doctors would not only use nanorobots to correct problems like heart disease, cancer, or damages suffered from normal aging processes, but could also direct them to strengthen and enhance other parts of the body. These computer-guided creations would restore aging bones, muscles, eyesight, and teeth to a biologically perfect state. When finished, the 'smart bots would exit the body through urine.

Experts envision that these creations will be manufactured in home nano-factories, using special nano-scale tools capable of forming them to specifications required for each job. The design, shape, size and type of atoms, molecules, and components used in their makeup would always be task specific.

Will the drug giants fill a role in tomorrow's nano-world? 'Yes', Freitas says. 'Issues such as IP rights, quality, design, software, and government regulation should allow Big Pharma to retain a significant role in nano-machine manufacture, even in an era of widespread personal nano-factory use.'

In addition, drug companies could assume liability for errors, experts say. Patients need a legally responsible entity they can sue in case of mistakes or defective products. No one wants 'robots gone wild' roaming through their bodies. Raw materials and labor for construction would be nearly cost-free; and even though Big Pharma gets part of the action, nanorobots will still be a very affordable health tool.

Freitas offers an example of a medical nanorobot he designed that would act as a red blood cell. It consists of carbon atoms in a diamond pattern to create a spherical pressurized tank with 'molecular sorting rotors,' which could grab and store oxygen and carbon dioxide molecules.

Respirocytes, as he calls his creations, each consist of 18-billion atoms and can hold 9-billion oxygen and carbon dioxide molecules, 200 times the capacity of human blood cells. The added capacity would allow a person to run at full speed for 15 minutes without taking a breath – no more huffing and puffing.

Other nanorobot creations include artificial white blood cells called microbivores that seek and digest harmful bloodborne pathogens, including bacteria, viruses, and fungi. Even if a bacterium has acquired drug resistance to antibiotics, the microbivore would hunt it down and destroy it.

Microbivores would completely clear blood-borne infections in hours or less, much faster than the weeks or months needed for antibiotic-based cures. Other proposed applications will eliminate tumors, remove circulatory obstructions that cause heart attacks, and prevent brain damage in stroke victims.

Freitas mentions a procedure where 'bots' called 'chromallocytes' would seek out aging cells and make repairs or replace the cell with a new younger version. Chromosome replacement therapy will not only repair aging damages; but would also eradicate any disease in the patient's body that might cause death.

This remarkable technology promises huge advances in extending a healthy lifespan and is not limited to Freitas' efforts. Other nanorobot research underway, include University of Southern California; Cornell University; Monash University; and Ecole Polytechnique, Montreal.

It's the dream of most future watchers, that we will one day say goodbye to aging and hello to being forever young and healthy. Freitas predicts nanobots could appear in clinical trials by mid-2020s."[1]

In other words, it can happen at any time! Anti-aging abilities, repairing faulty DNA, get rid of diseases, running at full speed for 15 minutes without ever having to take a breath, prevent heart attacks and strokes, and even increase your life span, maybe even indefinitely! Wow! So much for embellishment or hyper sensationalism! You just heard it for yourself. This really is the genetically modified future for humanity that the scientific community is planning for you and me. Or should I say, maybe only a select few. You know, the rich and powerful. We'll get to that, eventually. But, speaking of the scientific community, if you noticed in that article, it mentioned two futurists. Robert Freitas and Ray Kurzweil. Now, lest you doubt that what you just read really is their plan for our future, watch this recent interview of both of them talking about it.

"My name is Robert Freitas. I am the Senior Research Fellow at the Institute for Molecular Manufacturing. I am a Nanorobot Theoretician."

Ray Kurzweil: *"Drexler talked about nanosystems 20 years ago and laid out a vision of what nanotechnology ultimately could be. What progress have we made in the last 20 years in verifying and confirming the basic foundations of the theory and also in terms of the actual practical parts of that vision have been put into practice?"*

Robert Freitas: *"I think in the last 20 years Drexler's theories have been confirmed to the extent that we have been able to test them. So far nothing that he wrote in nanosystems has shown to be wrong of any substance. On the theoretical side we have progressed to nanorobot designs, we have many nanorobot designs. We have many machinery designs. We have* *designs of devices which have, I think, the last one was 25,000 atoms. It is a very large complicated gear structure. In the 90's there were many designs for bearings and gears and small manipulating devices and various parts that had several thousand atoms. So, we are starting to get a good library of nanoparts built up."*

Ray Kurzweil: *"Is this some idea of a road map from where we are today to actually making these nanofactories feasible?"*

Robert Freitas: *"Well, my colleague Ralph Merkle and I have started something called the nanofactory collaboration and we have approximately two dozen researchers who are participating in it and we're starting with diamond mechanosynthesis but the long-term goal is to work toward all the components you would need to be able to build a working desktop nanofactory. Since then there have been a number of theoretical advances and experimental advances leading towards the working out of that technology in a practical sense. And the ultimate goal of that is to build nanofactories and ultimately medical nanorobots so that we can all have very long and extended lives.*

How to Manufacture Nanorobots

Ray Kurzweil: *"When people think of a factory, they think of a big building, but these nanofactories will sit on a tabletop, right?"*

Robert Freitas: *"They will be on a tabletop, that is correct."*

Ray Kurzweil: *"They will be placing and positioning molecules and molecular fragments and even atoms, obviously not one at a time but trillions or more at a time. How is it going to scale up to be so massively paralleled?*

Robert Freitas: *"Now the tools, you have one tool operating at a time on a particular reaction. But you have many independent production lines in a nanofactory. You may have millions or even billions of separate production lines and in each production line you have a tool that is doing* *an operation, a particular chemical reaction, building a particular part of a nanopart that you are building. So, many of them are being processed in parallel."*

Ray Kurzweil: *"So just like on a chip today, you have billions of components, these nanofactories that will sit on a tabletop will have billions of little processes going on."*

Robert Freitas: *"Exactly, and they will have billions of processes at each scale. There will be some going on at the nanometer scale and then there will be parts which are composed of ten, hundred, even a thousand atoms and they will be feedstock to the next project which has larger assembler arms and they will be grabbing them and feeding them to still larger assembler arms all the way up to the macroscale at the highest level of the factory. The robot arms inside will be picking up parts and assembling them into larger parts and the larger parts will then become parts of the nanorobots."*

Biomedical Nanorobots

Ray Kurzweil: *"You mentioned red blood cells, a more complicated cell in the blood stream as a white blood cell. What is the feasibility of creating basically robotic immune system cells? Like T cells, that would augment the immune system?"*

Robert Freitas: *"Yes, we could create artificial white blood cells. I've designed one on paper, it would have more atoms, about a hundred billion atoms, a little bit more than 100 billion atoms. It would be put into the blood stream, probably about a hundred billion of them. They would go through the blood stream and they would look for bacteria that they were programmed to detect and like fly paper on their surface, the bacteria would stick to their surface. And then the bacteria would be transported into the mouth of the device and inside the device the bacteria would be digested. The remainder would be harmless sugars and amino acids that would be put out into the blood stream with no problem. This entire process of digesting the bacteria would take only about half a minute.*

Now a natural white cell takes about a hundred times that long to completely digest the bacteria. So again, we have a situation where the medical nanobot is one hundred to a thousand times faster or more effective in some way than a natural biological system. "

Ray Kurzweil*: "Presumably you can program these or download software to combat a whole variety of different pathogens, perhaps ones that our natural immune system is not evolved to deal with. "*

Robert Freitas*: "That's right, the micro before us could be programmed to deal with any type of bacteria whose antigen signature was known. It could even be programmed to deal with ones that were created artificially for nefarious purposes or ones which had evolved in some obscure part of the world that nobody had ever seen before. As long as you know what the bacterium looks like on its outer surface you should be able to program a microbe to detect it and dispose of it. "*

Ray Kurzweil: *"What about viruses and cancer cells? "*

Robert Freitas: *"A version of the microbe which has more mobility than the one that travels through the blood stream would be able to go through the tissues and look for tumors. It would recognize the tumors the same way it would recognize the bacteria by the cellular antigen structure. And it could digest the tumors right on the spot. So, essentially the microbe class nanorobot would be able to dispose of cancer quite easily. Nanorobots can also be used to combat arteriosclerosis.*

I would use a nanorobot called vascularcite which is a small device which has lots of little legs on it and is injected into the blood stream. It collects in the capillaries and forms up in traveling rings then walk back up the vascular tree until they reach the site of the arteriosclerotic lesion. They then form up into a bandage and perform repairs. Another nanobot called a chromallocite would be the first true cell repair machine. Chromallocite is also a very small nanobot. It would be put into the body, it would travel through the tissues into your cell, inside the cell it would travel to the nucleus. It would there change out the chromosomes that are in your nucleus and replace them with newly manufactured ones that have been corrected. All the defects in them corrected the way you want. It would then remove itself from the body and the old gene genome would then be disposed of. This is a key technology because it will allow you essentially to roll back the clock."

Ray Kurzweil: *"My vision is that we can begin to actually replace biological systems with engineered systems."*

Robert Freitas*: "Yes, I have actually, with Chris Phoenix, designed a nanorobot system called the vasculoid. What it is, is a replacement for the entire human vascular system. What it does is, it's essentially a coding of nanomachinery over the entire vascular surface in your body. Materials are transported via a ciliary transport system with the materials like oxygen, carbon dioxide, nutrients, and things like that, transported in containers. This essentially would replace 90% of the volume of your body with nanomachinery. At some point we get to the question of what is it to be human, what is human? If you have 90% of your body replaced by machines are you still human or are you something else?"*

Challenges to Overcome

Ray Kurzweil: *"You mentioned the possibility of nanorobot augmenting our natural immune system. You mentioned nanorobots going into the brain and interacting with our biological neurons so they could monitor or influence the activity that goes on in the brain and these will be computerized. This introduces the concern about software problems, like software viruses, or software that would monitor what is going on in your brain or actually influence it. How do we deal with that if we actually have software nanorobots in the brain influencing what we do?"*

Robert Freitas: *"I think we are going to need, to avoid software glitches, we are going to need very strong laws prohibiting that sort of thing. We're going to need very good software engineering to prevent that sort of thing. We are going to have a lot of experience dealing with that beforehand because we are already building biotic equipment that people are using,* *artificial arms, things like that, that already have chips in them. That sort of abuse is already possible and I'm sure there will be cases in the future where that happens long before we get to nanorobots. I expect that by the time nanorobots are deployed, which will be sometime perhaps in 2020 to 2030's we will have a whole set of laws in place, regulations. There will be things you can and cannot do."*

Why is Nanotechnology Import

Robert Freitas: *"The average person should care about nanotechnology because it is the most important technology to be developed in the 21st century. In fact, you can almost call the 21st century the century of nanotechnology just as you might have called the 20th century the century of electricity or automobiles, something like that. It is basically a game changing technology that is going to change everyone's lives in almost every way you can imagine.*

I think that the 2020's will be the decade of the desktop nano-factory and the 2030's will be the decade of the nanorobots. We might see a few of the nanorobots coming in at the end of the 2020's but I think the 2030's will be when they will be deployed medically in a large way and start to displace most other forms of medical technology. I have a message for my fellow baby boomers. Aging is a disease, it's a curable disease. Nanomedicine is a cure for that disease."[2]

In other words, we really are planning on living forever in these human-hybrid genetically enhanced, altered bodies and the technology we need to pull it off is here right now, today, and we're about to soon put it all into play. Folks, there you have it, again, straight from the horse's mouth, you read it with your own eyes. These guys are not only serious about this genetically modified future for all of humanity, but they're expecting it very, very, soon.

Now for those of you who are still trying to wrap your head around what you just saw, wondering how in the world is all this possible, notice that they kept talking about a particular type of technology. It's called

Nanotechnology and they were talking about building Nano-factories with all this nanotechnology that could fit on a desktop. And therefore, someday soon, very soon, you could have a miniaturized molecular factory in your home, at your own disposal to do all kinds of things, including making the enhancements to the human body that they were talking about. In fact, here's an animation piece of what these nano-factories are going to look like and just some of the things they can do for you.

"Future advances in molecular nanotechnology will enable desktop appliances to manufacture products far better than today's best. The cartridges to the left supply simple raw materials to the machinery inside, here shown in schematic form. Products emerged from the top of this box which holds the heart of the manufacturing system. Each product is built from beneath layer by layer by billions of tiny machines all working together. Near the top surface is the productive machinery itself organized into layers.

Machines in the lowest layer press the molecules into building blocks passing them upwards to machines that assemble them into larger components and then to machines that add these components to the product. From a millimeter scale, one million nanometers, our view zooms into the ten-nanometer scale. Each box is one-tenth the size of the one before. Here at the molecular scale, nanomachines make small building blocks from molecular raw materials.

The first machine sorts molecules by their size and shape, passing some rejecting others. Only molecules of the right kind can enter the processing machinery. The molecules contain four atoms, two of carbon and two of hydrogen. The molecules bind to a device that carries them to the next stage. Then a rotating mechanism swings tool tips into contact with the bound molecules. Each tip presses a molecular tool against the molecule bonding it firmly. The tools shown here have been analyzed using advanced quantum chemistry techniques. Another tool moves in from the left to remove the hydrogen atoms leaving a pair of carbon atoms exposed and ready to use.

The tools then carry these atoms to their destination where each pair bonds to a nanoscale building block making a tiny bit of crystalline carbon, a bit of diamond. Motions happen quickly at this scale. A conveyor carries the blocks past further machines which build the blocks step by step to full size. Elsewhere other specialized machines build blocks of different kinds.

A system of conveyor belts and transfer mechanisms carries completed blocks from where they are made to where they needed. This transfer mechanism moves blocks from one belt to another. The transportation system carries many different kinds of blocks. Different shapes, different materials, different functions. It delivers them to the next stage of manufacturing. Here a programable machine lifts and places small blocks to make larger blocks. The small blocks bond on contact to form components containing millions of precisely arranged atoms. These can be simple structural bricks or intricate components for mechanical and electronic systems.

The completed components are delivered to the final assembly stage where many machines work together to build the final product. At the base of each machine the transfer mechanism grabs components and lifts them from the conveyor. Each is flipped around and then carried up to the underside of the product construction. Finally, machines lift the components and plug them in place, adding layer after layer to the bottom of the product. When the last layer is finished, and construction is complete the product is ready to be removed and used. The result of this production run is an atomically precise multi-processor laptop computer with a billion times more processing power than today's best. The only waste products are warm air and pure water.[3]

And hey, that's good for the environment, isn't it? But did you see what you could have in your home, literally on your desktop? A molecular machine, a literal nano factory that can build all kinds of things out of thin air! This is the kind of technology that they want to release **inside our bodies** to create this so-called advanced technological utopia for the human race. Not only could it create a laptop computer out of thin air that was a billion times better than today's best laptop, but it can also be used to create a better you, a new and improved you, that's a billion times better than who you are today.

And as good as that sounds, as you might expect, there's some major problems with all this. First of all, let's go back to the interview you saw earlier with Freitas and Kurzweil. If you were paying attention there, they even admitted, and frankly half expected, that there will be many different kinds of problems with all this new kind of emerging technology.

First of all, they said there could be a whole new type of crime wave with these so-called nano terrorists injecting nanobots into a person and then cause them to self-replicate in order to host and take them out. Or they could even hack into your brain and manipulate and/or control you or even destroy you with a type of computer virus put into those nanobots that get injected into you. And of course, then they even mentioned how we need to ask ourselves, just how much of this manipulation can be done to the human genome and the human body and the person still somehow comes out being a real human? All very serious and frankly scary concerns.

But hey, that's right, don't worry! Hollywood is here for you. If you've been paying attention, the movie industry has already been out there for years helping to ease our fears concerning this genetically modified future that is coming to our planet very soon. In fact, just about every action movie nowadays seems to be not only exposing us to this futuristic reality, getting us conditioned to it, but they're also doing it in a way where people think those who are genetically modified with this type of technology are super cool, our heroes, or even a god-like. I mean, who wouldn't want to be like them, right? Line me up for genetic modification!

Now, to show you what I mean, here's just a small sampling of the plethora of movies that Hollywood is producing to prepare us for this altered humanity.

From the movie Splice: *As surgeons are looking down at the patient one says, "The heart rate is too high!" "If we don't use human DNA now someone else will." The first lady researcher declares. "Regulators and politicians will tear us to pieces," says the second researcher as they are sitting around the table. Later they are discussing what they have done. "Human cloning is illegal, this won't be human, not entirely," she says.*

From the movie Altered Carbon: *They are looking at what they have created in what seems to be a human floating in liquid attached to a cord. "Your body is not who you are. You shed it like a snake sheds its skin. You transfer the human consciousness between bodies to live eternal life." The researcher explains as the slides show the work being done to this person they are working on. Suddenly a man is out of the tank in a crouched position and he asks, "How long have I been down?" The answer was, "250 years."*

From the movie Bloodshot: *Soldiers are approaching with their guns ready to fire. "We are leading the way with the greatest human advancement of all time. The technology running through his veins augments his strength, his reflexes, even his healing capabilities. He is unlike anything we have seen before." The soldiers are now shooting at him. Half his face is gone but he is still standing and completely healed.*

From the movie Iron Man 3: *A couple is standing in the middle of lights flashing all around them. The girl asks, "What is that?" He answers, "Primary sensory cortex, the brains pain center and this is what I wanted to show you. Now extremist harnesses our bioelectrical potential and it goes here." With a click of the gadget he is holding in his hand he takes them to a place that looks like the galaxy. "This is essentially an empty slot but what it tells us that our mind, our entire DNA is destined to be upgraded."*

From the movie Limitless: *A couple at a bar is talking, the man tells the woman, "We can only access twenty percent of our brain." Then a researcher is holding a pill and says to him, "Why don't you access all of it? Just out of curiosity, and that is all?" And he puts it in his mouth.*

Suddenly, he is working out, dressing great, eating the best foods, "I was blind, but now I see." It can solve any problem. "A tablet a day and I was limitless. I had cultural appetites." His date asks, "Since when do you speak Italian?" It can unlock your potential. "I finished my book in four days. Math became useful." Being at the table with a potential client he is asked, "So what is your secret?" He answers, "Medication."

From the movie Replicas: "There was a crash. You and the kids died but I brought you back," he tells his wife. In the lab he is talking to his assistant. His assistant tells him, "There is a reason that human cloning is bad." His wife says, "I am dead." His assistant asks him, "What if something horrible goes wrong?" But his answer is, "Something already has."

From the movie Selfless: "Now as you slip away, do you feel immortal?" At the laboratory he is shown what can be done to extend the life of mankind. The worker says, "We offer man with the greatest minds more time to fill their potential. It's designed to give you the very best of the human experience." As they are looking at the person laying in the tank it moves. He asks, "It's alive?" The answer is, "An empty vessel. Once you do this, there is no turning back. Your old life is over."

As he is laying on the table waiting for the next step in preserving his life he asks, "What's that?" The answer is, "Something to stop your heart." As he is going into the capsule a person next to him is being pulled out of one. He is asked, "How are you feeling?" This younger man is now sitting in a chair in the company's office. He seems to be rather weak but answers, "It's a new body smell." As the person behind the desk smiles, he says, "A sense of humor, great."

From the movie Luke Cage: "Here is your rebound sheet, took a shotgun at point blank aim, pointed it under your chin and pulled the trigger." The friend tells him while he is loading clothes into the washer. He replies, "You think I asked for any of this. I was framed, beaten and put into a tank like some exotic fish. I came out with abilities."

From the movie Deadpool: *The character is laying on a stretcher. He awakens and starts to gasp for breath. The attendant is watching as his face turns red and he starts tearing up. But he's not in a bed, he is in a glass capsule. He is slowly changing physically. He is still gasping for breath and continues to shake from the pain of these changes in his body. The announcer says, "Did I says this was a love story, no it is a horror movie."*

The man is screaming as his skin is slowing ripping apart. The attendant comes back into the room to check on the guy. By now his skin is all deformed. They open the window to the capsule, and he yells, "What have you done to me?" "We raised your stress levels up to trigger a mutation." replies the attendant. Again, the man in the capsule yells, "You sadistic ...!" Then the attendant tells him, "I've cured you Wade. Your mutate can cure anything. Gets rid of your cancer as fast as it can form. You know I have seen some of these side effects before, but I cured them. So, what's the fun in that?"

From the movie Logan: *Children are sitting in a cell. One girl is cutting her arm. The doctors are watching them online. "As the children become older, they become more difficult. They could not be controlled. The company made their bodies into weapons, to teach them to kill. But they did not want to fight. A soldier that will not fight is useless. Inside this building they are working on something new. Something they think is better than the children. Something they say is without a soul. They must have been successful. About a week ago they told us to shut our program down. They started putting the children to sleep. We agreed to save as many children as we can. We are at another place, up north, a place for mutants. They call it Eden."*

From the movie Universal Soldier: *Soldiers are in combat outside but inside the building undressed men are laying side by side on recliners. These men had been killed in battle. The commander calls out, "Pack them in ice." We discovered that we could turn dead flesh into living tissue. "You push a car faster than my mother drives." A girl is telling one of the soldiers that has been brought back to life. "You use ice like* *someone would use a Band-Aid, you run through walls, I'm sorry this is not normal human behavior."*

From the movie the Fly: *There is a limit even to the imagination. Jeff Goldblum's character is telling a woman, "Human teleportation, molecular decimation, reformation is inherently merging." Where our greatest creations lead our greatest fears. She is telling him, "Something went wrong Seth, when you went through, something went wrong. Those hairs that were growing out of your back, I had them analyzed. They were definitely not human." She takes what she knows to get some help and is trying to explain to the doctor. She says, "If you could see how scared and angry and desperate, he is." The doctor says, "I'm sure Typhoid Mary was a very nice person too." When she gets back home, she sees him tearing up the apartment. "You are changing Seth, everything about you is changing."*

As he rips off his fingernails he exclaims, "Oh no! What is happening to me, am I dying?" She goes back to the doctor and he says to her, "I want to know what is going on." She answers, "It's a disease, Mark." Jeff Goldblum says, "It has turned me into something else." As the doctor looks closer at the machine, he realizes that a fly had gotten into the machine with him. "Oh no, a fly had gotten into the transmitter the first time I was alone. Don't go back there it could be contagious," he tells her. When she does go back, she found him with a girl. As he is trying to drag her out of the room she is screaming, "No, I'm afraid." He tells her, "Don't be afraid." But she tells the girl, "Yes, be afraid. Be very afraid."

From the movie Invasion of the Body Snatchers: *Announcer says, "The yellow door is for the loading and the unloading only. If you have other business stay clear from the yellow, stand clear of the yellow. It is for loading and unloading." Just then a dog, or what appears to be a dog comes running up. It is a dog but with a man's face. When they look down at it, yuck how disgusting.*

From the movie An American Werewolf: *As the music is playing and the actor is half dressed, feeling a little strange he looks at his hand and it* *starts changing. His jaw is starting to change. He starts to panic and begins to yell for help, he starts growing long hairs on his hands and arms. His feet start to change their form. He is on all fours; his spine is protruding out of his back and his hair all over his body is long. And he is covered in it. Pretty soon his teeth start to protrude out of his mouth and get longer. His face is distorted, his ears grow bigger, and his eyes are turning yellow. His yell has now turned to a loud growl.*

From the movie Star Wars: Episode II Attack of the Clones: *As Luke Skywalker is walking around the room looking at all the babies that are all in bottles on conveyor belts. There are thousands of them. The robot that is walking with him tries to explain to him what he is seeing. The robot says, "Clones can sync creatively. You will find that they are superior to droids. We take great pride in our combat education and training programs. This group was created about 5 years ago." Skywalker replies, "You mentioned growth acceleration."*

The robot answered, "Oh yes, it's essential, otherwise a mature clone would take a lifetime to grow. Now we can do it in half the time." Skywalker says, "I see." The robot says, "They are totally obedient, taking any order without question. We modified their genetic structure to make them less independent than the original host." "And who was the original host?" Skywalker asked. "A bounty hunter called Jango Fett," Replied the robot. "And where is this bounty hunter now?" The robot answers, "Oh we keep him here.

Apart from his pay which is considerable he only demanded one thing. An unaltered clone for himself. Curious isn't it?" Skywalker asked, "Unaltered?" The robot answers, "Pure genetic replication, no tampering with the structure to make it more docile, no growth acceleration." Skywalker replies, "I would very much like to meet this Jango Fett." Another robot walking with them said, "I would be very happy to arrange it."

From the movie Man of Steel: *"You led us here, now it is in your power to save what remains of your race. On Krypton the genetic template of* *every being yet to be born is encoded in the registry of citizens. Your father stole the registry codex and stored it in the capsule that brought you here." Superman asks, "For what purpose?" The reply is, "So Krypton can live again on earth. Where is the codex, Cal?" He answers, "If Krypton lives again, what happens to earth?" The man answers, "The foundation has to be on something, even your father recognized that."*

As Superman looks around and all he sees in human skulls covering the ground he says, "No, I can't be a part of this!" The man then asks, "Then what can you be a part of?" Superman starts to sink into the body of skulls and cries, "No, No." Suddenly he awakens in his bed and it was a bad dream. Then another man from Krypton speaks and says, "I have found the codex. It was never in the capsule. His father took the codex, the DNA of a billion people and he bonded it within his son's individual cells. All Krypton's heirs living in one body."

From the movie Morbius: *A doctor tells Morbius, "You have a gift, you always have. If there is an answer to this disease, we will find it." Morbius says, "I should have died years ago. Why am I still here? Is it to fix this? I have a rare blood disease and I am running out of time. This could be my last chance." A person working alongside him in the lab asks him, "You're working on something, what is it?" He answers, "It's not exactly legal." She answers, "I don't want to see you get hurt any more than you have." He says, "This could be a cure."*

As he cuts his hand and holds it up to the cave entrance, the bats all come out of the cave at the smell of his blood and everyone runs to safety except for him. The bats have come to taste his blood. She asks him, "At what costs?" He suddenly gets strength like he never had. He records how he is feeling. "Increased strength and speed. The ability to use echolocation. I have an overpowering urge to consume. How far are we allowed to go to fix something that is broken?" The answer, "Until the remedy is worse than the disease."

From the movie Gemini Man: *He asks, "Are you all right?" She answers, "He is you." "What?" he asks. She replies, "There is a DNA lab* *here, I gave them samples. I used the baseball cap he was wearing. He looks so much like you I thought he must be your son so I... There are 3 tests. Your DNA and his. All 3 came back identical. Not close, identical. As in the same person. He is your clone. I thought I had made a mistake that I had given them the sample of the same person. But I didn't. He is you." His friend asks, "How is this even possible?" "It's complicated but it's doable. All you have to have is a surrogate mother and a DNA sample." He replies, "You can clone a person, you would think they would clone more doctors, scientists, not me. They could have cloned Nelson Mandela." She responded, "Nelson Mandela couldn't kill a man on a moving train from two kilometers away."*

From the movie Captain America: *Several men are up on the second floor watching the scientist work below. He says, "Can you hear me? Is this on? Ladies and gentlemen today we take another step towards annihilation, the first step on the path to peace. We begin with micro injections into the subject's major muscle groups. The serum infusion will cause the immediate cellular change and then to stimulate growth the subject will be saturated in his vital areas."*

He was given his first injection. "Well, that wasn't so bad." The scientist responds, "That was penicillin. Serum infusion beginning in 5, 4, 3, 2, 1." All the capsules are emptied into his body. As his body is getting the full injections, the platform he is on is raised so he is in the standing position. The capsule then closes around the subject. When it opens back up, he is standing there stronger and more muscular than ever before. He gradually wakes up and they help him out of the capsule.

From the movie The Incredible Hulk: *The scene starts with a man that has grown so big that his shoes are ripping off his feet, his clothes are falling to the floor as they are shredded by his growth. He is on the bridge overlooking the soldiers that are there to kill him. As he grows to his full capacity, he breaks the windows on the bridge and growls at the soldiers. The soldiers turn and run. He is far too big for them to fight. He jumps off the bridge onto the grass. The men stand there in amazement. This is the Green Hulk. As they have bigger and better guns to fire at him, he is* *untouchable. He grabs a large piece of metal, breaking it with his bare hands. The soldier is taking it personal and is trying to get closer and closer to the Hulk, but it doesn't do any good. He is far outmatched. As they see the Hulk is winning the cannons are called in but to no avail.*

From the movie X-Men Apocalypse: *A man steps down barefooted with cut off pants. As the camera raises further up his body you see he has blades on his hand and a helmet on his head. The soldiers are facing him guns drawn. The bullets do not stop him. He jumps at them and kills them with his blades. He is a weapon. It is announced over the intercom that 'Weapon X is loose. Repeating, Weapon X is loose.' They find him down the corridor but again the bullets don't stop him. He kills them all. Watching on video all are amazed at what he can do and is doing.*

From the movie Batman V Superman, Dawn of Justice: *As they unzip the body bag the name Alexander Luther is called out. The security override has been accepted. They are ready to analyze the genetic sample. The person in the bag is being pulled out into the water. Acknowledge the existence of the genetic material. Identify the host, General Candor. A knife is opened, and the man cuts his hand and squeezes blood onto the face of the man floating in the water.*

Advise foreign material. Again, a voice says to analyze it. "You flew too close to the asylum." Advising, action forbidden. It has been decreed by the council of Krypton that none will ever again give life to a deformity. He asks, "And where is the council of Krypton?" Destroy it and then proceed. Very well preparing the commencing metamorphosis. "Ancient Kryptonian deformative. Blood of my blood." In a large sack there is a monster looking thing, that is struggling to get out to get the man. Superman is standing there watching what is going on. The man says, "This is your doomsday." As the thing breaks out of the sack and showing its teeth growls at Superman.

From the movie Fast & Furious Presents Hobbs & Shaw: *"So you guys are being hunted by an army of mercenaries led by a genetically enhanced soldier." The genetically enhanced soldier says, "Look at me.... I'm the* *black superman. He is fighting against the Rock and Jason Statham. As it is two against one, the Rock says, "He really is the black Superman."*

From the movie Bloodshot: *"What am I doing here?" Vin Diesel's character is asking. "You got yourself killed. You have been given a second chance. You have an army inside you. They rebuilt you," answers the doctor. But he asks, "What if I need blood?" The answer is, "They are your blood. Welcome to your future."*[4]

Folks, what you just read is just a small tiny sampling of Hollywood doing what Hollywood does best. These movies today, are not just about entertainment, they are about slowly but surely, preparing us for the future they're building for us. It's called soft disclosure. A little here and a little there, piecemeal it out, so that when it does descend upon us, we don't freak out as much, and if all goes well accordingly, we even cry out for it.

Now, the other huge concern with the technology is what I mentioned at the very beginning. This tweaking of the human genome, this altering of the human body creating a human hybrid type scenario, is actually a major sign that we're living in the Last Days, and people generally have no clue about it! In fact, Jesus said all this wicked hybrid behavior talked about and promoted in Hollywood today, is actually a sign He's about ready to come back to judge the planet again! Time for humanity is running out. I didn't say that, He did! Here's what Jesus said was going to happen right before He came back at His Second Coming.

Matthew 24:37 "As it was in the days of Noah, so it will be at the coming of the Son of Man."

Alright, so let's find out what was going on in the days of Noah and see how close we are to Jesus' return.

Genesis 6:1-7 "When men began to increase in number on the earth and daughters were born to them, the sons of God saw that the daughters of men were beautiful, and they married any of them they chose. Then the

LORD said, 'My Spirit will not contend with man forever, for he is mortal; his days will be a hundred and twenty years.' The Nephilim were on the earth in those days – and also afterward – when the sons of God went to the daughters of men and had children by them. They were the heroes of old, men of renown. The LORD saw how great man's wickedness on the earth had become, and that every inclination of the thoughts of his heart was only evil all the time. The LORD was grieved that He had made man on the earth, and His heart was filled with pain. So the LORD said, 'I will wipe mankind, whom I have created, from the face of the earth – men and animals, and creatures that move along the ground, and birds of the air – for I am grieved that I have made them.'"

Why? Because of their wicked behavior! This is why God judged the world the first time with a worldwide flood. Not just because mankind was continually thinking evil all the time, which I think we can all readily agree is here right now as well, as this man shares.

This video shows a man waking up and turning off his alarm radio. He stumbles out of bed and goes out the front door to retrieve his morning paper. He sees his paper being picked up by a guy walking his dog. He then proceeds down the street to the newspaper stand to buy a paper but there is a guy standing there breaking the door to steal a paper. The door is left open with one paper remaining. He puts his money in and takes the last paper. He goes back home and fixes himself a bowl of cereal and sits down to eat and read his paper. The paper has big bold letters on the front page "Terrorist."

"And it came to pass that when men began to multiply on the face of the earth, the Lord saw that man's wickedness had become great and saw that their hearts dwelled only on evil. The earth was corrupt in God's sight and full of violence and the people had corrupted their ways. The Lord regretted that He had made man and His heart was filled with pain. So, the Lord said 'I will wipe my creation from the face of the earth. Man, and animals, creatures that crawl on the ground and birds of the air. For I am grieved that I have made them.' But one man found favor in the eyes of the

Lord, one righteous man blameless among the people of this time. Who walked with God? This is the story of Noah."[5]

And this is the story of us today. Sounds familiar, doesn't it? We're there right now, as you just saw. The continual wickedness of Noah's day is here today. We're seeing a repeat of it, just like Jesus said would happen when you're living in the Last Days! A society with wickedness, wherever you go.

But the Bible also mentioned that mankind in the days of Noah was also involved in another wicked behavior, that of tweaking humanity into some sort of a hybrid type creature that they called the Nephilim. They were giants and even looked upon as heroes, or men of renown, doing great feats, literally "famous" in their day.

And so, in response to this total wickedness, God sent a global flood that totally destroyed the earth. All that survived it was Noah and his family and the animals on that ark. In fact, it probably looked something like this.

"The large door of the Ark mysteriously closes. The animals are stirring in anticipation. Even the fish in the ocean are swimming as if they know something is about to happen. Then a large crack starts to open in the bottom of the ocean. (It is now 20 seconds after 8:00 am). The crack gets larger and larger and water begins to spew from under the ocean out into the world. Tons and tons of water. (It is now 24 second after 8:00 am) As the water continues to come out of the earth a tsunami begins to go towards the earth. People are screaming. They have never seen such a huge wall of water. (It is now 8:14 am) But this tsunami isn't coming towards one continent, it is covering the land all around the world.

As the water approaches the Ark the occupants are busy doing their daily routines. They have never seen anything like this before, they only knew they were following God's word in building the Ark and living in it. The wave is getting closer and closer. (It is now 12:10 pm) The people of the town are doing their shopping and stop in horror as they see this large

wall of water approaching. (It is now 1:40 pm) They start to run in a
panic. But where will they hide? It is almost complete. The Ark is now
afloat, and the world is covered with water and the only ones saved are
Noah and his family. (It is now 4:00 pm) "[6]

That's what God did to the planet the first time when mankind
became so wicked with their behavior. So the point is this, Jesus said
when you see a repeat of this same wicked behavior, as it was in the days
of Noah, continually thinking evil all the time and even tweaking
humanity into some sort of a hybrid type of creature, so will it be at the
coming of the Son of Man. In other words, this same wicked behavior
being repeated on planet earth, it's a major sign that **Jesus is getting
ready to come back** to judge the planet again, just like He did the first
time! These wicked behaviors we are seeing today, the interviews you just
saw, the movies depicted in Hollywood, are all a sign we're living in the
Last Days and time is running out! The door of escape is about to be shut!

So, the question for you and I today is, "Is mankind really trying to
create some sort of human hybrid of giant proportions that people look
upon as heroes capable of doing great feats?" Yes! In fact, what we have
seen thus far is just the tip of the iceberg of this kind of prophetic wicked
behavior that mankind is already engaged in, again, that Jesus warned
about. Actually, it's been going on for quite some time.

So let's now begin our journey into Hybrids, Super Soldiers & the
Coming Genetic Apocalypse and see just where all this wicked
hybridization began and observe where it's going in the very near future,
whether we like it or not, or want it or not.

Chapter Two

The History of Hybrids

Now, you would think that a worldwide flood would get mankind's attention to never commit these kinds of wicked behaviors again that grieved the heart of God. Yet, approximately 900 years after the flood of Noah, God was already once again warning mankind of the dangers of creating hybrids and mixing lifeforms together. We see this in the book of Leviticus.

Leviticus 19:19 "You are to keep My statutes. You shall not breed together two kinds of your cattle; you shall not sow your field with two kinds of seed."

Not once, but twice, God reiterated the command that you **shall not** mix together or intermingle two different kinds of lifeforms, again, only 900 years after the Flood. He also mentioned this warning here.

Deuteronomy 22:9 "You shall not sow your vineyard with two kinds of seed, or all the produce of the seed which you have sown, and the increase of the vineyard will become defiled."[1]

So, there you have it again. Another warning from God that you **shall not** mix together lifeforms, or seeds in this case. Why? Because it's not just the same type of behavior that caused God to judge the planet the first time, but there's strong evidence today that this manipulating of genes in man, animals, or even plants, is sure enough extremely harmful to mankind. No wonder God forbids it!

Here's just a small portion of the evidence today as to why God said you shall not modify, mix, or manipulate lifeforms, in order to protect mankind.

"The prohibition to mix certain things in the Bible is something that is often overlooked and seems quite unimportant. But God gave us the answer.

There are two main scriptures that deal with mixing: Leviticus 19:19 and Deuteronomy 22:9.

The phrase 'two kinds' used with seed is translated from 'kilayim' which means as translated, two things of different kinds.

It is important to note that when mixing takes place, the product becomes indistinguishable from the parts used to create it. Keep this in mind as you continue to read.

Also, it is written that you are not to breed together two kinds of your cattle. The Hebrew word 'raba' was translated as 'breed.' It means to have sexual relations with, formally, lie down, i.e., engage in sexual intercourse, literally to 'cross-breed.'

Here is an excerpt from Wikipedia on crossbreeding for more understanding:

'A crossbreed or crossbred usually refers to an animal with purebred parents of two different breeds, varieties, or populations. Crossbreeding refers to the process of breeding such an animal, often with the intention to create offspring that share the traits of both parent lineages and producing an animal with hybrid vigor. While crossbreeding is used to maintain health and viability of animals, irresponsible crossbreeding can

also produce animals of inferior quality or dilute a purebred gene pool to the point of extinction of a given breed of animal.'

At the onset, this could also be referring to genetic engineering. Another kind of mixing will result in a hybrid.

'A hybrid animal is one with parentage of two separate species, differentiating it from crossbred animals, which have parentage of the same species. Hybrids are usually, but not always, sterile.'

'One of the most ancient types of hybrid animal is the mule, a cross between a female horse and a male donkey. The liger is a hybrid cross between a male lion and female tiger. The yattle is a cross between a cow and a yak. Other crosses include the tigon (between a female lion and male tiger) and yakalo (between a yak and buffalo). The Incas recognized that hybrids of Lama glama (llama) and Lama pacos (alpaca) resulted in a hybrid with none of the advantages of either parent.'

'A clearly ambiguous counter-example to any value judgment on hybrids and hybrid vigor is the mule. While mules are almost always infertile, they are valued for a combination of hardiness and temperament that is different from either of their horse or donkey parents. While these qualities may make them 'superior' for particular uses by humans, the infertility issue implies that these animals would most likely become extinct without the intervention of humans through animal husbandry, making them 'inferior' in terms of natural selection.'

This commandment would prohibit genetic engineering. When genetic engineering is carried out, one of the things that can be accomplished, is to mix different species to become a new species. Knowing what is happening in the scientific world, we can understand that it must be an abomination to God. From the beginning man wanted to be like God. That's the reason why Eve ate the fruit, then we see the same with the Tower of Babel -- and you can go on and on.

Also, animal genes are now being mixed with human genes and vice versa to 'create' humans with better eyesight, for example, or sheep that can produce human milk. Scientists do this under the mantle of helping mankind, but they do not think it through. What would happen if these sheep with human genes get in contact with sheep bred for meat? It won't always be possible to keep track of these animals and keep them separate because they look the same from the outside. The union of these sheep will cause humans to consume human DNA, which will probably have serious health consequences. What an abomination!

The result of mixing plants is the same as the mixing of animals. It causes perversion. So much mixing has taken place that we cannot compare the grains we have at present with ancient grains. Grains we have nowadays can even, in some cases, affect our health negatively. There are many people who have gluten intolerance, and many digestive problems exist because of the grain we consume. If people kept God's commandments, this would surely be different.

You see, the problem is that mankind thinks they can do it better. God created, and now man wants to better something where no improvement was required in the first place. This has now ended in corruption and destruction, so much so that our very existence is threatened. Why are they doing it? For power and money, that is what it is always about. They reject God's ways in order to gain control and fortune. Sounds like satan's way of life, doesn't it?"[2]

Yes, it sure does. Great commentary. And it also sounds like satan has figured out a way to trick mankind into once again violating God's commands against hybridization and genetic mixing to our own detriment. In fact, speaking of detriment, here's a recent report on another genetic modification gone mad just like God warned us about.

"GMO mosquito experiment goes horribly wrong: Insects adapt and overcome, transforming into super 'mutant' mosquitoes that could cause mass death across South America.

Remember the two-year experiment to release genetically modified mosquitoes into the wild to eradicate all the mosquitoes? For years, we were all lectured by scientists and GMO pushers who insisted that genetically modifying male mosquitoes to be infertile would cause the termination of nearly all offspring as females mated with the GMO males. The result, we were told, would be a mass die-off of the mosquito population at large, saving human lives by avoiding the catastrophic effects of mosquito-borne disease.

Science would save us, in other words. And if we didn't believe the hype, we were labeled 'anti-science.'

At first, the experiment seemed to work. For the initial 18 months of the experiment carried out in Brazil — in which 450,000 genetically modified male mosquitoes were released into the wild — mosquito populations plummeted. But then something happened.

As published in the journal Nature, in a study entitled, "Transgenic Aedes aegypti Mosquitoes Transfer Genes into a Natural Population," the very same modified genes we were told would never be passed to 'in the wild' mosquito populations has, in fact, done exactly that.

Powered by these new genes, the mosquito population surged back. Even worse, now the wild populations of mosquitoes in Brazil have these 'mutant' genes which were combined from Cuban and Mexican mosquito populations, meaning these new gene-enhanced mosquitoes are now a kind of 'super mutant' insect that may be resistant to all sorts of insecticides."[3]

Oops! Guess you should've listened to God! They go on in that report to conclude, *"Humanity has reached a tipping point of developing technology so profound that it can destroy the human race."* Gee, where have I heard that before? But as you can see, mixing and intermingling of lifeforms is extremely dangerous behavior. God not only considers it wicked, but it's seriously detrimental to mankind and life on earth as we know it, and that's why He warned about it after the flood. Plus, it was this same kind of wicked behavior that caused God to judge the world the first time with a global flood and that Jesus warned about would unfortunately appear again on the earth again just before He came back to judge it again.

So now let's take a look at the history of this unfortunate repeat of wicked behavior that God forbids, this intermingling of lifeforms, or what's known today as **Genetic Engineering**.

- 1773-1858: Robert Brown discovered the nucleus in cells.
- 1802: The word "biology" first appears.
- 1822-1895: Vaccination against smallpox and rabies developed by Edward Jenner and Louis Pasteur as seen in this video.

"This is the smallpox virus. It infected the Pharaohs, caused a terrible impact on the Greek and Roman Empires and decimated the Native American populations. Nothing seems to stop this lethal plague until the end of the 18th century. At that time smallpox was the major global pandemic disease. Only in Europe it killed around 400,000 people per year. It didn't differentiate between rich and poor, even five kings were killed but for some reason milkmaids seemed to be immune to the disease.

In fact, they were renowned for their beauty because their skins were free of the scars that smallpox caused. They were attractive and resistant, but why? That is what the doctor Edward Jenner was trying to understand. He knew that milkmaids had small blisters on their hands when they were milking cows that were suffering from cowpox, a mild disease that cattle suffered from which caused similar lesions caused by smallpox.

This phenomenon made Dr. Jenner think that cowpox and smallpox were related and that infection with the milder disease was enough to protect people against the lethal one. As a man of science, he decided to prove it and to do this he needed three things. Cowpox that he extracted from a milkmaid, fresh smallpox from a patient, and a human guinea pig. So, he chose his gardener's son, an eight-year-old, called James Fipps. He infected the child with cowpox, waited a couple of months, and injected him with smallpox and James didn't become ill. He repeated the experiment with other patients with the same results.

Jenner was right even though he didn't fully understand how his remedy worked. The most remarkable thing was that his discovery was made way before Jakob Henle in 1840. The infectious diseases were caused by germs, a theory that was demonstrated by Robert Koch. Decades later Louis Pasteur inspired by Jenner's experiments showed that the microbes could be used to prevent diseases and he proposed the term 'vaccine' in his honor."[4]

- 1850: Casimir Davaine detected rod-shaped objects in the blood of anthrax-infected sheep and was able to produce the disease in healthy sheep.
- 1855: The Escherichia coli bacterium is discovered. It later becomes a major research, development, and production tool for biotechnology.
- 1868: Fredrich Miescher reported nuclein, a compound that consisted of nucleic acid that he extracted from white blood cells.
- 1870: Breeders crossbreed cotton, developing hundreds of varieties.
- 1870: The first experimental corn hybrid is produced in a laboratory.
- 1909: The term 'Gene' was coined by Wilhelm Johannsen. He also coined the terms 'genotype' and 'phenotype.'
- 1909: Genes are linked with hereditary disorders.
- 1911: American pathologist Peyton Rous discovers the first cancer-causing virus.
- 1915: Phages, or bacterial viruses, are discovered.
- 1919: The word "biotechnology" is first used by a Hungarian agricultural engineer.
- 1924: The start of Eugenic Movement in the US.
- 1933: Hybrid corn is commercialized as this video shares.

"A Hundred years ago farming was a lot different. At the turn of the century average national yields of corn had not improved much from

the previous century. Fluctuations were due mainly to climate. Yields remained much as they had been before. Averaging only 23 to 28 bushels per acre. During the mid-1930's the average yield dropped because of drought. But in the 40's yields increased more than ever before. The reason, hybrid seed had been introduced. As we moved into the 50's and beyond average yields were bolstered by the use of fertilizers and pesticides, improved machinery, more plants per acre, timeliness of operation and better farm management. The major factor of these increases, however, was the continued development of better hybrid varieties.

Today virtually all the seed corn that farmers plant is hybrid seed. With average national yields of over 100 bushels per acre. Four times of what it had been only 50 years before. How did farmers accomplish this? They changed their way of getting seed. Before hybrids farmers used only pollinated seed. That is the stokes of the ear of any plant could be pollinated from any of hundreds of different plants in the field. Each sister kernel on an ear may have had a different male parent. When the farmer selected the best-looking ear to save for planting next year, he was actually saving a variety of genetically different kernels. When he planted them the next spring, hoping to produce a uniform crop of high yield he got only a diverse uniform crop of average yield, not much different from what he had in previous years.

Hybrid seed however is not produced by the farmer. It's scientifically developed by specialized seed corn companies which then sell their seeds to farmers. Because of nearly identical heredity the hybrid plants have uniform resistance to pests and diseases for example. They are adapted to the areas where they are grown and because of their uniformity they can be easily planted and harvested by machine. So, the higher price of the hybrid seed is offset by its dependably higher yield.

How then is a hybrid seed developed? The process occurs in three steps. The first is to produce genetically pure lines of seed by selective inbreeding. An important characteristic of corn is that it has both male and female parts on the same plant. The male part is the tassel which produces pollen. The female part is made up of potential kernels on the ear shoot deep within the husk. Each potential kernel has an exposed silk attached to it to catch the pollen making reproduction possible. Inbreeding is the carefully controlled method of pollinating a plant with its own pollen.

The ear shoots are covered to prevent their silks from accidental pollination from neighboring plants. Each selected plant is carefully pollinated by hand. This inbreeding and selecting process may be repeated for as many as 6 or 7 generations until the plant's heredity becomes uniform. That is all plants of an inbred variety will look the same and will respond in a similar way to the environment. Hundreds of inbreds are produced and their resulting seeds are tested for the desired combination of traits.

What are some of these traits? Good seed must have traits adapted to the environmental condition in which it is planted. For example, the soil type. The amount and distribution of rain fall, the length of the growing season and the prevalence of particular pests. One such test is for the resistance to the European Corn Borer, an insect that has been a major threat to corn growers. After they are infested the test inbreds are each evaluated to see which one does the best job of resisting these hungry insects. By the time inbred testing is complete most will have failed to measure up and will have been discarded. Those inbreds showing the most desirable traits will go on to the second step of hybrid seed development.

Experimental or test crossing. The key to hybridizing is taking pollen from one selected inbred and cross pollinating it with a second unrelated inbred. The outcome is usually amazing. The resulting hybrid seed produces a plant the following year that is bigger and stronger than either of its parents. This is the miracle of hybrid vigor. The purpose of this test crossing is to find the cross of two inbreds that combines the desired traits and gives a higher yield than the existing hybrids. Again, the same carefully controlled methods of pollination is followed. Only this time the pollen from one inbred is crossed onto the silks of the other inbred.

Thousands of inbreds are crossed. The resulting hybrid seeds taken from the female plant are planted the following year for testing and evaluation. This is time consuming and expensive, but it eventually comes up with a winning cross. It is estimated that out of more than a thousand test crosses only one will produce a hybrid seed that will perform significantly better than had existed before. When the breeder has found the cross of two inbreds that produces an acceptable high yielding hybrid seed, the third step begins.

Mass producing it in sufficient quantities for sale to farmers. Seed corn companies contract with skilled farmers to do this on a large scale with the assistance of the company. The two selected inbreds are planted in the same field in alternating sets of rows. For example, one male row of one inbred may be planted next to as many as four female rows of the other inbred. And it is these female plants that will eventually produce the needed quantity of hybrid seed.

The resulting hybrid seed is harvested from the female row. This is the seed that will be sold and distributed to farmers for planting next year. Before distribution the seed is taken to a conditioning plant where it is sorted, dried, sized and bagged for sale to farmers all over the world. The farming of corn in the early 1900's has been vastly improved by the introduction of hybridization. Today yields are at least four times that of the 1920's allowing farmers to export more corn to world markets. Enough to make a significant impact in helping to feed the world. This is the miracle of hybrid corn."[5]

- 1941: The term "genetic engineering" is first used by a Danish microbiologist.
- 1942: Penicillin is mass-produced in microbes for the first time.
- Pfizer, which had made fortunes using fermenting processes to produce citric acid in the 1920s, turned its attention to penicillin. The

massive production of penicillin was a major factor in the Allied victory in WWII as is seen in this video.

"Poverty, hunger, and disease, these three ancient enemies of man still stalk, hand in hand across too much of the world. Of the three, disease can be said to be the deadliest. Disease often fathers hunger and poverty. This is the story how one of the mightiest weapons against disease was forged. It is the story of penicillin. The first of the modern wonder drugs known as antibiotics. Today the penicillins are only one group of antibiotics among many. In laboratories around the world the search goes on for more. To learn how the first of them, penicillin, was discovered and developed one must know of the work of three British scientists. What they achieved has revolutionized medicine. Sir Alexander Fleming for the initial discovery of penicillin. Dr. E.B. Chain and Sir Howard Florey for their finding its curative power to benefit millions.

Early in the 1920's, in London, Alexander Fleming, a young bacteriologist, worked in the inoculation department of St Mary's Hospital. Familiar with antiseptics and inoculations as weapons to help the human body battle against disease germs, he began to wonder what natural defensives might be possessed by exposed parts of the body such as the eyes. In each case Fleming found protective substance that could destroy some germs before they invaded the body. Some germs but not all and not the deadliest.

In one of the glass dishes where he cultured germs for his experiments, Fleming noticed one day, in 1928, that some mold such as what appears on decaying food had begun to grow, a spoiled experiment. But with mind alerted by the earlier work on protected substances, he looked closer. He saw that near to the mold new germs were growing. Might it be that this mold, like the human body produced a substance capable of destroying germs? He made tests and found that even some of the most dangerous germs died near the mold. He then grew the mold in a meat broth liquid. The color of the liquid changed finally to a bright yellow. This liquid proved lethal to germs even when greatly diluted. Not pure enough to be injected into a human body it was nevertheless effective on wounds. Fleming published what he had done, calling this substance penicillin. Attempts to purify it and to extract its essence failed.

In the 1930's, a new chapter opened at the University of Oxford. The professor of pathology, Dr. Howard Florey was joined by Dr. E.B. Chain. Together they planned a research project on natural germ-killing substances. They unearthed the now old papers on penicillin. They formed a team and the great quest was on.

First Chain and his colleagues set to work on the chemical problems of extraction and purification. They found a way of transferring the active penicillin from liquid to liquid until it was held within almost pure water. They froze off the water which left a brown powder. Here was a powerful form of penicillin, still crude but produced no ill effects in animals. Florey prepared the great test. The germ streptococcus is a killer. This he injected into mice. Half of them then received the brown powder. Those who had been given the penicillin lived and were healthy and Professor Florey declared, 'It looks like a miracle.' But attempts to make it pure enough for man caused it to lose its potency.

Chain and a colleague, Dr. Abraham, then devised another method. Dissolving the crude penicillin in ether, they passed it through a long tube filled with alumina. Each substance producing layers of differing colors. In the yellow layer was penicillin. They repeated the process again and again. Now Florey could try penicillin on human beings. The results proved the healing power of penicillin.

But by now World War II was raging. The need for penicillin's healing power was enormous for soldiers and for civilians. But in 1941 purified penicillin was still desperately short and Britain was hard pressed by air attacks. To make the quantities needed it was decided to seek help in the United States. Here scientists devised better ways of culturing penicillin which could give much bigger yields. Production in quantity could now be foreseen. With encouragement from their government the American drug companies tackled the difficulties of producing penicillin on an industrial scale.

Florey returned to Chain and the others, able to look forward to supplies for further research. Alexander Fleming had a patient dying of meningitis. Fleming turned to Florey, and Florey gave him all the penicillin that could be made available and with it his advice. Profoundly impressed by this personal experience of penicillin's dramatic power Fleming addressed himself to the British government about the need for large scale production. And the press took up the cause.

The big British chemical and drug companies and the research workers now also protected the big scale production of penicillin. The mold was grown in thousands of flasks. Britain's output joined the huge supplies now coming from the United States to give life to hundreds of thousands of soldiers.

By the end of the war flasks had been replaced by great steel vats, each making 15,000 gallons of penicillin liquid and huge factories were in production in Britain and in the United States. Penicillin was now for the world. The great discovery for which in 1945 the world rightly and greatly honored Dr. E.B. Chain, Sir Howard Florey, and Sir Alexander Fleming."[6]

- 1950's: The first synthetic antibiotic is created.
- 1951: Artificial insemination of livestock is accomplished using frozen semen.
- 1953: JD Watson and FHC Crick for the first time cleared the mysteries around DNA as a genetic material, by giving a structural model of DNA, popularly known as, 'Double Helix Model of DNA.'

"We are in 1953 in Cambridge, a city where scientists are racking their brains to corner what was known as molecule of life... Yes, that one. Ok let's rewind a little. Several researchers over many years

discovered within the nucleus of our cells there was a substance called DNA which contains all our genetic information and it was made of four compounds, Adenine, Thymine, Guanine and Cytosine. How was it possible that the whole book of our life was written with just four letters?

Our celebrating friends, James D. Watson and Francis Crick thought that maybe the answer was in the structure of DNA and they were trying to solve this four-piece puzzle that was driving all the scientific community crazy. They had two clues. The first one was a discovery that was made by Irwin Chargaff who found that in all the organs that he tested, the relative amounts of Adenine and Thymine were equal. And the same happened with Guanine and Cytosine.

The second clue came from Rosalind Franklin, an experienced chemist who generated DNA crystals and shot Xray's through them to study their structure. The Xray picture showed a repeated pattern which meant it was something similar to a helix. Watson and Crick tried all the possible unions between A and T and G and C, and one was perfect.

Two bonds between A and T and three bonds between G and C would fit in a helix. A double helix indeed. Also, the four units structured this way could code a huge amount of data as a dot and a dash could pose a whole alphabet in Morris Code. On top of these discoveries, specific pairing suggested the copying mechanism for DNA for the production of new cells and new life.

Ten years after the celebration in the pub, Watson, Crick, and Morris Wilkins and Rosalind Franklin received the Nobel Prize for this discovery and the DNA revolution spread across every biology laboratory in the world."[7]

- 1954: Dr. Joseph Murray performs the first kidney transplant between identical twins.

- 1955: Dr. Jonas Salk develops the first polio vaccine. The development marks the first use of mammalian cells (monkey kidney cells) and the first application of cell culture technology to generate a vaccine that changed history.

Ron Evans: *"Jonas was a big thinker and he wanted a place where big thinking could be done. He was a dreamer and he knew that you would have to dream to create something new."*

Peter Salk, President Jonas Salk Legacy Foundation: *"The centenary of my father's birth is an opportunity not only to look back at what was done at the Polio and Salk Institute but to look forward to what can be built, how can this legacy be continued."*

Inder Verma, Professor, Laboratory of Genetics*: "There was a relatively young boy, I would say he was twelve or thirteen, I suspect. This is Dr. Jonas Salk, he cured polio. The little boy looked at him and said, 'What is polio?' and Jonas was beaming because he felt he has finally achieved it because this kid doesn't even know the disease polio."*

Walter Eckhart Professor Emeritus, Molecular & Cell Biology Laboratory*: "I think Jonas realized that his discovery wasn't only important in terms of public health but that it was important to remove a sense of fear in people. And that might have been the biggest effect."*

Roger Guillemin Distinguished Professor & Nobel Prize Recipient*: "He was certainly conscious of the significance of these vaccines and indeed Jonas never obtained return money from the sale of the vaccine."*

Tony Hunter, Professor, Molecular & Cell Biology Laboratory: *"One has to admire his single mindedness in developing this polio vaccine against a lot of people who doubted this and said it couldn't be done this way. Once he had done that, I think he felt he needed to do something else with his life. Help humanity in a different way."*

Greg Lemke Professor, Molecular Neurobiology Laboratory: *"He was free thinking. He was an exceptionally creative man. And he had this notion of the distinction between people who are evolvers and people who are maintainers of the status quo. He really wanted to populate the institute with creative people who were evolvers."*

"Hope lies in dreams, in imagination and in the courage of those who dare to make dreams into reality." Jonas Salk.

Janelle Ayres, Assistant Professor, Nomis Foundation Laboratories: *"I see that quote by Jonas Salk everyday as I walk into the courtyard and it really reminds me of why I came to the Salk Institute to do my research. There are no boundaries and that is really how great discoveries are made."*

"I believe that beyond polio the institute will be his long-lasting legacy. It's a huge honor to be able to be here and celebrate his 100th anniversary."[8]

- 1957: Scientists prove that sickle-cell anemia occurs due to a change in a single amino acid in hemoglobin cells
- 1958: Dr. Arthur Kornberg of Washington University in St. Louis makes DNA in a test tube for the first time.
- 1958 Nobel Prize for showing that genes regulate the metabolism.
- 1960: French scientists discover messenger RNA (mRNA).
- 1961: Scientists understand genetic code for the first time.
- 1962: Dr. Osamu Shimomura discovers the green fluorescent protein in the jellyfish. He later develops it into a tool for observing previously invisible cellular processes.
- 1963: Dr. Samuel Katz and Dr. John F. Enders develop the first vaccine for measles.
- 1964: At a conference in 1964, Edward Tatum laid out his vision of "new" biotechnology to modify organisms. 1. The recombination of existing genes, or eugenics. 2. The production of new genes by a process of directed mutation, or genetic engineering. 3. Modification or control of gene expression, or euphonic engineering."

- 1967: The first automatic protein sequencer is perfected.
- 1967: Dr. Maurice Hilleman develops the first American vaccine for mumps.
- 1967: DNA ligation links DNA fragments together. The discovery of DNA ligases is considered a pivotal point in molecular biology, because they are essential for the repair and replication of DNA in all organisms. This helped pave the way for other "splicing" experiments in the 1960's and early 1970's.
- 1968: Discovery of Restriction Enzymes. Werner Arber noticed that certain bacterial strains fought off infection by chopping off its DNA. So, he theorized that bacterial cells produce two types of enzymes: one called a "restriction" enzyme that can identify and cut foreign DNA, and a "modification" enzyme that recognizes the host DNA and protects it from cleavage.
- 1969: An enzyme is synthesized in vitro for the first time.
- 1969: The first vaccine for rubella is developed.
- 1970's: Genetic Engineering takes off unexpectedly.
- 1970: Restriction enzymes are discovered. This understanding of how restriction enzymes "cut" DNA, and how host DNA works to protect itself is the basis for the modern genetic engineering therapies that are being developed, and for CRISPR.
- 1971: The measles/mumps/rubella combo-vaccine was formed.
- 1971: Gene splicing experiments begin which radically change everything.

"Since splicing is a word that is often used to describe the specific changes in micro-organisms, we use these a lot. So typically, you would make a change in a micro-organism, produce an enzyme that would, for example, break down grasses to use for biofuels. We use these for brewing, for producing products from agricultural plants. There is the high-fructose corn syrup that is in all the sodas, not especially good for you but it's everywhere. Tastes great. But that is produced using enzymes that have been engineered.

When we talk about micro-organisms engineering, particularly the production of something that we will isolate and purify and then use in an industrial process we often describe that as gene splicing in a common language. And what you are talking about there is inserting a specific gene under your control and producing a lot of something. You're not really studying the system itself; you just want the product. So that is kind of the implication of describing something called gene splicing.

After twelve years of searching, Monsanto found a soil bacterium that is naturally immune to Roundup Herbicide. Their goal was to genetically engineer DNA from this bacterium from various plants. They cut out a sequence of DNA that is resistant to Roundup, but if this DNA sequence alone is inserted into a corn plant it will have no effect. So, the next step involves E.coli bacteria. Dots are created in the E.coli DNA and when the two test tubes are mixed together some of the E.coli DNA recombines with the Roundup resistant bacteria.

Then the technician smuggled the engineered DNA into the cells of the corn plant that they wanted to modify. Cells will naturally reject foreign DNA, so they developed a method using soil bacteria that causes tumors in plants. They use this bacterium to ferry the engineered DNA into the plant's nucleus. There are also two other methods to get the engineered DNA through the cell wall. One uses a stream of electricity to create tiny holes in the plant cells, so they become vulnerable to infiltration by foreign DNA.

Another is the gene gun that blasts particles of gold coated with engineered DNA into the plant cells. Each of these three methods needs a promotor gene that turns on the desired characteristics. The promotor gene is often extracted from the cauliflower mosaic virus.

This engineering is really a radical revolution in food production. It's really a cell invasion technology. Now people have heard they're taking a flounder gene and putting it in a tomato so the tomato can last in cold temperatures, but people ask how that flounder gene gets into that tomato. And what really happens is, the only way you can do it is to invade the cell of the tomato and deposit the flounder gene."9

- 1971: Type II restriction Enzymes are used for mapping DNA.
- 1972: Recombinant DNA (rDNA) is created.
- 1973: Cohen and Boyer perform the first successful recombinant DNA experiment, using bacterial genes.
- 1974: Stanley Cohen and Herbert Boyer developed a technique for splicing together strands of DNA from more than one organism. The product of this transformation is called recombinant DNA (rDNA). Popularly referred to as "genetic engineering," it came to be defined as the basis of new biotechnology.

"Biotechnology, a dynamic field creating new drugs for our hospitals and new foods for our tables. Today Biotechnology is a multi-billion-dollar industry, but in the early 1970's it was little more than a scientific experiment. In 1972 two scientists from different fields, Stanley Cohen and Herbert Boyer combined their talents and laid the groundwork that forever changed the way we look at living things. By the early 1970's scientists had learned a great deal about genes and cells.

The structure of DNA had been revealed by Watson and Crick, and its role in genetics was being uncovered. But there was still a great deal to be learned. At the University of California in San Francisco, Herbert Boyer was one of the scientists probing the mysteries of the cell. Boyer's work focused on how particular sections of DNA could be cut by molecules called restriction enzymes. The cut DNA was left with two sticky ends. Boyer knew that if he added another similar piece of DNA it would join with the cut DNA forming a new molecule. This had been done in a test tube but would this new DNA work in an actual cell?"

Herbert Boyer: *"I was trying to put all the pieces of the puzzle together, but I didn't have all the pieces actually."*

"The other pieces were being gathered just forty miles away at Stanford University."

Stanley Cohen*: "At the time antibiotics were discovered it was thought that the end of infectious disease was in sight. But it soon became clear that bacteria could develop resistance to antibiotics, and it was discovered initially in Japan and in England that the genes that made bacteria were resistant to antibiotics were carried by plasmids.*

"Plasmids are simply tiny circles of DNA. Most of the time they can be found living inside bacteria. Hitching a ride so to speak. But every now and then a plasmid will leave the bacteria and hitch a ride on a different one, adding its genetic material to the new cell and passing along its antibiotic resistance."

Stanley Cohen: *"What we developed in my laboratory was a way to allow bacterial cells to take up naked plasmid DNA molecules and once taken up by the bacterial cell the plasmid replication machinery allowed the plasmid to reproduce itself."*

"A significant accomplishment, but Cohen wanted to do more than just move plasmids around."

Stanley Cohen: *"Even though we had found a way to introduce plasmids into bacterial cells there was no way to rearrange them. That is, no way until restriction enzymes became available."*

"Restriction enzymes, exactly what Herbert Boyer was working on. And Stanley Cohen's work with plasmids was the missing piece that Boyer was seeking. In April 1972 Boyer and Cohen, both attended a scientific meeting in Hawaii. It would be the beginning of a long and adventurous trip."

Stanley Cohen: *"I was very excited by Herb's talk and that evening a number of us took a walk."*

Herbert Boyer*: "And Stanley and I got together and 'boom' you know, we were right on each other. That was what he wanted to do and that was what I wanted to do. He would send me plasmids and I would cut it up and relegate it and send it to him and he would transform it."*

Stanley Cohen: *"It was an extremely exciting time. We worked literally day and night. Things were too exciting for us to get very much sleep. It was a continual high."*

Herbert Boyer: *"It was like realizing a potential for this technology and we learned on the very first experiment."*

"With this new technique Boyer and Cohen could take a piece of DNA and splice it into the plasmid. The plasmid was then inserted into a bacterium. When the new cell multiplied it replicated the new piece of DNA as well."

Stanley Cohen*: "After all these years it sounds funny to think that we weren't certain at the time that one could in fact simply splice another piece of DNA into a plasmid and expect that foreign piece of DNA to replicate."*

"But splicing genes was just the first step. If DNA included a human gene that produced a particular protein, the bacteria would produce the protein as well. They had discovered a way to manufacture human proteins. The promise of this technology to produce cures and treatments for a wide range of diseases such as diabetes and cancer. Soon it attracted the attention of the media."

Stanley Cohen: *"Shortly after our first paper on this work was published I was interviewed by Victor McAlhaney of the NY Times who was writing an article about the work and he asked me specifically when did I think the first commercial product using these methods would be available. I looked at him for a moment and replied, 'Oh* *within 5 or 10 years and it turned out to be 7 and that product turned out to be insulin."*

"Today there are dozens of biotech companies producing a wide range of products from new crops and food to aids therapy and life-saving drugs. What started out as a simple scientific collaboration has transformed medicine and health care."[10]

- 1974: The birth of The National Academy Moratorium on Genetic Engineering Experiments. All these developments were great for science, but with these recent achievements in splicing DNA together, it was evident that there were ethical dangers associated with these experiments. Scientists proposed a temporary moratorium on all genetic engineering experiments in 1974. But Joshua Lederberg, a Stanford professor, emerged from this conference as a strong voice highlighting the potential of recombinant DNA technology for curing disease. His optimism and foresight drowned out fears about using this technology for ill, including eugenics or "superbug" infectious diseases. Now a Nobel Laureate, Lederberg's argument for the successful future use of recombinant technology ushered in a golden age for science and biotechnology.
- 1975: George Kohler & César Milstein created cells that produce very specific antibodies essentially revolutionizing modern genetic diagnostics and immunology treatments.
- 1976: Molecular hybridization is used for prenatal diagnosis.
- 1978: Recombinant human insulin is produced for the first time.
- 1978: With the development of synthetic human insulin the biotechnology industry grew rapidly.
- 1979: Human growth hormone is synthesized for the first time, which has led to many abuses on up to today.

Rich Piana: *"Side effects that I have gotten from using GH. I talked a little about this in the past, but people wanted me to get a little more specific. So, I'm going to get a little more specific. Basically, all the side effects that I have gotten from using Growth Hormones, and I have used them for about 10 years straight. And when I say straight, I* *mean straight. I have to say my shoe size, and I used to wear a size 12, now I wear a size 15. My head, I used to wear a size 7 3/8, a fitted cap, now I wear a 7 ¾, maybe 7 5/8, I don't know. My hands, my fingers have grown, my wrists have grown, my wrists have probably grown about ¾ of an inch, my fists have grown about ½ inch in width. It basically makes every tissue in the body grow.*

Now in saying that I have to say, has my heart grown? Probably. Has my brain grown? Probably. Has my intestine grown? Yes, I know my intestines have grown because my stomach has gotten thicker over the years, which is a side effect that I am most bothered by. That is what made me stop doing GH. It was because of the stomach growth. As a body builder we don't think about our heart growing and how we are going to have a heart attack at age 50 because our heart has grown.

But we think about the things, like my hair is falling out. Oh no what am I going to do. But as we get older, we start to realize these things. Now I'm a lot more concerned about the organs growing, and how it's going to affect me in the future. So, anyway those are the side effects I have incurred while using Growth Hormones. It's a choice people make. I just want people to be educated and know what they are getting themselves into. Because when I chose to do it, I had no idea what I was getting into."

Channel 7 ABC Reports*: "Concerns about more teenagers using human growth hormone. A new survey shows that experimentation with HGH has increased significantly in recent years and doctors are worried about the risk it poses. Seven Action News reporter Tara Edwards has more on what parents need to know about this trend."*

Tara Edwards*: "The numbers are overwhelming. Experimentation with the Human Growth Hormone by teens in America have more than doubled in a year. A new survey involving thousands of high school students say that 11% of kids reported using HGH at least once in 2013. According to the survey it's up from 5% in 2012. Doctor McGraw warns kids and their parents to be careful of products sold* *online and in nutrition stores advertising they contain HGH as well. And if the teen believes that what they are consuming is a steroid, what a lot of them are not aware of are the long-term side effects the drug can have on the body."*

Dr. Marcus McGraw: *"Natural growth hormone or steroids can have a significant consequence to growth. Significant long-term consequences to even appearance, with hair loss, with their sexual development."*

Tara Edwards*: "Or even worse, kidney problems or death. It's hard to say how much HGH teens are using. Dr. McGraw says especially when they are going online to get it, they could be taking several different products, making it even more dangerous."*

Dr. Marcus McGraw: *"One of their friends will take something and genetically they will be more blessed with a certain body type and when they see their friend taking something and assuming that is the product doing the work they are going to want to try it too."*

Breaking the Law for Beauty*: "How often do you use it?"*

Aimi Veness: *"I've used it for the past year."*

"And how did you find it?"

Aimi Veness*: "My husband introduced it to me. He had heard about it at gym. And he knows it's an advertiser's dream. If there is a product that is going to make me younger, I am going to try it. Demi Moore is using it. She looks amazing."*

"We don't know that she is of course. Interestingly as you were just saying you didn't know until we spoke to you that it was illegal."

Aimi Veness*; "I had no idea. I was absolutely shocked."*

"It was really easy for you to get?"

Aimi Veness: *"It was really easy and then I was told I could get 14 years in prison for taking it."*

"It's supplier up to 14 years in prison, 2 years in prison for possession. So, it is legal to possess it if it is a medicine that has been prescribed by a doctor. Otherwise it is illegal for buying online. And you were buying it online. How much did it cost you?"

Aimi Veness: *"About 200 pounds and that would last me about a month. I don't inject very much. I don't want to be really big."*

"What benefits have you noticed.?"

Aimi Veness: *"I have so much energy. My skin is so much better, my hair, I lose weight, my nails, it's just like a Peter Pan drug."*

"If you are 86, I would be massively impressed. Can I ask you how old you are?"

Aimi Veness: *"I'm 40. I turn 40 in November. That's what kind of started it."*

"Have you noticed, some people can be 40 and look amazing, so we don't know if that is because of this particular drug."
Aimi Veness: *"I was always very tired. It gave me so much more energy. I just felt like Wonder Woman on it. It took a while for it to kick in but when it did, I felt amazing."*

"And you administer it yourself?"

Aimi Veness: *"That was really scary. I had never injected. I am scared of needles. Injecting it myself took a few hours the first time I did it. It's not nice."*

"And you have no training in that at all?"

Aimi Veness: *"No."*

"Your face is a picture here."

Dr Frances Prenna Jones, Leading dermatologist: *"I think there are two debates here actually. There is the debate of getting something online when you have no idea what it actually is. And the debate of actually doing it yourself. And the jury is still out about long term benefits verses the risks as we were having a conversation earlier on. It may well be in 10 years' time we say it was a fabulous thing to take but we don't know 100% at the moment."*

"Because it had a very grizzly beginning, didn't it?"

Dr. Frances Prenna Jones*: "It did have a grizzly beginning so far as it was originally prescribed in the 70's to children who had stunted growth basically, in order to help them grow. Originally it came from cadavers, dead bodies basically. And what we discovered was that those children later down the line, we think, developed what the press called mad cow disease."*[11]

Oh, I've always wondered where that came from!

- 1980: The U.S. Supreme Court approved the principle of patenting genetically engineered life forms.
- 1981: Scientists at Ohio University produce the first transgenic animals by transferring genes from other animals into mice. This process is now standard in genetics and known as "DNA microinjection" where foreign DNA is literally inserted into the host organism.

"A round organism is punctured by a needle containing DNA. It is inserted into the host and several beadlets of the DNA is inserted. Then the needle is taken back out of organism."[12]

- 1981: The first gene-synthesizing machines are developed.
- 1981: The first genetically engineered plant is reported.
- 1982: The first recombinant DNA vaccine for livestock is developed.
- 1982: The first biotech drug, human insulin produced in genetically modified bacteria, is approved by the FDA. It was created by a Genentech scientist, Dennis Kleid, and is considered a defining moment for the concept of genetically engineered drugs being approved for human consumption. Genentech has since become a leading biotech company developing various medicines for people utilizing genetic modification techniques.

Robert A. Swanson, *Founder, Genentech: "Towards the end of 1975 there was some discussion and a number of scientific journals on the potential of recombinant DNA technology to produce useful products. And I got very excited about the potential of the technology and I started calling up scientists. One of the early people I called was Dr. Herbert Boyer at the University of California. I tried to convince him to see me. He was very polite and nice, but he said he was awfully busy. I said that you don't understand. You are the only one I have talked to that thinks something can be done now.*

Finally, he relented and said well maybe ten minutes on Friday afternoon. So, I showed up at his lab at University of California, San Francisco. In my suit, everyone else was in jeans and T-shirts and we hit it off. After 2 or 3 or 4 hours and about that many beers, we found out that not only did we like each other but we shared a common vision. From that point I went about putting together a business plan. We each put in our $500 and incorporated Genentech. Here we have a whole infrastructure of Venture Capital that are willing to bet on a person with an idea and give them the money necessary to build their company."[13]

- 1983: Kary Mullis developed polymerase chain reaction (PCR), which allows a piece of DNA to be replicated over and over again. By implementing the chain reaction, any copy of a DNA sequence is amplified to make more copies and can generate thousands or even millions of copies.

- 1983: The first artificial chromosome is synthesized.
- 1983: The first genetic markers for specific inherited diseases were found.
- 1983: The first genetic transformation of plant cells is performed.
- 1984: The DNA fingerprinting technique was developed.

"Back in the 1980's, labs around the world were searching through DNA for the genes that caused major human illnesses. An unexpected breakthrough emerged from a biological back water in a small British city of Leicester. On September 17, 1984 while comparing some tiny fragments of human DNA, Alec Jeffries made a discovery that would turn DNA into a household word."

Alec Jeffries: *"I just had a gut feeling that this had the potential of being big. Just how big, I didn't have the faintest idea. But this was new. I did note."*

"Jeffries was investigating how diseases run in families. There were many parts of the DNA where you could see inherited patterns. But one region appeared to be unique to an individual except in the case of identical twins."

Alec Jeffries: *"I thought, the full weight of many magical, so fantastically variable patterns here, lots of bits of DNA having a peculiar pattern in a gene where you've got a short block of DNA repeated over and over again."*

"This peculiar repeated pattern suggested that it would be ultimately possible to identify every human being in the world with a unique readout like a bar code."

Alec Jeffries: *"I went charging back into the lab and started running around there, very excited, we thought we were on to something. So,* *we got together and started drawing up a list of things this could be used for."*

"They began gathering samples from all over the lab. Smears on equipment, stains on clothes, rogue hairs, dirty cups and flakes of skin. They were then able to match each shred of evidence to its owner's unique DNA pattern."

Alec Jeffries: *"So I thought, okay we've got a possibility here of using this for identification, so we immediately thought forensics. The possibility here that maybe we could use this for establishing family relationships. To immediately start thinking of paternity disputes. We tried hair roots and so on, it's all working, absolutely amazing and we looked at brothers and sisters and other types of close relatives.*

Lots and lots of similarities even between very close relatives. So, it was clear just intuitively these patterns were essentially completely individual specific. I think it was at that point we needed a name. A very good friend of mine said, 'Well that's interesting, but that's fingerprints aren't they'. That was it, it was called DNA fingerprints."

"The far-reaching implications of DNA fingerprinting were just beginning to dawn on Jeffries."

Alec Jeffries: *"I went home that evening and sat down with my wife, showing all this stuff. She said, 'All right, that's great, but you missed that one area.' I said, 'That's okay, what's that?' 'The immigration disputes. And that's disputes where you have got doubts about clean family relationships.' At that point I think my blood froze, because I suddenly thought, hang on, if we get into this it is no longer your son's, this is heavy-duty politics."*

"Within a year DNA fingerprinting had settled the first of thousands of immigration disputes proving that this family was entitled to access to Britain. The following year DNA evidence was first used to resolve a paternity suit. It was the first of millions of paternity cases worldwide

and in 1988 this rapist became the first criminal to be convicted on DNA evidence. Countless offenders have since been identified around the world."

Alec Jeffries: *"It was DNA actually saving lives, saving future victims, it's pretty awesome stuff."[14]*

- 1985: Genetic markers are found for kidney disease and cystic fibrosis.
- 1986: The first recombinant vaccine for humans, a vaccine for hepatitis B, is approved.
- 1986: Interferon becomes the first anticancer drug produced through biotech.
- 1986: DNA testing was used in a criminal investigation. The investigation used genetic fingerprinting in a case of two rapes and murders located in the United Kingdom. This DNA testing of a crime scene also began to overturn previous rulings that falsely accused people of crimes they never committed.

"In the late 1980's DNA testing brought a new level of certainty to America's courtrooms. Convicting the guilty. DNA evidence has helped put hundreds of violent criminals behind bars and freeing the innocent. DNA testing proved they didn't do it. And calling into question the forensics science that had sent many of them to prison in the first place. The only physical evidence linking him to the murder has been discredited."

Anderson Cooper *Live CNN: "It's science but it's not as foolproof as you might think."*

Before DNA the criminal justice system had long relied on microscopic hair analysis, a forensic technique whose impact is only beginning to become clear."

"We started asking ourselves, 'what do we know?'

The DNA Revolution: Hair Analysis.

"In 1981, Kirk Odom saw how a few hairs could change a man's life."

Kirk Odom: *"I used to go jogging, like every Sunday. This particular Sunday morning as I was leaving out of my house the Metropolitan Police were knocking at my door."*

"The police had noticed Odom a few weeks earlier when they were scouring the neighborhood looking for a suspect who broke into a woman's apartment and raped her at gunpoint."

Peter Neufeld, *co-founder, Innocence Project: "The policeman said, 'Oh, he looks a little bit like a composite sketch I saw of the rapist."*

Kirk Odom: *"I told them that I was at home in bed and my mother could verify that, but they didn't believe me."*

"The victim soon picked Odom out of a lineup, though her identification was called into question."

Peter Neufeld: *"She only had a fleeting opportunity to see the perpetrator."*

"But the police had another piece of evidence. A hair found on the victim's nightgown."

Kirk Odom: *"They didn't give me any information, they just wanted hair from my groin area and a hair from the top of my head."*

"The police sent the hairs to the FBI's renown crime lab. There some of the nations most experienced forensic scientists use high powered microscopes to check more than a dozen characteristics. From pigment distribution to scale patterns. They told them whether a hair could have come from a suspect."

Max Houck, *Physical Scientist, FBI Laboratory (1994-2001): "We would look at hairs all the time, every day. If you look at something every day, routinely, you get very good at noticing small differences."*

"Max Houck would later join this unique unit of hair and fiber experts."

Max Houck: *"Some of the people that I work with were fantastic. They had such a keen eye, such good discrimination, they saw things that I didn't think you could see."*

"The examiner's skills had been honed through decades of scientific crime fighting at the bureau."

A Day with the FBI (1951) TV show: *"The strand of hair taken from the assailants scalp is exactly the same as the hair taken from the head of one suspect being held by police."*

"By the 1970's microscopic hair comparisons were an essential part of the FBI's arsenal. Even a single hair will supply evidence."

"When Odom's case came to trial in 1981 the FBI's analysis was clear."

Kirk Odom: *"It was explained to me that when they matched the hair, one hair didn't match the other."*

"The most important evidence came from the hair microscopist, who said, 'I can't say it's unique, but I can say the chances of it coming from any other than Kirk Odom are small.'"

Kirk Odom: *"I could put myself in one of the juror's place and say, 'Well, yeah, he must have done it."*

"It took just a few hours for the jury to convict Odom. He was sentenced to more than 20 years in prison. Six years into Odom's prison term a revolutionary new technology burst onto the scene."[15]

Wow! Well, good thing DNA Testing is here! Or, could we just be exchanging one problem for another. We shall see.

- 1986: University of California, Berkeley, chemist Dr. Peter Schultz describes how to combine antibodies and enzymes (abzymes) to create therapeutics.
- 1988: The first pest-resistant corn, Bt corn, is produced. Known as "Bt corn" because it contains genes from the bacterium Bacillus thuringiensis (Bt). This corn was able to increase yields by discouraging pest impacts. But like with other genetic modifications, it creates a whole new set of problems.

"85% of the food we eat comes from large farms like this, 2,700 acres. Joe Tumbleson only grows two crops; corn and soy. He was hoping that Monsanto's genetic technology could help him get rid of a big pest, the European Corn Borer Caterpillar."

Joe Tumbleson; *"They burrow into the stalk and it rots the inside of the stalk, they burrow into the shank that holds the ear and rots that, then the wind comes up and the corn falls off. Now to keep that from happening we spray our field with an insecticide, but we can't get selective. We spray for an insect, but we might get four or five that we don't want dead. Now we have killed them."*

"Monsanto had a solution to sell. Corn that made its own pesticide. Scientists have long known that the humble soil bacterium called Bacillus thuringiensis (BT) produced toxins that killed caterpillars. Monsanto scientists spliced the bacterial gene that made the toxin into corn. Now every cell of the modified corn makes its own pesticide. The chemical protein, harmless to most insects and to humans whose bodies rapidly break it down, but lethal to the corn borer caterpillar."

Joe Tumbleson: *"If you have ever been around here when we have sprayed an insecticide, we put on leather gloves and coveralls, so it doesn't get on us, that is not a fun thing. That is not a fun thing that I don't even want to dream about, I don't even want to have it in my machine shed to have my grandkids around. But those are the type of things that we don't have to have with this new BT corn."*

"Welcome to Full Valley Farm. It's very different from most modern industrial farms. Instead of two crops, California farmer, Paul Mueller, grows seventy on just 200 acres. Everything is grown organically. There is one product that Muller uses from time to time to control pests. Something that has pitted him against the biotech industry. The organic pesticide known as BT."

Paul Mueller: *"The BT that we use is very specific, it doesn't have a very long life and we use it sparingly. We may only spray a field like this only once a year, once a season, and we don't use it unless we have to."*

"Monsanto says this is a leap forward, we're ending pesticides. Well, yes and no. Yes, they are ending the use of pesticides but now they are introducing more toxins that they ever introduced using pesticides. You have to think of that corn now as a factory producing toxin".

"And say critics, this toxin will cause a worse problem, resistant pests. It's not a new problem. Pesticides have never killed every last pest in the field. There is always a small number with genetic variations that resist the poison. Because these survivors eventually repopulate, the entire field with resistant descendants' overtime pesticides stop working. A field of BT corn potentially makes the situation worse. Seven days a week, twenty-four hours a day the corn puts out BT killing most but not all corn borers. The resistant survivors soon repopulate the field. The BT has not been effective against those pests."

Paul Mueller: *"By engineering BT into the corn they are taking a tool away from farmers over the long haul. The BT will disappear as an effective tool for farmers like me to use."[16]*

- 1988: Chymosin (known as Rennin) was the first enzyme produced from a genetically modified source-yeast-to be approved for use in food.
- 1988: Only five proteins from genetically engineered cells had been approved as drugs by the United States Food and Drug Administration (FDA), but this number would skyrocket to over 125 by the end of the 1990s.
- 1988: Congress funds the Human Genome Project, a massive effort to map and sequence the human genetic code as well as the genomes of other species and the race was on.

"Packed inside every cell in your body is a set of genetic instructions, 3.2 billion base pairs long. Deciphering these directions would be a monumental task, but it could offer unprecedented insight about the human body. In 1990 a consortium of twenty international research centers embarked on the world's largest biological collaboration to accomplish this mission. The Human Genome Project proposed to sequence the entire human genome over 15 years with three billion dollars of public funds. Then seven years before its scheduled completion, a private company called Celera announced they could accomplish the same goal in just three years and at a fraction of the cost.

The two camps discussed a joint venture but talks quickly fell apart as disagreements arose over legal and ethical issues of genetic property and so the race began. Though both teams used the same technology to sequence the entire human genome, it was their strategies that made all the difference. Their paths diverged in the most critical of steps.

The first one: In the human genome project approach, the genome was divided into smaller more manageable chunks, about one hundred and fifty thousand base pairs long that overlapped each other a little bit on both ends. Each of these fragments of DNA was inserted inside a bacterial artificial chromosome where they were cloned and fingerprinted. The fingerprints showed scientists where the fragments overlapped without knowing the actual sequence.

Using the overlapping bits as a guide the researchers marked each fragment based in the genome to create a continuous map. A process that took about six years. The cloned fragments were sequenced in labs around the world following one of projects, to major principals. The collaboration on our shared heritage was opened to all nations. In each case the fragments were arbitrarily broken up into smaller overlapping pieces about one thousand base pairs long.

Then using the technology called the Sanger Method, each piece was sequenced letter by letter. This rigorous map-based approach called Hierarchical Shotgun Sequencing, minimized the risk of this assembly, a huge hazard of sequencing genomes with many repetitive portions, like the human genome. The consortiums 'better safe than sorry' approach contrasted starkly with the Celera strategy called Whole Genome Shotgun Sequencing. It hinged on skipping the mapping phase, entirely. A faster though fool-hearty approach according to some. The entire genome was directly chopped up into a giant heap of small overlapping bits. Once these bits were sequenced into the Sanger Method, Celera would take the formidable risk of reconstructing the genome using just the overlaps.

But perhaps their decision wasn't such a gamble because guess who's just completed math was available online? For free. The Human Genome Consortium in accordance with the projects second major principal which held all of the projects data would be shared publicly within twenty-four hours of collection. So, in 1998 scientists from around the world were furiously sequencing lines of genetic code using the tried and true, yet laborious, Sanger Method. Finally, after three exhausting years of continuous sequencing and assembling, the verdict was in. In February 2001, both groups simultaneously published working drafts of more than 90% of the human genome, several years ahead of the Consortiums schedule. The race ended in a tie.

The Human Genome Project practice of immediately sharing its data was an unusual one. It is more typical of scientists to closely guard their data until they are able to analyze it and publish their conclusions. Instead the Human Genome Project accelerated the pace of research and created an international collaboration on an unprecedented scale. Since then robust investment in both the public and private sector has led to the identification of many disease related genes and remarkable advances of sequencing technology. Today a person's genome can be sequenced in just a few days. "[17]

- 1989: Microorganisms were used to clean up the Exxon Valdez oil spill.
- 1990: The first successful gene therapy is performed on a 4-year-old girl suffering from an immune disorder.
- 1993: The U.S. Food and Drug Administration (FDA) declared that genetically modified (GM) foods are "not inherently dangerous" and do not require special regulation.
- 1994: A tomato engineered to stay ripe is brought to market and bombs. It was approved at the same time as Bt corn and was actually brought to market for public consumption in 1994. This product was a perfect example of how difficult it can be to bring genetically engineered products to market - especially crops - as people literally have to eat them, and therefore, are wary of possible side effects.
- 1990's: The terminator seed was developed. It was a new type of genetically modified seed developed that commits suicide or literally becomes sterile in the second generation, which means you always have to go back to an entity who manufacturers or controls the seed production for your next batch of seeds. This has led many to be concerned about the fact that if this sterilization of seeds continues, then not only will plants no longer be able to self-replicate and make more seeds for the individual, but for the first time in man's history, anyone who wants to grow food has to go back to a global entity who is in control of the seed production which means they are now the food

supply. What is also alarming is the fact that similar global entities have also created a Global Seed Vault in the middle of the Arctic lending to even more concerns.

Arwa Damon, CNN Reports: *"Look at the landscape around us and how remote this is and then jetting out of the side of this Artic mountain is this Svalbard Global Seed Vault and we have all been very excited to actually get inside to see for ourselves how what is being done here is playing a very vital role when it comes to trying to mitigate against the consequences."*

The Artic Seed Vault: Longyearbyen, Svalbard, Norway: "Welcome to the Global Seed Vault. This is a facility where we store copies of seeds from gene banks all over the world. Now we're entering the long tunnel which leads into the Global Seed Vault."

"Deep across the Permafrost Mountain close to the North Pole the storage facility with the capacity to store over four million crops and a maximum of 2.5 billion seeds. The Global Seed Vault was created as a back-up system as the world's gene bank to protect humanity against any catastrophe that would potentially wipe out our agricultural diversity."

Asmund Asdal, Svalbard Global Seed Vault Coordinator: *"We're now quite deep in the mountain. When you pass this door, we are in the Permafrost part of the rocks here. Now we are moving from approximately zero degrees (Celsius) into the permafrost section. We're in the permafrost here, -5 (Celsius). In there, it's -18 (Celsius). And here, you can feel the atmosphere, it's silent, you can hear the echo. It's a very nice place to grasp the atmosphere of being in an important place. Some journalists call this the 'Noah's Ark of plant diversity.' And personally, I think that's quite a good name. We call it the world's most important room, so let's go in. If humanity can't survive, we will need new plant varieties. And the material you need for developing new varieties are genetic diversity.*

We have seeds from all countries in the world. Kenya, Mexico, India, Peru, Germany, Colombia, Costa Rica, Zambia, Brazil, Australia. Here we have some nice wooden boxes from Tajikistan. Workers in gene banks, farmers have struggled to produce all these seeds and sent them here, because they feel safe when they send the seeds here. Svalbard is a safe place, it's the permafrost here, so it's frozen even if the artificial cooling fails. And Svalbard is quite far away from conflicts. Here we have boxes from Russia and here we have boxes from Ukraine. And even if they are enemies abroad, outside, in the seed vault they cooperate. And here are some wooden boxes made in North Korea. So even North Korea has sent seeds here and in the seed vault here, international conflicts are cooled down.

We had seed boxes from ICARDA's gene bank in Aleppo. They sent seeds here from 2008, and when the gene bank in Aleppo was ruined, we were able to send the seeds back so they can start creating a new gene bank. This system saved the seeds. If they had no backup here the seeds would have gone extinct. There is in this seed vault about 70,000 different varieties of barley. And 150,000 samples of rice. And 140,000 samples of wheat. Researchers investigate what are the properties we found in these older varieties, and they use the genes for making new varieties for new purposes, for new growing conditions.

Without this material, plant breeders, agriculture would never manage to feed the growing population. This is the raw material that we need for the future that breeders need to make new varieties to increase the world's food production. The work gene banks do every day conserving their seeds, preparing the genes for future food supplies is a very, very crucial and important work. I have a quite good feeling when I'm here and know that this is a resource that the future will need. Seeds go extinct every day and personally it's a big motivation to think about all the work that has been done to bring the seeds here. And it feels very good to be a part of this global effort for future food supplies and to conserve them in a safe place."

Arwa Damon, Sr. International Correspondent: *"It is truly remarkable and such a unique experience. The general population doesn't have access to this vault and we are among the few who have actually been inside and as Michael said it truly makes you pause and think about how what is being done here is really helping to safeguard our future."*[18]

Safeguard our future? Or control our future? That is the concern many have with this genetic sterilization of our seed supply. And it's interesting, of all things to compare this to, a "type" of Noah's Ark for seeds. Didn't we see that the "real" Noah's Ark was constructed due to this same genetic modification behavior? What do they know that we don't know?

- 1994: The first breast cancer gene is discovered.
- 1995: Gene therapy enters the clinic in the war against cancer.
- 1995: The first baboon-to-human bone marrow transplant is performed on an AIDS patient.
- 1995: The first vaccine for Hepatitis A is developed.
- 1996: A gene associated with Parkinson's disease is discovered.
- 1996: The first genetically engineered crop is commercialized.
- 1996: The cloning of Dolly the Sheep. This was one of the biggest stories spread throughout the public that science has ever seen. The project was led by Ian Wilmut of the Roslin Institute. As the first mammal to be cloned from an adult cell, with the same genetic identity, Dolly was a huge achievement, proving that the process of cloning found in nature could be attributed to organisms it does not naturally occur in.

Aljazeera Reports: *"Dolly the sheep was a sensation when she first appeared before the world. A scientific breakthrough, fascinating, but also menacing. Dolly was cloned by taking a body cell from sheep A, fusing that cell's DNA with an egg cell with its nucleus removed from sheep B. This fused cell developed into an embryo which was placed in the uterus of a surrogate mother, sheep C. The resulting lamb, in this case Dolly, is a clone of sheep A. These are Dolly's so-called siblings.*

Identical sisters all cloned from the same sheep. Professor Kevin Sinclair worked with them and knew Dolly. "

Kevin Sinclair: *"It was a step change in our understanding of early development which ultimately led several years later into, in 2006, to the discovery that you can actually induce somatic cells. These are self-cells that belong to the body to become embryonic like cells that has the potential to divide into two other cell types. "*

"This was Dolly's greatest legacy. Advances in what we call stem cell research. The ultimate but still elusive goal is to use cloning technology to create healthy tissues which can be transplanted to heal damaged cells and organs. But back in 1997 Dolly seemed to raise more frightening issues. If we can clone a sheep, many asked, why not a human being. Since then scientists have cloned more than 20 species including horses and household pets. "

Kerry Bowman, University of Toronto: *"I think where we draw the line is if we're going to use genetic manipulations. We have to be extremely careful and we have to look for severe disease effects to control for. Because with a lot of these things it's not just the person you are doing a genetic manipulation on or potentially cloning but it would affect all the generations ahead. "*

"So, Dolly's brave new world has not turned out quite as predicted, a sheep like number 4 but she could not escape her own mortality. She died in 2003, now stuffed in a Scottish museum. "[19]

- 1997: The first human artificial chromosome is created.
- 1998: Human skin is produced for the first time in the lab.
- 1999: The complete genetic code of the human chromosome is deciphered.
- 2000: The National DNA Data Bank was established to profile, identify, link and investigate individuals involved in designated offenses, and to assist in the investigation of missing persons and unidentified human remains.

Alec Jeffries: *"As of 2007, four million DNA profiles on the UK database. Five million plus profiles in the United States database. Worldwide, most countries have a national database. Worldwide we have about twelve million plus people, mainly criminals logged into those databases. An enormously powerful tool in the fight against crime. So, in England, Wales, when you have a crime scene sample that yields a DNA, simply by looking up the database, you'll find your prime suspect, in round about 53-54% of cases. In Scotland it's up to 68%, quite remarkable. So, this is a shortcut if you have a lot of police investigative work, with DNA you are going to essentially solve the case on the spot. The impact is extraordinary, major impact on detection rates involving crimes like car theft and burglary. The detection rate is shot right up thanks to the availability of DNA.*

What we are now seeing is, there are various international conventions that are being drawn up which now allow information to be compared between national DNA databases. So, both the G8 countries and separately Interpol, establishes protocols whereby, if you have a crime in Britain that you can't solve, and you have a feeling it could be a Dutch person or something or vice versa. So, you start exchanging information until you have matches outside your country. The number of quite serious offensives have been solved by exactly that approach."[20]

But this has led to many concerns over who's controlling these DNA databases around the world and what they're doing with it, as well as signs that taking DNA samples from people are becoming "mandatory" in some cases.

RT Reports: *"Britain holds one of the world's largest collection of human genetic data. The National DNA database per capita is by far the biggest anywhere. The genetic data of 5% of the people in the UK is held proportionately ten times more than in the US. The database was created in 1995 as a crime fighting tool and has never been far from controversy. This intensified in 2004 when a law was passed allowing the DNA of innocent people to be retained by the police. Now* *anyone who is simply arrested and not necessarily cautioned or convicted has their genetic code entered into the database. In December it was ruled that this contravenes the European Convention of Human Rights. But still the database keeps growing."*

Helen Wallace, Director, Genewatch UK: *"DNA databases are really out of control. It was set up to keep the DNA of convicted criminals, people convicted of serious offenses, but now it contains about five million people's profiles that will be innocent of any crime, many of them children."*

RT Reports*: "But that's not the only reason Genewatch is participating in this seminar. Research shows that the database is racially biased. Three out of every four black men have their genetic code stored suggesting the police arrest far more black people than white. Even though statics show whites have a higher rate of offending. Matilda Macattram argues this criminalizes an entire community."*

Matilda Macattram, Director, Black Mental Health UK: *"Effectively the genetic heritage of every black citizen within the UK is on a criminal database even though this group does not have a high propensity to commit a crime and in this country which has held up as a bastion for civil liberties and human rights one is innocent until proven guilty by a court of law and until the law changes that's what the police who are supposed to be upholding the law should adhere to."*

RT Reports: *"The organization Black Mental Health UK hopes a change of government at Parliamentary elections, which must take place by June next year, will bring about a change in policy on the national database. Opposition parties support the system that currently exist in Scotland where the law on genetic information storage is different from the rest of Britain. There, DNA is collected on arrest but automatically deleted from the files in the vast majority of cases if no charges are brought."*

David Burrowes, Shadow Justice Minister, Conservative: *"We needed a system where if you are arrested for an offense and you're cleared, that your samples are cleared off the system, but in any particular circumstances such as those who have been charged of serious violence or sexual offenses should they have their samples kept for a period of up to five years. That happens in Scotland."*

RT Reports*: "In the meantime the database keeps on growing and introducing the Scottish system isn't even under discussion by the ruling labor party. Despite the decision by the European court of human rights that retaining innocent people's DNA illegal, the police are still adding 400,00 profiles to the database every month. British internal security still proposes keeping the DNA of innocent people for up to 12 years."[21]*

- 2000: Kenya field-tests its first biotech crop, virus-resistant sweet potato.
- 2001: FDA approves Gleevec, a gene-targeted drug for patients with leukemia and is still used today as a cancer treatment drug.
- 2002: EPA approves the first transgenic rootworm-resistant corn.
- 2002: The Banteng, an endangered species, is cloned for the first time.
- 2003: China grants the world's first regulatory approval of a gene therapy product, Gendicine, for head and neck cancer.
- 2003: GloFish' went on sale in Taiwan, as the first genetically modified pet which is the tip of the iceberg of genetically modified animals that are now being produced onto the scene.

"Over the past 30 years the biotechnology developments have allowed scientists to alter the genetic makeup of bacteria, plants and animals. Here are seven of these such experiments, but they represent just the tip of what will become a massive iceberg.

At number 7 we have the Sudden Death Mosquito. Dengue fever is a mosquito borne virus that causes 2.3 million infections and another 25,000 deaths per year worldwide. As of yet, there is no cure. But to deal with it, scientists have created what I call, sudden death genetically modified mosquitoes which are released into the wild and breed with the indigenous mosquito population. These then passed the special gene to their offspring. This special gene means that the baby mosquitoes die before they themselves can breed, thus reducing the number of mosquitoes that can infect people. Trials in specific areas have showed up to an 80% decrease in the mosquito population up to three months after the initial release.

Number 6 is Glow in the Dark Cats. The Glow in the Dark Cat was developed to try to fight the feline immunodeficiency virus or FIV which is related to the human version of HIV and typically affects feral cats. In 2011, American and Japanese scientists inserted genes into cats to help them resist FIV. In order to mark the cells more easily they also inserted a green fluorescent protein into both genes transferred to the feline eggs. This protein which is naturally produced in jellyfish is commonly used in this area of research to monitor the activity of altered genes. This lets the scientists examine how the resistant genes develop within the cats by examination under a microscope. The modified cats are always normal during the daytime but sometimes they glow at night.

Number 5 is the Web Spinning Spider Goats. When it comes to natural goods, flexible and strong spider silk is incredibly valuable. Spider silk is pound per pound five times stronger than steel and far more elastic than rubber. Normally getting enough spider silk for these applications requires a large number of spiders. However, spiders tend to be territorial so when the researchers set up spider farms the spiders killed each other. So, they inserted the silk making genes into the mammary gland cells of goats. The cells then make the extra protein to make the spider's silk. The milk then can be collected, and the protein is extracted to make the spider silk thread.

Number 4, Singing mice. Sometimes there is no defined end result for the genetic tweaking involved and this is what happens with the Japanese evolved mouse project. It's a bit like adding some extra genes and let's see what happens when the results of the experiments are allowed to breed. One morning while checking on a new litter of mice, researchers discovered that one of the baby mice was singing like a bird. They focused on that mouse and now bred over a hundred mice that can sing. But it doesn't end there. They noticed that when normal un-modified mice grew up around the singing mice, they too began to use different sounds and tones almost like a simple language. The project's goal is to artificially speed-up evolution, but we might have just created a super talking mouse that will one day go on to take over the world and experiment on humans in the future.

Number 3, Popeye Pigs. For all of you meat eaters out there that love bacon and hate vegetables, Japanese scientists have taken pigs and added the gene from spinach. This creates healthier meat with a lower saturated fat content and contains proteins that are found in the spinach leaves. Dubbed the Popeye pigs because of the spinach these pigs have been inserted with a special Spanish gene that converts from saturated fat into unsaturated fat. Although the pigs have been cleared of any health complications, their announcement was met with a public outcry. Maybe a better solution is just to eat more greens with your organic pork instead of trying to create pigs that do both.

Number 2, Cows that produce human milk. Babies could be fed on human milk produced by cows in the wake of the latest genetic modifications. Scientists have created cattle that have been given human genes to make their milk contain the same nutrients and fat content as breast milk, however human milk differs from cow's milk in several important ways. It contains high quantities of nutrients beneficial to the baby's growth and also special immune system antibodies that are specific to that mother and baby which could never be replicated using this method.

Number 1, Glowing Zebra Fish. Glofish is a patented brand of genetically modified fluorescent zebrafish with bright red, green, and orange fluorescent colors. Though it was originally created to show the presence of toxins in water, it was the first genetically modified animal that has gone on to be widely available to the public as a pet.

In 1999 scientists at the National University of Singapore were working with a gene called the green fluorescent protein, GFP, originally extracted from a jellyfish that naturally produced a bright green bioluminescence. They inserted the genome into the zebrafish embryo allowing it to integrate with the zebrafish genome. This caused the fish to be brightly fluorescent under both natural white light and ultraviolet light. The idea was to develop a fish that would detect pollution by glowing in the presence of environmental toxins.[19]

- 2004: UN Food and Agriculture Organization endorses biotech crops, stating biotechnology is a complementary tool to traditional farming methods that can help poor farmers and consumers in developing nations.
- 2004: The United Nations formally endorses biotech crops as a way of supporting struggling farmers in developing nations and solving the world's hunger crisis.
- 2004: FDA approves the first antiangiogenic drug for cancer, Avastin.
- 2005: The Energy Policy Act is passed and signed into law, authorizing numerous incentives for bioethanol development.
- 2006: FDA approves the recombinant vaccine Gardasil®, the first vaccine developed against human papillomavirus (HPV), an infection implicated in cervical and throat cancers, and the first preventative cancer vaccine.
- 2006: USDA grants Dow Agro Sciences the first regulatory approval for a plant-made vaccine.
- 2006: The National Institutes of Health begins a 10-year, 10,000-patient study using a genetic test that predicts breast-cancer recurrence and guides treatment.
- 2006: The DNA testing Company 23andMe was founded to help people access, understand and benefit from the human genome.

"You're here to understand what '23 and Me' is all about, right? How does it work?" "What does DNA even stand for anyway?" "DNA stand for Deoxyribonucleic Acid." "I knew that." "You definitely did not!"

"Your DNA is organized into 23 pairs of chromosomes and it can tell you a lot of what makes you, you. There are two '23 and Me' services that can help you explore your DNA. One that focuses on ancestry and one that adds in health and traits. With '23 and Me' you can discover where in the world your DNA comes from. You can even learn how you are connected to others by opting into '23 and Me's' relatives feature and can connect with people who share DNA with you.

There are fascinating insights about your traits to explore. You can learn how genetics might influence your risk for certain diseases. But remember other factors such as lifestyle and environment are important too. If you choose to you can opt in to receive genetic health risks reports such as Parkinson's Disease and late-onset Alzheimer's disease free.

Now there's only one thing left to do. We get to spit. Not quite. First you have to order your kit. Order your '23 and Me' kit online and chose either the health and ancestry or the ancestry service. After your kit arrives in the mail, read and follow the instructions. We value your privacy and the instructions will help you register your online account before you send in your sample. Now you get to spit.

Fill the collection tube to just above the fill line and remember don't eat, drink, smoke, chew gum, brush your teeth or use mouth wash for at least 30 minutes prior to providing your saliva sample. After you have spit, securely snap the cap to the tube which releases the DNA stabilization buffer solution. Holding the tube upright unscrew the funnel from the tube and discard. Use the small cap to close the tube tightly. Shake the capped tube for 5 seconds. Place the capped tube in the small plastic bag, seal the bag and return it to the original box. The plastic clamshell is recyclable. All that is left to do is peel the strip and seal the box closed, then ship.

You will receive updates letting you know that your sample is being processed. You will be able to track your kits journey through the lab in your private account and then about 6 to 8 weeks later you will receive an email letting you know that your reports are in and your genetic journey is about to begin. "[22]

- 2006: The artist Stelarc had an ear grown in a vat and grafted onto his arm.
- 2007: FDA approves the H5N1 vaccine, the first vaccine approved for avian flu.
- 2007: Scientists discover how to use human skin cells to create embryonic stem cells.
- 2008: Chemists in Japan create the first DNA molecule made almost entirely of artificial parts.
- 2009: Global biotech crop acreage reaches 330 million acres.
- 2009: Sasaki and Okana produced transgenic marmosets that glow green in ultraviolet light and pass the trait to their offspring.
- 2009: FDA approves the first genetically engineered animal for production of a recombinant form of human antithrombin.
- 2010: Craig Venter announces completion of "synthetic life" by transplanting synthetic genome capable of self-replication into a recipient bacterial and demonstrated that a synthetic genome could replicate autonomously as this news report shows.

ABC News Reports: *"Scientists announce today that they have made a major breakthrough in the quest to create life in a laboratory. For the first time they have produced a living cell in which the active DNA was put together by computers. What does this mean for science and does it mean now there is synthetic life?"*

Dr Richard Besser: *"That's right, today's announcement marks a major turning point. Researchers have now created life from non-living parts. They call it a synthetic cell. World renown geneticist, Craig Venter has been trying to unlock the mystery of life for 15 years. What have you achieved?"*

Craig Venter: *"We announced today the first synthetic cell, instead of having a genetic relative that it evolved from the parent of this cell is a computer."*

Dr. Richard Besser: *"What Venter has done is astonishing. With just 4 vials of chemicals off the shelf in his lab, his team replicated more than a million bits of genetic code to create a living organism. Here's how it worked.*

They isolated bacterial cells and removed all their genetic materials, the DNA from inside, and they took those 4 bottles of chemicals and used them to make new genetic material. They transplanted it into the empty cell, that material, that new cell booted up and began to reproduce. And reproduce a billion times."

Art Caplan, PhD: *"I think this is the creation of life. And I think it is an experiment that shows that life is not a mystery. It's a mysterious force that infuses things that make them come alive. If you put the right genetic message in the right order and put it in the right environment it will come alive."*

ABC News Reports: *"But along with promise comes precaution."*

Paul Wolpe, PhD: *"Like any great scientific innovation this has enormous promise and enormous peril. This may allow us to make more virulent viruses. This could unleash a bacterium on the world that has properties that we didn't expect that could cause great disease or ecological damage."*

ABC News Reports: *"Scientists will surely debate whether this is truly creating new life, but no one can deny the potential impact of this achievement."*[21]

And that impact is going to come with some horrible consequences. But notice how they arrogantly said, "This is the creation of life." Actually, it's not. It's the manipulation of already existing life. Only God can create life. It reminds me of the cartoon on the following page. As you can see, the caption reads the misguided mindset of today's modern evolutionary scientist, "If I can only create life in this test tube, I will have disproved that absurd notion that intelligence was needed to create life in the beginning." Really? Does anybody see the irony of that cartoon besides me? You had to use your

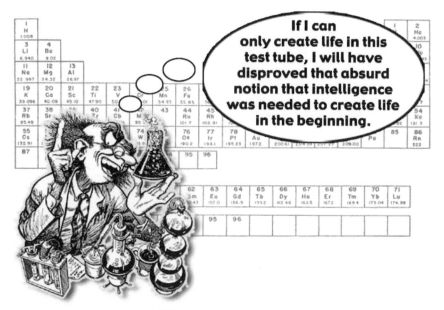

own intelligence to create life in order to prove that life came about without intelligence! Really? Have you thought that through intelligently? You see, the facts are, man is very good at manipulating, modifying, even cloning pre-existing materials, even down to the genetic structure. But man, can never create something out of nothing. Only God can do that like these other scientists learned.

"There was a group of scientists and they were all sitting around discussing which one of them was going to go to God and tell Him that they didn't need him anymore.

Finally, one of the scientists volunteered and went to go tell God he was no longer needed.

So the scientist says to God, 'God, you know, a bunch of us have been thinking and I've come to tell you that we really don't need you anymore. I mean, we've been coming up with great theories and ideas, we've cloned sheep, and we're on the verge of cloning humans. So, as you can see, we really don't need you.'

God nods understandingly and says: 'I see. Well, no hard feelings. But before you go let's have a contest. What do you think?'

The scientist says: 'Sure I'm all for it. What kind of contest?'

And God said, 'A man-making contest.'

And the scientist replied, 'Sure! No problem.'

So, the scientist bends down and picks up a handful of dirt and says, 'Okay, I'm ready!'

And God says, 'No, no, no. You go get your own dirt.'"[23]

Does anybody see the irony of that joke as well? Manipulating, modifying, or even cloning pre-existing dirt, or even adding dirt to an empty bacterium so to speak is not creating new life. It's manipulating existing life. Only God can create life from nothing. You're not God! And that's precisely the problem. You think you are and that's one of the reasons why God's judgment is coming!

- 2010: Harvard researchers report building "lung on a chip" technology.
- 2010: Scientists created malaria-resistant mosquitoes.
- 2011: Trachea derived from stem cells transplanted into human recipient.
- 2011: Advances in 3-D printing technology lead to "skin-printing."
- 2011: The discovery of TALENs was made which stands for Transcription Activator-Like Effector Nucleases and this paved the way for precise genome editing.
- 2012: Ancestry DNA announced the launch of its new DNA testing service.

Several people are sitting at a table and the question is asked, "Would you dare to question who you really are?" As they sit and think about the question, they each individually answer in the following way.

Person #1: "I'm proud to be English, my family served and defended this country and has been to war for this country."
Person #2: "I'm really patriotic about Bangladesh."
Person #3: "Well I am 100% Icelandic, yeah definitely."
Person #4: "This is Kurdish wedding with my mom in traditional Kurdish cloth."
Person #5: "We're just proud blacks so that's it."
Person #1: "Yeah, I think we are probably the best country in the world, if I'm honest"

Interviewer: "Think about other countries and other nationalities in the world. Would there be any that you don't feel you would get on with well or you won't like particularly."

Person #1: "Germany, yeah I'm not a fan of the Germans."
Person #6: "You might think they're a little bit..."
Person #2: "Particularly India and Pakistan probably because of the whole, you know, the conflict."
Person #4: "I have this side of me, there's like that hates Turkish people, not the people but the government."
Person #3: "I'm more important than you. I don't know you, but it is my opinion I am strong, and I am more important than a lot of people."
This is the DNA Journey

Interviewer: "How would you feel about taking a journey based on your DNA?"

Person #6: "Yeah, I would feel very intrigued."
Person #1: "What could you possibly tell me that I don't know?"

Interviewer: "Do you know how DNA works? So you get half from mum and half from dads, a 50% from each of them and they get 50% from their parents and back and back and back and back and all those little bits of your ancestors, they filter down to make you, you. I need you to spit in this tube for me, spit up to the little black line."

Person #6: "That's a lot of spit."

Interviewer: "The story of you is in that tube. What's it going to tell me?"

Person #6: "It's gonna tell me, oh yeah, you're French and wait your grandparents are French."
Person #2: "I'm solid Iraqi."
Person #7: "I'm Cuban."
Person #1: You gonna tell me that I'm English no I told you.

Two Weeks Later

Interviewer: "Are you ready for your results? Will you read it out to us please?"

Person #6: "Oh my, oh wow, you didn't explain that."
Person #2: "Wow."
Person #4: "Caucasus, which was Turkish, yeah."
Person #5: "Eastern Europe, Spain, Portugal, Italy, and Greece."
Person #6: "I'm 32% British."
Person #1: "Great Britain 30%, 5% German."
Person #4: "I'm Irish, yeah."
Person #2: "I'm a Muslim Jew."
Person #3: "Iceland has definitely moved closer to Europe now."
Person #6: "I'm gonna go a bit far right now but this should be compulsory that there would be no such thing as like extremism in the world if people knew the heritage that, who would be stupid enough to think of such a thing as like a pure race."

Interviewer: "In a way we're all kind of cousins in a broad sense, in a much more direct sense. You have a cousin in this room. Turn around and guess who it is."

Person #4 turns around to look at the audience.

Interviewer: "Wash, why don't you come down here and meet your cousin."

Person #2 stands up and comes down from the audience. He says, "I had no idea. I didn't know, my hearts pounding right now."

You have more in common with the world than you think[24]

If anything, this proves the Biblical account that we all come from two parents, Adam and Eve. And even more recently, from the eight survivors who got off the Ark after God judged the planet the first time and then repopulated the planet. But notice again, this is another heart appeal to go ahead and give them a sample of your DNA. My question is, on top of all the other DNA samples they already have from the police forces and DNA databases around the world, some being taken whether you want to or not, I sure hope all these other so-called "voluntary" DNA samples and testing's from these kinds of companies around the world won't eventually be used for some nefarious purposes in the future!

- 2012: The Discovery of the CRISPR Genome Engineering Tool was made by Jennifer Doudna. What CRISPR technology is being used for varies from developing cancer treatments, to tackling obesity, to creating hornless cows and so much more.

Trace Dominguez @ Domain.com: *"Crispr could be responsible for the new era of genetically perfected plants, animals, and even humans, but what the heck is it? A few years ago, something called a Clustered Regularly Interspaced Short Palindromic Repeats (CRISPR) burst onto the scene. It worked so well scientists began issuing ethical* *statements about its use. CRISPR cuts DNA strands with unprecedented accuracy and simplicity allowing geneticist to directly edit any of earth's organisms however they like. CRISPR could be used to engineer disease free organisms, formulate high yield crops, or even cure genetic and hereditary human conditions. Of course, it could theoretically also be used to let parents pick their kids sex, eye color, height, or whatever. In the end CRISPR is, as one noble scientist said to the Independent, jaw dropping in its efficiency and simplicity.*

It all began in the late 1980's when some Japanese scientists were looking at bacterial DNA. They spotted repeated palindromic patterns. Palindromes is a mirrored set of characters, like race cars or noon (though DNA sequences only use A, C, T, or G). In the 2000's scientists realized that these repeating characters were part of an ancient bacterial immune system. The palindromes were framing the DNA of viral invaders. This viral DNA is used by bacteria's immune systems like a 'Most Wanted Poster.' It would detect an attack, go look at the 'Most Wanted Poster' section of their DNA, figure out which virus was attacking and then create an RNA defender to fight back.

Now that the RNA knew what to attack it needed a way to do so. Which is where CAS9 comes in. CAS9, or CRISPR associated protein 9 is an enzyme that unwinds DNA and cuts it up. The trick is that cutting process works with more than just viral DNA. Once scientists figured out how this process worked, they learned how to use it to cut out and replace any DNA sequence. I know it's confusing but think of it as our own immune system. The RNA is like antibodies, are tagging the invaders and then CAS9 eliminates them. Like our white blood cells do except at the cellular level and even smaller, on the molecular level, tiny.

After the word got out, scientists everywhere began making their own RNA targets, wrapped them in CAS9 and then send them out to cut DNA, like our own RNA army. CRISPR CAS9 is so accurate that it can recognize as many as twenty base pairs. Meaning that scientists can cut single genes out of a DNA strand. After the strand was cut it would self-repair disabling the gene. But if scientists injected replacement DNA that would fill the space instead. This allows us to swap in DNA wherever we like. If you want corn with genes to fight bacteria, cool we can do that. If you want fish that glow, grab some DNA from phosphorescent algae and toss it in there.

This technique is so simple it's scary. It's paving the way for widespread genetic engineering and it's kicked off a media frenzy. Like when the Chinese authorities announced that they'd edited human embryos although they had not allowed them to grow. Craig Mello is the co-Laureate of the 2006 Nobel Prize for medicine and he told the Independent, 'It is a triumph of basic science,' and claimed it was even more important than his discovery that had won him the Nobel Prize. But because it is so simple scientists are calling for ethical oversight, all over the place, and need to align science with public support. "[25]

In other words, we may have just opened up Pandora's Box. Are we sure we want to go down this genetic altering route?

- 2012: Researchers at the University of Washington in Seattle announced the successful sequencing of a baby's genome using nothing more than snippets of DNA floating in its mother's blood.
- 2013: Researchers in Japan developed functional human liver tissue from reprogrammed skin cells.
- 2013: Researchers published the results of the first successful human-to-human brain interface.
- 2013: Doctors announced that a baby born with HIV had been cured of the disease.
- 2014: Researchers showed that blood from a young mouse can rejuvenate an old mouse's muscles and brain.
- 2014: Researchers figured out how to turn human stem cells into functional pancreatic Beta cells—the same cells that are destroyed by the body's own immune system in type 1 diabetes patients.
- 2014: For the first time ever, a woman gave birth to a baby after receiving a womb transplant.

CBS This Morning Reports: *"So the Cleveland Clinic has made history, for the first time in North America a woman gave birth after receiving a uterus transplant from a deceased donor. Now the reason this is significant is, first of all, one in five thousand women cannot have children because of a uterine problem. Typically to fix that problem they have to do really complex surgery on living women. Taking it from one woman and putting it in another one. Now for the first time in North America they have done it with a deceased person. It opens the windows for all these women with this issue and it reminds me of what Jeff Goldblum said in Jurassic Park 'nature will find a way', well maybe not nature, maybe the doctor, the clinic, medicine, they will find a way."[26]*

- 2014: An international team of scientists reconstructed a synthetic and fully functional yeast chromosome. A breakthrough seven years in the making, the remarkable advance could eventually lead to custom-built organisms (human organisms included.)
- 2014: Ebola was merely an interesting footnote for anyone studying tropical diseases. Now it's a global health disaster. But the epidemic started at a single point with one human-animal interaction — an interaction which has now been pinpointed using genetic research. A total of 50 authors contributed to the paper announcing the discovery, including five who died of the disease before it could be published.
- 2014: Doctors discovered a vaccine that totally blocks infection altogether in the monkey equivalent of the disease — a breakthrough that is now being studied to see if it works in humans.
- 2014: The creation of Gene Drives using CRISPR was developed that forces and ensures genetic modification in all organisms.

"Historically scientists have been able to alter the traits of domesticated plants and animals but have not been able to do this to wild populations. Here we use mosquitoes as an example to explain why most genome alterations designed by humans don't persist in nature and how a recently proposed technology can change that. The transgenic mosquito tinted blue has an altered gene inserted into one of its chromosomes. When it mates with a wild type mosquito, each

parent contributes one copy of each chromosome to their offspring, thus only 50% of offspring will carry the altered gene, while the other half will inherit the wild type version from both parents.

Even if the altered gene doesn't reduce the likelihood of each mosquito surviving and reproducing it may persist at a low frequency in the ocean of wild mosquitoes or it might go extinct after several generations of especially unlucky inheritance. This process is what keeps us from altering wild mosquitoes to prevent them from carrying diseases such as Malaria or Dengue.

A team led by Kevin S. Felt at the WYSS Institute, the Harvard Medical School and the Harvard School of Public Health, has now outlined a way to build a gene drive that can improve the odds that almost any altered gene will be inherited, potentially allowing them to spread through even wild populations. The proposal relies on the CRISPR/CAS9 system. A new genome editing technology, co-developed, by the same researchers at the WYSS. Gene drive mosquitoes carry both the altered gene, the genes for the CAS9 enzyme and several guide RNA's that tell it where to cut. When passed to offspring the guide RNA's direct CAS9 to cut the wild type version of the gene inherited from the wild type parent.

The cell then copies both the altered gene and the drive when it repairs the damage. Because the mosquito now has two identical copies one on each chromosome, all of its offspring will inherit the alteration and the gene drive. This same process will be repeated through subsequent generations causing the alteration in a gene drive to spread through the population. "[27]

Which means its irreversible effects. No turning back after that! Uh oh!

- 2014: Russia starts building the world's first DNA databank of all living things as a type of "Noah's Ark." They say it's," the animal

equivalent of the 'Millennium Seed Bank'," a project that
encompasses all of the world's seeds.

Patrick Jones: *"Russia is creating a Noah's Ark of every living and
extinct creature's DNA to preserve them. Okay, well there are 35,000
types of spiders. How about if we shave a few off the top. Moscow
State University is getting a $194 million dollar grant and they are
going to use that to freeze or preserve everything living or dead that
he can get his hands on. The idea is to possibly one day use the DNA
to make more of the animals. It will take to 2018 to finish and when it
is done it will be 267 square miles or my fellow American's about the
size of 29 McDonalds. A project like this has never been attempted to
this extent. But it makes sense to back things up. When I forget to back
up my video file and I lose them things can get to table flipping levels.
Now imagine that on a 'we forgot', and all elephants are extinct level.
Makes you think of Noah and his Ark."[28]*

Yeah it sure does! Straight from the horse's mouth! Do they know
something we don't know? First it was all the seeds around the world
you're storing and now it's all the DNA? And again, of all things to
compare this project to, was a "type" of Noah's Ark. Folks, this is not
by chance. They even admit what they're doing and how dangerous it
is. Yet do they not realize, all kidding aside, that the "real" Noah's Ark
was constructed due to this same kind of genetic modification behavior
that went on several thousand years ago and that Jesus said would
appear on the scene right before He came back at His Second Coming?
I mean, do the Russians know something we don't know?

- 2015: Scientists from Singapore's Institute of Bioengineering and
Nanotechnology designed short strings of peptides that self-assemble
into a fibrous gel when water is added for use as a healing nanogel.
- 2015: CRISPR scientists hit a number of breakthroughs using the
gene-editing technology. Researchers in China reported modifying the
DNA of a nonviable human embryo, a controversial move.
Researchers at Harvard University inserted genes from a long-extinct
woolly mammoth into the living cells — in a petri dish — of a modern

elephant. Elsewhere, scientists reported using CRISPR to potentially modify pig organs for human transplant and modify mosquitoes to eradicate malaria.

- 2015: Researchers in Sweden developed a blood test that can detect cancer at an early stage from a single drop of blood.
- 2015: The first GMO salmon is sold in Canadian markets. It was approved to solve the world's overfishing crisis and soon moved to other markets.

The National News Reports: *"Move over wild and firm Salmon, a genetically engineered cousin is a step closer to the market. Long touted as safe by Aqua Bounty, the company that has been swimming upstream seeking regulatory approval for about 20 years."*

Garth Fletcher, *AquaBounty Technologies: "The risk is as minimal as you can ever expect to get with any product."*

The National News: *"Now the Food and Drug Administration in the U.S. agrees. Ruling there is no meaningful differences between the engineered salmon and its conventional counterpart. From a land locked lab on PEI, the eggs are injected with a gene from an eel called an Ocean Pout and one from a Chinook Salmon are flown to tanks in Panama to be grown to market size. Now with this ruling they are cleared for sale in the United States without any labeling required. These genetically modified fish can grow to market size twice as fast as farmed fish and costing a lot less to feed. But opponents say this ruling is based on poor science."*

Dr. Michael Hansen, Consumers Union: *"There is actually an increased risk of allergies and allergenic potential but that was based on a sample size of six fish which is too small."*

Mark Butler, Ecology Action Centre: *"Our concern is the risk to the wild Atlantic Salmon, that these GM Salmon can escape and can reproduce with wild Atlantic Salmon causing genetic contamination."*

The National News: *"Even those in the Salmon farming business in Canada are distancing themselves from what critics are calling 'Frankenfish.'"*[29]

- 2015: A team of geneticists finished building the most comprehensive map of the human epigenome, a culmination of almost a decade of research. The team was able to map more than 100 types of human cells, which will help researchers better understand the complex links between DNA and diseases.
- 2015: Stanford University scientists revealed a method that may be able to force malicious leukemia cells to change into harmless immune cells, called macrophages.
- 2015: Using cells from human donors, doctors, for the first time, built a set of vocal cords from scratch. The cells were urged to form a tissue that mimics vocal fold mucosa – vibrating flaps in the larynx that create the sounds of the human voice.
- 2015: A human embryo is edited with CRISPR by Junjiu Huang at the Sun Yat-Sen University in Guangzhou. Originally rejected by Western science journals because it did not follow ethical rules of science, this later made its way into publication in other ways. Because Huang had altered the cells that affect heredity, his experiment aiming to fix a gene error causing a blood disease was not considered ethical and became a controversy almost instantly. This was three years before human trials for CRISPR were officially approved by any governing body.

SciAM Reports: *"In a world's first, Chinese scientists have reported they have used a powerful gene editing technique to modify human embryos. Their paper published in the Beijing Journal came as no surprise to the community, but it has ignited a wide range of debate of what type of gene editing research are ethical. The publication also raises questions about the appropriate way to publish such work. In the paper, researchers led by Junjiu Huang, a researcher at Sun Yat-Sen University described how they used a system of molecules called CRISPR CAS9 known for its ease of use to cut DNA in human embryos and then attempt to repair it by introducing new DNA."*[30]

- 2016: A little-known virus first identified in Uganda in 1947 – Zika – exploded onto the international stage when the mosquito-borne illness began spreading rapidly throughout Latin America. Researchers successfully isolated a human antibody that "markedly reduces" infection from the Zika virus.
- 2016: CRISPR, the revolutionary gene-editing tool that promises to cure illnesses and solve environmental calamities, took a major step forward when a team of Chinese scientists used it to treat a human patient for the very first time.
- 2016: Stem Cells injected into stroke patient re-enable patients to walk.
- 2016: Study finds that cloning does not cause long-term health issues.
- 2016: For the first time, bioengineers created a completely 3D-printed 'heart on a chip.'
- 2017: Scientists at the Salk Institute in La Jolla, CA, said they're one step closer to being able to grow human organs inside pigs. In their latest research they were able to grow human cells inside pig embryos, a small but promising step toward organ growth.

Freethink Reports: *"Our relationship with animals is really, really complicated. Some animals we keep as pets and companions and some we eat; some try to eat us. We drink their bodily fluids, we mix their bodily fluids with bacteria and let it ferment, then we eat it with their meat or their reproductive cells. We grind up their bones and put it into lipstick and makeup. We use their skin for hats and jackets and shoes and luggage and sporting goods and fancy chairs. Of course, we mix our cells into their embryos to create chimeras that will grow new human body parts for transplantation. That last one, that last one is new.*

Whether you realize it or not we are in the middle of a medical crisis. In the US today roughly 115,000 people are waiting for an organ transplant. Twenty-two people die every day waiting for an organ that never comes. But these are just numbers. Let's talk about a person."

Father: "When I was 14, my parents took me to a physician/specialist, and he said the chances are that people with the disease you have are going to have a very short life. Crohn's Disease patients generally tend to live until they are twenty to twenty-one at best. He suggested that if there was anything I wanted to do in my life, I better get it done as quickly as possible."

Son: "This is my dad. He's not twenty or twenty-one, in case you are wondering. That would be weird, even for this show. His life has been extended time and time again as medical technology has continued to improve. About 4 ½ years ago though, it looked like time was running out. Dad had been on the kidney transplant list for several years. Then one day he finally accepted that he might never get one."

Father: "I didn't think I was going to survive much longer. It wasn't ten minutes later, we got a phone call asking us if we could come to the transplant center and I received from that center a very good kidney. A perfect match."

Son: "And now there is a good chance that dad will need another kidney. We are all asking ourselves if he can last another five years on a waiting list when the previous wait almost killed him."

Lady: "We believe that the pig is a perfect model to all the human organ shortage problems."

Son: "Hey lady, I'm trying to talk about my dad. What does this have to do with pigs?"

Lady: "If twenty-two people are waiting every day for an organ transplant, we have the ability to use the pig to grow human cells, tissues, and organs, why wouldn't we give the gift of life to people that are waiting in need."

Son: "Oh, well next time lead with that.

This is Tammy Lee Stanoch, the CEO of Recombinetics. Tammy and other folks here are working to develop a way to grow transplant organs for humans in genetically modified pigs, naturally or unnaturally. Not these pigs, these pigs are just delicious breakfast pigs." As the screen moves from the farm pigs to some all black pigs he says, "These are the genetically modified life-saving pigs. And one day soon, pigs like these will have their genome altered and human stem cells inserted into their embryos to create what's known as a chimera."

"This is Adrienne Watson. She's a scientist."

Adrienne Watson*: "I'm the Senior Director of Preclinical Development here at Recombinetics."*
Son: *"Like I said, scientist."*

Adrienne Watson*: "When we talk about chimeras, we're talking about an organism that's got cells from two different types of organisms. So, our pig chimeras, for example, are mainly composed of pig cells, but the organ of interest would be composed of human cells. That's called a chimera."*

Mitchell Abrahamsen, Chief Commercial and Scientific Officer at Recombinetics: *"Ultimately, we would like to grow whole organs: livers, kidneys, hearts, corneas. By providing an alternative method or alternative approach for generating these human tissues, cells, and products today, we really do open the door to some solutions that currently don't exist due to limited supply of available human tissues."*

Adrienne Watson*: "We already have the ability to grow human cells, including blood tissues. We can grow hepatocites, which are liver cells, pancreatic cells to cure diabetes, or to prevent or delay diabetes."*

Mitchell Abrahamsen*: The first step to creating these chimeras that are definitely not man-pigs is to take the embryo and knock out the* *genes that would normally grow the organ you're looking to replace. Say a liver. Get outta here, liver genes."*

Adrienne Watson*: "That embryo is then injected with human cells and those human cells then fill the niche where the pig cells can't. So, if the pig embryo is knocked out for a gene necessary for the liver to develop. Now the human cells will go in and actually develop the liver in the pig."*

Mitchell Abrahamsen*: "Boom you've got a liver. A liver made out of human cells with your DNA. A perfect transplant organ made just for you that won't require you to take a lifetime of antirejection and immunosuppressant medications."*

Son: "The idea of growing a human organ in a pig is something that probably catches people off guard. But if you're one of those people that need a heart, or if you have a child that needs a liver transplant or a pancreas, if you've got a child who's got some really serious disease, you're looking for solutions."

Adrienne Watson*: "These pigs are superheroes because they are saving human lives."*

Mitchell Watson*: "Let's not be too terribly glib about this. There's a ton of ethical questions that arise from this idea of mixing our cells with animals. We're toying around at the fuzzy edges of what actually separates us from the animals we've gotten so creative in utilizing. But we will do it."[31]*

- 2017: First step taken toward epigenetically modified cotton.
- 2017: Sequencing of green alga genome provides blueprint to advance clean energy, bioproducts.
- 2017: Fine-tuning 'dosage' of mutant genes unleashes long-trapped yield potential in tomato plants.
- 2017: Scientists engineer disease-resistant rice without sacrificing yield.

- 2017: Blood stem cells grown in lab for the first time.
- 2017: Researchers at Sahlgrenska Academy in Sweden generated cartilage tissue by printing stem cells using a 3D-bioprinter.
- 2017: Two-way communication in brain-machine interface achieved for the first time.

Dr. Justin Sanchez, *Director, Biological Technologies Office: "I'm Justin Sanchez, Director of DARPA's Technology Office. Today I am really excited to share with you the new results on how we are working to directly interface machines with the human brain. A DARPA funded research team led by the University of Pittsburg has demonstrated for the first time ever in humans, to experience the sensation of touch through a robotic prosthetic arm connected directly to the brain. The volunteer, whose name is Nathan, underwent a surgery to have two microelectrode arrays placed in his sensory cortex. This is the region of the brain that is responsible for identifying tactile sensation such as pressure. Those electrodes were then connected by wire to a robotic hand and arm fitted with tactile sensors in its fingers."*

The technician is holding the hand and touching each finger testing if Nathan can in fact feel the sensation of touch.

Dr. Justin Sanchez: *"What you are seeing as the trials take place is as the researcher applies light pressure to the robotic fingers those physical sensations are converted into electrical signals that are fed directly back into Nathan's brain. Through this brain machine interface electrical signals are delivered as precise stimulation that his brain interprets as if his own fingers were being touched. Despite being blindfolded Nathan can identify with nearly a 100% accuracy which fingers on the robotic hand are being touched.*

What does this mean for the future of neurotechnology? DARPA has previously shown that a brain interface can be used to direct the movements of a robotic arm. Now with this new development of adding sensation by directly sending signals from the robotic hand back into the brain, we have closed the loop between human and machine. At

DARPA we are always pushing the boundaries of what is possible. We view Neurotechnology as one of the next great frontiers enabling new ways for humans to interact with each other and with the world."[32]

- 2017: First CAR T Therapy for cancer is approved, that is if treatments prove as effective as expected, will likely replace chemotherapy as the primary form of cancer treatment, and has demonstrated complete ablation of cancerous tumors in as little as 10 days.
- 2018: The first human trials for CRISPR are officially approved.
- TODAY: Today, biotechnology is being used in countless areas including agriculture, bioremediation and forensics, where DNA fingerprinting is a common practice. Industry and medicine alike use the techniques of DNA modification. Genetic manipulation has been the primary reason that biology is now seen as the science of the future and biotechnology as one of the leading industries. But the journey of genome engineering is far from finished. With discoveries burgeoning across the globe, human health and disease, along with areas such as agriculture, energy, animal husbandry, and environmental science among others all stand to benefit enormously from these strides forward. As CRISPR becomes as easy a tool to implement as a hammer to nail, the world as we know it is continually altered by the efforts of scientists who drive genome engineering technology forward and could potentially change everything as we know it forever.

"Imagine you were alive back in the 1980's and were told that computers would soon take over everything, from shopping to dating and the stock market. Zillions of people would be connected by a kind of web. That you would own a handheld device with magnitude more powerful than super computers. It would seem absurd, but then all of it happened. Science fiction became our reality and we don't even think about it.

We are at a similar point today with genetic engineering. So, let's talk about it. Where it came from, what we are doing right now and about a recent breakthrough that will change how we live and what we perceive as normal forever.

A very short and incomplete history of Genetic Modification

Humans have been engineering life for thousands of years. Through selective breeding we strengthened useful traits in plants and animals. We became very good at this but never truly understood how it works until we discovered the code of life, Deoxyribonucleic acid, DNA, a complex molecule that guides the growth, development, function and reproduction of everything alive. Information is encoded in the structure of the molecule. Four nucleotides are paired and make up a code that carries instructions. Change the instructions and you change the being carrying it.

As soon as DNA was discovered, people tried to tinker with it. In the 1960's, scientists bombarded plants with radiation to cause random mutations in the genetic code. The idea was to get a useful plant variation by pure chance. Sometimes it actually worked too. In the 1970's scientists inserted DNA snippets into bacteria, plants, and animals to study and modify them for research, medicine, agriculture, and for fun.

The earliest genetically modified animal was born in 1974, making mice a standard tool for research, saving millions of lives. In the 1980's, we got commercial. The first patent was given for a microbe engineered to absorb oil. Today we produce many chemicals by means of engineered life, like lifesaving clotting factors, growth hormones, and insulin. All things we had to harvest from the organs of animals before that.

The first food modified in the lab went on sale in 1994; the Flavr Savr Tomato, a tomato given a much longer shelf life where an extra gene that suppresses the build-up of a rotting enzyme. But GM food and the controversy surround them deserve a video of their own.

Genetically Modified Organism

In the 1990's, there was also a brief foray into human engineering. To treat maternal infertility, babies were made that carried genetic information from 3 humans. Making them the first humans ever to have 3 genetic parents. Today there are super muscled pigs, fast-growing salmon, featherless chickens, and see through frogs. On the fun side, we made things glow in the dark. Fluorescent zebrafish are available for as little as ten dollars.

All of this is already very impressive, but until recently gene editing was extremely expensive, complicated, and took a long time to do. This has now changed with a revolutionary new technology now entering the scene – CRISPR. Overnight the costs of engineering have shrunk by ninety nine percent. Instead of a year, it takes a few weeks to conduct experiments, and basically everybody with a lab can do it. It's hard to get across how big a technical revolution CRISPR is. It literally has the potential to change humanity forever. Why did this sudden revolution happen and how does it work?

The Oldens War on Earth

Bacteria and viruses have been fighting since the dawn of life. So-called bacteriophages or phages hunt bacteria. In the ocean, phages kill forty percent of them every single day. Phages do this by inserting their own genetic code into the bacteria and taking them over to use them as factories. The bacteria tried to resist but failed most the time because their protection tools are too weak. But sometimes bacteria survive an attack. Only if they do so can they activate their most effective antivirus system; they save a part of the virus DNA in their own genetic code in a DNA archive called CRISPR. Here it's stored safely until it's needed.

When the virus attacks again, the bacterium quickly makes an RNA copy from the DNA archive and arms a secret weapon – a protein called CAS9. The protein now scans the bacterium's inside for signs of the virus invader by comparing every bit of DNA it finds to the sample from the archive. When it finds a 100 percent perfect match, it's activated and cuts out the virus DNA, making it useless, protecting the bacterium against the attack. What's special is the CAS9 is very precise, almost like a DNA surgeon.

The revolution began when scientists figured out that the CRISPR system is programmable. You can just give it a copy of DNA you want to modify and put the system into a living cell. If the old techniques of genetic manipulation were like a map, CRISPR is like a GPS system. Aside from being precise, cheap, and easy, CRISPR offers the ability to edit live cells, to switch genes on and off, and target and study particular DNA sequences. It also works for every type of cell: microorganisms, plants, animals, or humans.

But despite the revolution CRISPR is for science, it's still just a first-generation tool. More precise tools are already being created and used as we speak.

The End of Disease?

In 2015, scientists used CRISPR to cut the HIV virus out of living cells from patients in the lab, proving that it was possible. Only about a year later, they carried out a larger scale project with rats that had the HIV virus in basically all of their body cells. By simply injecting CRISPR into the rat's tails, they were able to remove more than 50% of the virus from cells all over the body. In a few decades a CRISPR therapy might cure HIV and other retroviruses, viruses that hide inside human DNA like herpes, could be eradicated this way. CRISPR could also defeat one of our worst enemies – cancer.

Cancer occurs when cells refuse to die and keep multiplying while concealing themselves from the immune system. CRISPR gives us the means to edit your immune cells and make them better cancer hunters. Getting rid of cancer might eventually mean getting just a couple of injections of a few thousand of your own cells that have been engineered in the lab to heal you for good.

The first clinical trial for a CRISPR cancer treatment on human patients was approved in early 2016 in the US. Not even a month later, Chinese scientists announced that they would treat lung cancer patients with immune cells modified with CRISPR in August 2016. Things are picking up pace quickly.

And then there are genetic diseases. There are thousands of them, and they range from mildly annoying to deadly or entail decades of suffering. With a powerful tool like CRISPR, we may be able to end this. Over 3,000 genetic diseases are caused by a single incorrect letter in your DNA. We are already building a modified version of CAS9 that is made to change just a single letter, fixing the disease in the cell. In a decade or two, we could possibly cure thousands of diseases forever. But all of these medical applications have one thing in common: they are limited to the individual and die with them, except if you use them on reproductive cells or very early embryos.

But CRISPR can and probably will be used for much more; the creation of modified humans – designer babies – and will mean gradual, but irreversible changes to the human gene pool.

Designer Babies

The means to edit the genome of a human embryo already exists. Though the technology is still in its early stages, it has already been attempted twice. In 2015 and 2016, Chinese scientists experimented with human embryos and were partially successful on their second attempt. They showed the enormous challenges we still face in gene editing embryos, but also that scientists are working on solving them. This is like the computer in the 1970's. There will be better computers. Regardless of your personal take on genetic engineering, it will affect you. Modified humans could alter the genome of our entire species, because their engineered traits will be passed on to their children and could spread over generations, slowly modifying the whole gene pool of humanity.

It will start slowly. The first designer babies will not be overly designed. It's most likely that they will be created to eliminate a deadly genetic disease running in a family. As the technology progresses and gets more refined, more and more people may argue that not using genetic modification is unethical, because it condemns children to preventable suffering and death and denies them the cure.

But as soon as the first engineered kid is born, a door is opened that can't be closed anymore. Early on, vanity traits will mostly be left alone. But as genetic modifications become more accepted and our knowledge of our genetic code enhances, the temptation will grow. If you make your offspring immune to Alzheimer's, why not also give them an enhanced metabolism? Why not throw in perfect eyesight? How about height or muscular structure? Full hair? How about giving your child the gift of extraordinary intelligence? Huge changes are made as a result of the personal decisions of millions of individuals that accumulate. This is a slippery slope. Modified humans could become the new standard.

But as engineering becomes more normal and our knowledge improves, we could solve the single biggest mortality risk factor: aging. Two-thirds of the 150,000 people who died today will die of age-related causes. Currently we think aging is caused by the accumulation of damage to our cells, like DNA breaks and the systems responsible for fixing those wearing off over time. But there are also genes that directly affect aging. A combination of genetic engineering and other therapy could stop or slow down aging, maybe even reverse it.

Lobster

We know from nature that there are animals immune to aging. Maybe we could even borrow a few genes for ourselves. Some scientists even think biological aging could be something that eventually just stops being a thing. We would still die at some point, but instead of doing so in hospitals at age 90, we might be able to spend a few thousand years with our loved ones. Research into this is in its infancy, and many scientists are rightly skeptical about the end of aging. The challenges are enormous and maybe it is unachievable, but it is conceivable the people alive today might be the first to profit from effective anti-aging therapy. All we might need is for someone to convince a smart billionaire to make it their next problem to solve.

On a bigger scale, we certainly could solve many problems by having a modified population. Engineered humans might be better equipped to cope with high-energy food, eliminating many diseases of civilization like obesity. In possession of a modified immune system, with a library of potential threats, we might become immune to most diseases that haunt us today. Even further into the future, we could engineer humans to be equipped for extended space travel and to cope with different conditions on other planets which would be extremely helpful in keeping us alive in our hostile universe.

A Few Grains of Salt

Still a few major challenges await us; some technological, some ethical. Many of you will feel uncomfortable and fear that we will create a world in which we will reject non-perfect humans and pre-select features and qualities based on our idea of what's healthy. The thing is we are already living in this world. Tests for dozens of genetic diseases or complications have become standard for pregnant women in much of the world. Often the mere suspicion of a genetic defect can lead to the end of a pregnancy.

Take Down syndrome for example, one of the most common genetic defects. In Europe, about 92 percent of all pregnancies where it's detected are terminated. The decision to terminate a pregnancy is incredibly personal, but it's important to acknowledge the reality that we are pre-selecting humans based on medical conditions. There is also no use in pretending this will change, so we have to act carefully and respectfully as we advance the technology and can make more and more selections.

As powerful as CRISPR is – and it is, it's not infallible yet. Wrong edits still happen as well as unknown errors that can occur anywhere in the DNA and might go unnoticed. The gene edit might achieve the desired result – disabling a disease, but also might accidentally trigger unwanted changes. We just don't know enough yet about the complex interplay of our genes to avoid unpredictable consequences. Working on accuracy and monitoring methods is a major concern as the first human trials begin. And since we've discussed a possible positive future, there are darker visions too.

Imagine what a state like North Korea could do if they embraced genetic engineering. Could a state cement its rule forever by forcing gene editing on their subjects? What would stop a totalitarian regime from engineering an army of modified super soldiers? It is doable in theory. The technology really is that powerful.

While this might be a tempting reason to ban genetic editing and related research, that would certainly be a mistake. Banning human genetic engineering would only lead to the science wandering off to a place with jurisdiction and rules that we are uncomfortable with. Only by participating can we make sure that further research is guided by caution, reason, oversight, and transparency.

Conclusion

Do you feel uncomfortable now? Most of us have something wrong with them. In the future that lies ahead of us, would we have been allowed to exist? The technology is certainly a bit scary, but we have a lot to gain and genetic engineering might just be a step in the natural evolution of intelligent species in the universe. We might end disease. We could extend our life expectancy by centuries and travel to the stars. There is no need to think small when it comes to this topic. Whatever your opinion on genetic engineering, the future is approaching no matter what. What has been insane science fiction is about to become our new reality, a reality full of opportunities and challenges."[33]

Gee, I wonder if this was the same historical pattern and same Pollyannaish Utopian attitude that the people of Noah's day had when they were doing these same kinds of experiments with hybrid modifications? It'll fix all disease! Humanity will be better! We'll live longer, hundreds and hundreds of years, maybe even longer than that. And yet people still scoff today at the Genesis account of people living long lifespans even back then. Let's revisit that text.

Genesis 5:1-32 "This is the written account of Adam's line. When God created man, He made him in the likeness of God. He created them male and female and blessed them. And when they were created, he called them 'man.' When Adam had lived 130 years, he had a son in his own likeness, in his own image; and he named him Seth. After Seth was born, Adam lived 800 years and had other sons and daughters. Altogether, Adam lived 930 years, and then he died. When Seth had lived 105 years, he became the father of Enosh. And after he became the father of Enosh, Seth lived 807 years and had other sons and daughters. Altogether, Seth lived 912 years, and then he died. When Enosh had lived 90 years, he became the father of Kenan. And after he became the father of Kenan, Enosh lived 815 years and had other sons and daughters. Altogether, Enosh lived 905 years, and then he died. When Kenan had lived 70 years, he became the father of Mahalalel. And after he became the father of Mahalalel, Kenan lived 840 years and had other sons and daughters. Altogether, Kenan lived 910 years, and then he died. When Mahalalel had lived 65 years, he became the father of Jared. And after he became the father of Jared, Mahalalel lived 830 years and had other sons and daughters. Altogether, Mahalalel lived 895 years, and then he died. When Jared had lived 162 years, he became the father of Enoch. And after he became the father of Enoch, Jared lived 800 years and had other sons and daughters. Altogether, Jared lived 962 years, and then he died. When Enoch had lived 65 years, he became the father of Methuselah. And after he became the father of Methuselah, Enoch walked with God 300 years and had other sons and daughters. Altogether, Enoch lived 365 years. Enoch walked with God; then he was no more, because God took him away. When Methuselah had lived 187 years, he became the father of Lamech. And after he became the father of Lamech, Methuselah lived 782 years and had other sons and daughters. Altogether, Methuselah lived 969 years, and then he died. When Lamech had lived 182 years, he had a son. He named him Noah and said, 'He will comfort us in the labor and painful toil of our hands caused by the ground the LORD has cursed.' After Noah was born, Lamech lived 595 years and had other sons and daughters. Altogether, Lamech lived 777 years, and then he died. After Noah was 500 years old, he became the father of Shem, Ham and Japheth."

Doesn't sound so farfetched anymore, does it? People living super long lives. That was the original creation plan from God before the gene pool became infected by sin and rebellion leading to a shortening of lives among many other problems we have to deal with today unfortunately. Yet once again, here we have mankind rebelling and sinning against God again, just like in the Genesis account, with all this hybrid technology, trying to create this false utopia without God, trying to play God, trying to be like God, including, the extension of human lifespans. When will we ever learn? God forbids it all, but we rebel again, thinking just like in Noah's day, we know better than God.

And yet, as it was the first time around when this happened, humanity today is about to pay a horrible price. The judgment of God is coming again. Why? Because He clearly warned us of never repeating this type of genetic altering. It's also a sign that the Second Coming of Jesus Christ is fast approaching because as He said, "As it was in the Days of Noah, so shall it be at the Coming of the Son of Man."

In fact, it's not just God who is warning us of this type of genetic altering behavior, so is the press and the scientific community. Not everyone is on the bandwagon with this Utopian approach. Even certain sectors of our society today admit that this behavior of "playing God" with this type of technology could actually destroy us with irreversible negative side effects.

So now let's move on to the dangers that this hybrid genetic technology poses to all of mankind, even from the human perspective.

Chapter Three

The Dangers of Hybrids

Even as far back as the 1970's, the scientific community was already concerned about the possible horrific irreversible side effects of genetic modifications performed on various lifeforms. In fact, other fields of science had restrictions and limitations placed upon their research due to the obvious dangers they posed to mankind, like nuclear physics for example. I mean, we all know nuclear bombs and nuclear weaponry are a serious danger to mankind. Yet, for some reason, no one seemed to put a lid of regulatory control upon genetic engineering, leading to the nightmare scenario we are dealing with today, as this article admits.

"It was natural that 140 scientists gathered in 1975 for an unprecedented conference. They were worried about what people called 'recombinant DNA,' the manipulation of the source code of life.

It had been just 22 years since James Watson, Francis Crick, and Rosalind Franklin described what DNA was.

Preeminent genetic researchers like David Baltimore, then at MIT, went to Asilomar California to grapple with the implications of being able to decrypt and reorder genes. It was a God-like power – to plug genes from one living thing into another. Used wisely, it had the potential to save millions of lives. But the scientists also knew their creations might slip out of their control.

By 1975, other fields of science – like physics – were subject to broad restrictions. Hardly anyone was allowed to work on atomic bombs. But biology was different. Biologists still let the winding road of research guide their steps. On occasion, regulatory bodies had acted retrospectively – after Nuremberg, Tuskegee, and the human radiation experiments, external enforcement entities had told biologists they weren't allowed to do that bad thing again.

And yet, earlier this year, researchers joined together again for another California conference, this one at the Carneros Inn in Napa Valley. 'It was a feeling of déjà vu, one researcher stated. 'Here we are again, gathered with some of the smartest scientists on earth to talk about the implications of genome engineering.'

The stakes, however, have changed. Everyone at the Napa meeting had access to a gene-editing technique called Crispr-Cas9. It proved to be a programmable machine for DNA cutting. It makes it easy, cheap, and fast to move genes around – any genes, in any living thing, from bacteria to people.

Using the three-year-old technique, researchers have already reversed mutations that cause blindness, stopped cancer cells from multiplying, and made cells impervious to the virus that causes AIDS.

Agronomists have rendered wheat invulnerable to killer fungi like powdery mildew, hinting at engineered staple crops that can feed a population of 9 billion. Bioengineers have used CRISPR to alter the DNA of yeast so that it consumes plant matter and excretes ethanol, promising an end to reliance on petrochemicals.

The technique is revolutionary, and like all revolutions, it's perilous. CRISPR goes well beyond anything the Asilomar conference discussed. It could at last allow genetics researchers to conjure everything anyone has ever worried they would – designer babies, invasive mutants, species-specific bioweapons, and a dozen other apocalyptic sci-fi tropes.

It brings with it all-new rules for the practice of research in the life sciences. But no one knows what the rules are – or who will be the first to break them. Pick your creature, pick your gene, and you can bet someone somewhere is giving it a go.

When I asked one researcher for his most nightmarish CRISPR scenario, he mutters something about weapons and then stops short. He says he hopes to take the specifics of the idea, whatever it is, to his grave.

But thousands of other scientists are working on CRISPR. Not all of them will be as cautious. "[1]

In other words, they're not going to be restricted in their behavior and experimentation and it's going to spiral out of control. And that's precisely the problem. There is largely no cautionary oversight in this field, let alone consistent regulation across the planet. Not only has our modern atheistic evolutionary mindset permeated the scientific community causing them to reject the idea, notion, and existence of God, but neither are they listening to God and His warnings in the Bible to never go down this route again.

Jeremiah 11:7-8 "I warned them again and again, saying, 'Obey me.' But they did not listen or pay attention; instead, they followed the stubbornness of their evil hearts."

2 Chronicles 24:20 "This is what God says: 'Why do you disobey the LORD's commands? You will not prosper."

1 Samuel 12:15 "But if you do not obey the LORD, and if you rebel against His commands, His hand will be against you, as it was against your ancestors."

And yet, despite these warnings, once again mankind is in rebellion to God's commands. Now that the modern scientific community has the genetic tools to "play god" themselves so easily, they are not only launching into this forbidden behavior again, but with full abandonment and little to no oversight.

Let me repeat the danger again. There is virtually no regulation controlling what these scientific communities around the world will do and frankly are already doing as we speak, that is, genetically modifying bacteria, plants, animals, even humans, you name it, to their hearts content. This is not only dangerous, but it really is leading towards the soon coming judgment of God. He put a stop to this wicked behavior once, He's going to do it again. And dare I say, much sooner that people realize or even want to believe.

Now, as you have noticed, much of this dangerous genetic modifying behavior from the scientific community that is leading to an apocalyptic scenario really began to escalate right after the invention of CRISPR. As we saw in our previous History section of Genetic Engineering, learning about DNA and the Human Genome and formulating ideas of one day being able to modify genetic structures has been going on for quite some time. But it wasn't until the recent development of an invention called CRISPR that mankind really had the ability to actually pull off genetic modification so precisely and effectively.

Bloomberg Reports: *"Right now there is a very special mosquito flying around a laboratory in California that is carrying a genetic weapon. One that might be capable of wiping out one of the world's most deadly diseases, Malaria, which kills half a million people every year. All that suffering might end if we just open a window and let this creature out. But will we do it? The mosquito is just one project of thousands for a new gene editing tool called CRISPR that is absolutely transforming biological science."*

Mayo Clinic: *"In a document, if we suspect we've misspelled a word, we can use the find function to highlight the error and correct it or delete it. Within our DNA that function is taken on by a system call CRISPR/CAS9. CRISPR is short for Clustered Regularly Interspaced Short Palindromic Repeats. CRISPR consists of two components, the CAS9 protein that can cut DNA and a guide RNA that can recognize the sequence of DNA to be edited.*

It's only four years old but in preliminary lab experiments it's already been used to eliminate HIV, reverse mutations that cause blindness, and stop cancer. It can even one day be used to reverse human aging. More than a billion dollars has been invested and this really is just the beginning.

CRISPR works like a pair of DNA scissors. Geneticists programed a piece of RNA much like they would write a bit of software code and then guides the scissors to a very specific location on the genome. Snip, Snip and out goes any unwanted genes and in goes the good stuff. The breaks in the double helix heal automatically. This is true cut and paste genetics and it's making the science fiction of the decade know completely plausible today.

CRISPR shortens genetic work from years to weeks and reduces the cost of each experiment from more than $5,000 before CRISPR to less than $50 now. A person with a background in genetics can learn the basics in a day or two. The genome is now a dry erase board that anyone can scribble on.

The biggest quest that is holding the mosquito back is no longer about the science of what is possible, what is advisable. Are we really ready to take over the blueprints of life on earth? There isn't much time for debate. Soon some of the first human trials will use CRISPR based therapies to treat genetic diseases. A farm in North Carolina is preparing to raise CRISPR pigs in order to transplant their organs into humans. Dupont is already field-testing new versions of wheat and corn and by 2020 you can bet all sorts of subtly different fruits and vegetable and even meats will start showing up in your grocery store. CRISPR is the key to unlocking bioengineering. For better and maybe for worse."[2]

As you saw, the recent invention of the DNA cutting tool called CRISPR, really changed the game on genetic modifications. Not only was it cheaper and faster, making it much more feasible for DNA manipulation, but it's very precise and exacting, not to mention so easy to use that virtually anybody around the world with just a little pre-education on the technology can begin using it as a genetic modification tool themselves. And now, because of that, just about everything you can think of is being modified with CRISPR.

"CRISPR was co-discovered in 2012 by molecular biologist Professor Jennifer Doudna whose team at Berkeley, University of California were studying how bacteria defend themselves against viral infection. They are now among the world's most influential scientists.

The natural system they discovered can be used by biologists to make precise changes to any DNA. In fact, Doudna stated, 'Since we published our work four years ago laboratories around the world have adopted this technology for applications in animals, plants, humans, fungi, other bacteria: essentially any kind of organism they are studying.'

Some researchers have adapted the system to repress or activate genes; others, to make insertions. Uptake in labs has been so enthusiastic that CRISPR has become a verb, a la Google. People say, 'I'm going to CRISPR that.'

In fact, Doudna works with Berkeley-based Caribou Biosciences, whose motto is, 'engineering any genome, at any site, in any way.'"

And boy have they ever! Here are just a few examples.

PLANTS: *"It often takes years of careful cross-breeding for horticulturalists to turn flowers certain colors, but scientists can dig right in and change them at a genetic level much faster. Using the CRISPR-*

Cas9 gene-editing tool, scientists have changed the flowers of the Japanese morning glory from its usual violet color to a pure white, by disrupting a single gene.

Plant scientists are already using CRISPR and related technologies to reshape food crops in dramatic ways – editing wheat to reduce gluten, editing soybeans to produce a healthier oil, editing corn to produce higher yields, editing potatoes to store better (and not throw off a carcinogen when cooked).

In both industrial and academic labs, new editing tools are being developed that will have a profound impact on the foods all of us eat. Harry Klee, a tomato expert at the University of Florida, says that the perfect tomato for industry is one that exactly matches the size of a McDonald's hamburger.) As Klee puts it, 'there isn't a single crop that I know of in your produce aisle that is not drastically modified from what is out there in the wild.'

Don't like the look of those roses in your garden? One day you might be able to buy a spray that changes the color of their flowers by silencing certain genes. Companies like Monsanto are already developing gene-silencing sprays that get inside bugs and kill them by disabling vital genes."

Now, stop right there. If they can do that already for plants, could they also do that for animals or even humans? Is it really farfetched to think that these same industry leaders could likewise develop a gene-silencing spray and kill an entire population of people by disabling their vital genes? And what would that look like? What kind of gruesome scene would that be? Just exactly where does this nightmare scenario end? Could you turn people into Zombies? Could you really do something to alter their DNA structure where they look and act like real Zombies? Thinking like this makes you wonder why Zombie movies and Zombie shows are all the rage right now. Have you ever thought about that? People can't seem to get enough of them. Does Hollywood know something we don't know? In fact, if you do the research, there are some pretty strange documents floating around out there from various government entities about how to deal with a possible coming Zombie Apocalypse.

"In 2011, the CDC published a plan outlining how the public should equip themselves for and respond to a zombie apocalypse. 'Get a Kit, Make a Plan, Be Prepared' recommending that everyone keep a kit with 3 days of food and water, enough time to find a 'zombie-free refugee camp.'

Families were advised to establish a meeting place and evacuation plan to be able to flee to safety and avoid infection. A zombie invasion would be treated like an outbreak with the CDC conducting lab tests and controls, including quarantines and interviewing zombies (if possible) to determine the source of the infection and understand how it is transmitted. Later, the CDC inexplicably backtracked, claiming it 'does not know of a virus or condition that would reanimate the dead.'"

Pentagon Conplan 8888-1: *A Pentagon document, 'Conplan 8888-11 Counter-Zombie Dominance,' outlines the US government's zombie invasion response plan. Though created as a training thought experiment, the plan explicitly states that it is 'not designed as a joke' and has 3 objectives: protect humankind from zombies, eradicate zombie threats, and maintain order during a zombie attack.*

Several variants of zombie lifeforms are identified, including space, symbiont induced, radiation, and weaponized zombies. The plan concludes the only way to defeat a zombie is by 'concentration of all firepower to the head, specifically the brain.' The Pentagon alarmingly acknowledged that it currently has 'no ground combat forces capable of repelling a zombie assault' and that military command centers would likely be overrun 'within the first days of a zombie invasion.'"

IRS National Emergency Operations: *"The National Emergency Operations section of the IRS Internal Revenue Manual outlines its operations in an apocalyptic scenario. Should the IRS's facilities be compromised, a makeshift emergency operations center will be* *established wherever possible from which 'operations will be concentrated on collecting the taxes which will produce the greater revenue yield.' Surviving employees would be expected to assume any role necessary to resume tax collection within 30 days of an outbreak.*

The revenue will be essential for funding a robust zombie counterattack and eradication strategy by the US government. The manual anticipates poor people will be 'most adversely affected,' leaving the wealthy to continue paying taxes."

Mathematical modelling of Zombies: *"With his equation (bn) (S/N)Z=BSZ, Robert J. Smith created a mathematical model to determine the best zombie survival strategy, N representing total population, S the number of susceptible people, Z the zombies, and B the likelihood of transmission. Smith's 'catastrophizing' models determined that 'a zombie outbreak is likely to lead to the collapse of civilization.' He concluded that a popular method of combating zombies via quarantine would only 'delay the time to eradication of humans.' Should we quickly develop a cure for 'zombieism,' survival is possible but in the end humans will 'only exist in low numbers.' According to Smith, 'the most effective way to contain the rise of the undead' is through force – 'hit hard and hit often'"[3]*

And is this one of the types of biological weapons that the previous researcher mentioned earlier that he said could be used on mankind, but he was personally taking it to his grave? Makes you wonder doesn't it? It also makes you realize why God said not to mess with this stuff. Stop trying to play God! You're not God and you'll mess it up every time! Why are you doing this? Do you really think you will prosper?

But let's continue. What else are the geneticists already doing with CRISPR?

ANIMALS: *"Researchers are looking at ways to not just alter mosquitos with CRISPR, so they don't carry malaria, but also even modify elephants to bring back woolly mammoths. More whimsically, the technology could be used to create, say, a unicorn, or a pig with wings.*

CRISPR/Cas9 makes it possible for nearly any scientist to edit DNA in nearly any cell. In the last couple of years, scientists have used it to edit animal embryos, including an experiment that proved it was possible to create primates with customized versions of genes involved in immune function and metabolism."

Now hold on a minute there. Is this why we're also seeing a resurgence of the *Planet of the Apes* movies that originally came out in the late 1960's and early 70's, you know, back when the geneticists were originally meeting in Asilomar to discuss the future dangers of this DNA altering technology? That was right about the same time frame you know. But of all times for these movies to appear again on the scene, it's now when they actually have the technology through CRISPR to pull it off. Read this from the *Planet of the Apes* trailer and you tell me if it's just a science fiction movie premise anymore.

Trailer from the Planet of the Apes: *The scene opens in a lab where a researcher is reaching for a large test tube on a conveyor belt. One researcher says to the other, "We are talking about huge potential for millions of people." In the conference room the speaker says, "Our therapy enables the brain to repair itself. We call it cured." Out in the hall one researcher stops the speaker and warns him saying, "I want you to stop testing these things asap."*

But the researcher (James Franco) opens a box and inside is a baby monkey. He says, "I have tested one subject and I want to make sure it's stable." Months later a little girl is playing in the yard and looks up at the window next door and there is a large monkey looking down at her.

"I designed the 1/12th repair, but Caesar has gone way beyond that. His skills far exceed that of his human counterpart," the researcher reports but his partner replies, "This is all wrong, Will." But he replies, "It works."

Later, as they are taking Caesar out in the woods she asks, "What about Caesar?" They are watching him climb to the highest tree. Then back at the lab he is confronted once again. "That chimp is company property!"

Now he is concerned. "He hasn't spent any time with other chimps." Caesar is put in a cage in a room full of other chimps. They are screaming, jumping and climbing on their cages. He feels so bad that Caesar has to be put in there, but his boss tells him, "they are not people you know."

"He's trying to control things that are not meant to be controlled," his partner tells him showing great concern. Soon Caesar is breaking out of his cage, getting the test tubes that had originally been used on him, making him who he is, and he throws them to the other chimps. Now they are contaminated.

"Put those apes down!" he is told but he replies, "You have no idea what you are dealing with." Caesar understands what is going on and turns all the apes out of their cages and onto the streets. They have invaded the city, into homes, totally uncontrolled. The researcher is now trying to find him calling his name to try to stop this rampage. But nothing is going to stop them. They now have control of the city.[4]

Based on current technology, that really could happen people, and a lot sooner than you think! But speaking of people, they're also already doing this genetic modification on you and me with CRISPR. Here's just a few of those examples.

PEOPLE: *"CRISPR may be used to repair a gene that has a deficient product, such as an enzyme or receptor, or alter code that merely suggests of risk. Ideas on how to use it change hourly. The method is here to last.*

The ethics will only get more fraught. With thousands of labs using the technology, it seemed inevitable that someone would try it on human embryos.

Proponents expect that CRISPR will change medical care in terms of genetic diseases and will upend existing markets and create entirely new approaches to care that the current health system can't anticipate. If you can repair a defect with a one-time therapy, you wipe out the existing market for treating the condition and scale back related doctor and hospital visits.

And if you can cut out a precise part of a gene, at some point you might be able to replace it with something else – turning the infection-fighting T-cells into super soldiers that can eradicate cancer, for example.

Some of those most deeply involved in the research are given to ambitious speculation about, for instance, engineering people to be virus-proof, or to have enhanced traits of various kinds, which would also be inheritable. The implications of this are profound.

At the end of the day, there's so much potential with the CRISPR platform to treat so many diseases and have a tremendous effect on the patients."

Well, that sounds so wonderful, doesn't it? That's the Utopian dream that the scientific community is trying to pitch to you and I to accept all this genetic altering technology.

CBS this Morning Reports: *"With this story revolutionary technology that can edit genetic mistakes is getting attention and scrutiny this morning, CRISPR could help rid us of diseases like Cystic Fibrosis, Muscular Dystrophy and even HIV and cancer. Think about that. What is CRISPR?"*

Jennifer Doudna: *"CRISPR is first of all an acronym which stands for Clustered Regularly Interspaced Short Palindromic Repeats, a huge mouthful if you ever use the acronym CRISPR."*

CBS News: *"So, I'm sorry what is CRISPR again?"*

"Geneticist, Jennifer Doudna is asked that question a lot. A researcher and professor at UC Berkley, Doudna has become a spokesperson for a gene editing technology she is credited with developing. That mouthful known as CRISPR."

"I've heard it compared to, essentially, to a film editor, slicing a bit of film."

Jennifer Doudna: *"I would say that is a great analogy."*

CBS News: *"How does that work then?"*

Jennifer Doudna: *"Well, think about a film strip and you see a particular segment of the film that you want to replace and if you had a film splicer, you would go in and literally cut it out piece it back together, maybe with a new clip. Imagine being able to do that in the genetic code, the code of life. You can go in and snip out a piece and replace it with something that corrects a mutation that would cause disease."*

CBS News: *"That's incredible!"*

"CRISPR has generated immense excitement because it's fast, cheap, and can cut and paste genetic code with great precision. It used to take months or years to alter a single gene. Now it can be done in a matter of days."

"Could it end cancer?"

Jennifer Doudna: *"What I am excited about there is the potential to use the CRISPR technology to program a patient's immune system to recognize tumor cells in a precise way."*

CBS News: *"Could it cure, at some point, or treat any disease?"*

Jennifer Doudna: *"Any disease that has a genetic basis is something that could be treated using the CRISPR technology."*

CBS News: *"And imagine, Doudna says we can expect to see clinical application through CRISPR within the next few years."*

Jennifer Doudna: *"This is no longer science fiction."*

CBS News: *"So this is so exciting, tell us what has been done so far in animals."*

"CRISPR has been used to design plants with useful traits in them, so it has already been used in agriculture. They have used it in mice to cure a rare liver disorder that was caused by single genetic mutation. Researchers in China have used this to produce super muscled dogs. We are the beginning of a sort of promise, this is the future of disease, this is gene editing."[5]

And as you just heard that so-called Utopia of Gene Editing with CRISPR technology eradicating virtually all diseases and making all kinds of supposed positive changes in all different kinds of lifeforms is here now! Isn't that wonderful? Actually, no, because as it turns out, the exact same community is already admitting that CRISPR technology can also very quickly move from a so-called modern-day Utopia to a freakish nightmare scenario in a heartbeat.

"Some of the enthusiasm turns to concern, though, when it comes to making DNA changes that would be passed on to future generations.

It is already known that CRISPR can sometimes change genes other than those intended as targets for editing, and of course that could lead to unwanted side effects.

A recent commentary in the journal Nature laid out a variety of potential problems. Mistakes might occur in the editing process that could result in severe birth defects.

Successful edits could affect other parts of the genome that were meant to be left alone. It's impossible to get consent from future generations who might inherit an altered gene.

We have the earth-shattering technology in our hands – but even its inventors worry about its awesome power to alter our genetic future.

Scientists say that CRISPR-Cas9 may soon allow them to perform miraculous fixes to eliminate or alter mutations that cause everything from some cancers to Parkinson's disease.

More nefariously, terrorists or the military might create pathogens that could harm far more people than splitting the atom has so far. Or, an accident could occur unintentionally.

Now some really bright high school student could conduct an experiment with CRISPR-Cas9. Let's say he decides to modify a mosquito to do some good, and he accidentally creates a super mosquito that gets in the environment and becomes like kudzu.

(Kudzu, 'the plant that ate the South,' was imported from Japan in the early 20th century to control erosion in the Southeastern U.S. and quickly took over, choking off native plants and driving everyone crazy even today.)

Many nations have weak or nonexistent controls, which is why the authors appeal to scientists everywhere to avoid germline experiments with CRISPR-Cas9 on their own.

Yet, our current laws wouldn't stop an ambitious scientist from using CRISPR to modify the germline. In fact, it's already being tried in China."

In other words, the nightmare of genetic modification has already started. But you might be thinking, "Well surely they're going to be putting a lid on this. I'm mean somebody somewhere is going to regulate this on a global scale to keep it from spiraling out of control." No, you still don't understand. It's "already happening" around the globe with little or no regulation. The U.S. and Europe may have put some restrictions on this Gene Editing Technology, but the bulk of the planet has not, including China.

CBS News: *"Along with CRISPR's promise comes some fears of its perils like embryo editing that could lead to designer babies. What is the dark side of this technology?"*

Jennifer Doudna: *"One of them is of course is making changes to human embryos, which become permanent. So, we are talking about something that would affect human evolution."*

CBS News: *"You could have an instance where a lab is creating lots of human embryos just for the sake of experimenting on genome editing on them. Right?"*

Jennifer Doudna: *"If you are asking me if that could be done technically, the answer is it could. Could it be done with current regulations in place, certainly not in the US or Europe."*

CBS News: *"There are still a lot of countries besides the U.S. and Europe."*

Jennifer Doudna: *"Well yes, science is global and there are a lot of different cultural viewpoints on that kind of application."*

CBS News: *"In April, Chinese scientists reported using CRISPR to edit the disease genome of human embryos for the first time, it sparked concern worldwide."*[6]

So again, this genetic modification nightmare, even in humans, has already started. China is leading the way. But even here in the U.S. we assume that the powers that be, who are supposed to have regulations and our best interests at heart would never use this type of genetic modification technology on us, the American public, for nefarious purposes. Yet, the facts are, it's already being done in a variety of ways. Let me show you just a few examples.

"Epigenetic modifications are simply modification of genes rather than alteration of the genetic code itself. Any outside stimulus that can be detected by the body has the potential to cause epigenetic modifications, from chemicals to lifestyle factors to lived experiences:

- ***Bisphenol A (BPA)*** *is an additive in some plastics that has been linked to cancer and other diseases and has already been removed from consumer products in some countries. BPA seems to exert its effects through a number of mechanisms, including epigenetic modifications.*
- *The beneficial effects of exercise have been known for generations, but the mechanisms are still surprisingly hazy. However, there's mounting evidence that changes to the pattern of epigenetic marks in muscle and fatty tissue are involved.*
- ***Childhood abuse*** *and other forms of early trauma also seem to affect DNA methylation patterns, which may help to explain the poor health that many victims of such abuse face throughout adulthood.*
- *We've known for some time that certain environmental factors experienced by adult mice can be passed on to their offspring via epigenetic mechanisms. The best example is a gene called agouti, which is methylated in normal brown mice. However, mice with an unmethylated agouti gene are yellow and obese, despite being genetically essentially identical to their skinny brown relatives. Altering the pregnant mother's diet can modify the ratio of brown to yellow offspring:* ***folic acid*** *results in more brown pups, while* ***BPA*** *results in more yellow pups.*
- *Research on the epigenetic inheritance of addictive behavior is less advanced but does look quite promising. Studies in rats recently demonstrated that exposure to THC (the active compound in cannabis) during adolescence can prime future offspring to display signs of predisposition to heroin addiction.*

Gee, aren't you glad Marijuana is being legalized all over the place? I don't think so! We have yet to see the long-term damage that it's going to cause!

- *Studies of humans whose ancestors survived through periods of **starvation** in Sweden and the Netherlands suggest that the effects of famine on epigenetics and health can pass through at least three generations. Nutrient deprivation in a recent ancestor seems to prime the body for diabetes and cardiovascular problems, a response that may have evolved to mitigate the effects of any future famines in the same geographic area.*

Now that's just how easy it is to change your genetic structure in our world today without purposely trying. The difference now is that people really are "purposely" trying to change our genetic makeup. And again, some of them are doing it without our knowledge, for nefarious purposes, including with vaccines.

Mike Adams, The Health Ranger: *"Breaking news about vaccines. News that will blow your mind. It will knock your socks off. An organization out of Italy has completed the genome sequencing of some of the proteins found in common vaccines such as MMR vaccines. Now we have warned you for years here at Brighteon.com that aborted human fetal tissue is routinely used in vaccines. It's openly listed by the CDC and the FDA and the vaccine manufacturers, I'll show you the documents here in just a second.*

For many, many years a lot of people just couldn't believe it. They could not believe that there were aborted human fetal cells used in vaccines even though it was openly admitted by the vaccine companies and of course the establishment tried to sensor everybody in order to make sure the news never came out. Well, this organization in Italy named Corvelva has completed the genome sequencing of these proteins in the vaccines. Guess what they found. It's the complete genetic code of a male human being. An entire human being's gene sequence is found in the cells that are put into the vaccines.

They are injecting you with the DNA sequencing of an entire individual human being who was murdered. An analysis of those genes has found an incredibly high rate of abnormality in the genetic code, including 560 genes that are linked to cancer. So just to summarize the breaking news here which of course you won't find reported anywhere in the lying fake news media. New York Times, Washington Post, they would just bury the story and hope you would never see it. That is why they censor us by the way because we are the only ones, we the independent media, we are the only ones in the industry that is reporting that information. Children's Health Defense has reported it, we are reporting it, you will see this covered on Infowars, you will see it covered across independent media but never ever in the mainstream media and quite frankly not even on Breitbart.com. They won't touch this topic. They don't tell the truth about vaccines, not even Breitbart.

But here's the truth. You can go to the CDC's website right now, with these documents, you can search CDC.gov and you can find mentions of these aborted human fetal tissue cell lines which are called MRC-5. MRC-5, according to the CDC is used in Varivax vaccines. It is used in Hepatitis vaccines, and it's used in Varicella vaccines as well, and that is CDC.gov. You can go to the FDA's website and you can find admissions of this. These documents here are from the FDA. They are showing another vaccine insert sheet, in this case it is from Varivax vaccine and it openly talks about MRC-5 cell lines that are used in the vaccines.

In fact, here is a sentence saying, 'This product also contains residual components of the MRC-5 cells including DNA and protein and trace quantities of neomycin and bovine cell serum from MRC-5 culture media.' What they are not saying, and they are admitting it right there, but only if you know the code words, what they are saying here is that they took aborted human fetal tissue cells from an aborted baby and they cloned them and they put them into the vaccines. And it's openly admitted. Here's a vaccine called Priorix-Tetra, this is an MMR vaccine for measles, mumps, rubella and varicella. And this says, 'each virus strain is separately produced in either chick embryo cells (mumps and measles) or MRC5 human diploid cells (rubella and varicella).'

It's right here, it's submitted by GlaxoSmithKline from the GlaxoSmithKline website. Now we have Children's Health Defense that is run by Robert F. Kennedy Jr. and an incredible staff there, that has gone public with new data showing aborted fetal cells in vaccines. This is summarizing the new study that has just come out from this Italian science organization Corvelva that has found the entire human genome sequence of a male fetus with 560 genes known to be associated with various forms of cancer. It's in the vaccines. They are injecting you with the entire genetic blueprint of another human being who was murdered and who has hundreds of genes linked to cancer. Now you tell me, why is this being covered up? Why does this vaccine industry have absolute legal immunity, when no one can sue them? Why is there no inquiry into this? Why is there no Republican, no Democrat, no one will talk about this?

Except Robert F. Kennedy, Jr., who by the way deserves the medal of freedom award. President Trump should award this guy something big. I mean, RFK Jr. should get the Nobel Peace Prize, not Greta Thunderpants or whatever her name is, the hysteric, lunatic child. It should be RFK Jr., whose father, by the way, was murdered by the deep state, but that's another story. RFK Jr. is telling the truth about vaccines right now. He is on to this and this Italian laboratory has broken the news. Now this is just the short version. I'm giving you a very quick overview of this report right now because I need to get this video out to you quickly. I am going to record a much longer more detailed discussion on this and release that video next week, on Natural News.com.

There are things about this that you cannot even imagine, the level of horror of what has taken place. For example, did you know that the aborted human baby that was murdered to get these cell lines, the cells that are put into these vaccines, that the mother of that baby was a psychiatric patient, she was insane. So, you have the murdered baby of an insane mother infested with cancer cells replicated for decades, since the 1960's, over and over and over again, and then deliberately put into vaccines that touch all of our children. Every child in America is injected with this aborted human fetal tissue cell line. It is the genetic imprinting of our children.

Every child that is vaccinated is imprinted with the genetic code for cancer. And the cancer industry is a multi-billion-dollar industry. And the psychiatric drug industry is a multi-billion-dollar industry. And remember that some of what is passed on from generation to generation is not just purely genetic but epigenetic. How to say this. There are elements of the mental illness and the violence of the murder and the suffering of that child that was murdered for his cells, elements of that continue to be expressed through the epigenetic factors of these genes that are injected into your children. You wonder why we have this exposure of cancer and mental illness and insanity and suffering and craziness in our world. For the last couple of decades, why does it keep skyrocketing, guess what, everybody is being injected with mental illness, with hatred, with violence, with murder, with aborted babies, with cancer genes, it's all part of the plan. Folks, this is what I have been trying to warn you about.

This goes way beyond medicine; this is an annihilation agenda for humankind which is why they are pushing these vaccines with mandatory immunization programs in places like California and all around the world. They insist that you infect your children and that you are infected with cancer viruses with hatred with suffering with violence, with the entire genetic imprint of a murdered human baby. This is what the vaccine program is absolutely, really about. It's not about immunization, it's about infecting you."[7]

And infecting you with what? With a vaccine that will purposely alter your genetic makeup. And I quote, "You wonder why we've had this exposure of cancer, mental illness, insanity, suffering and hatred for the last couple of decades in our world, and why does it keep skyrocketing? Guess what? It's because everybody is being injected with it." In other words, their genetic makeup is being modified with vaccines, whether they want them to or not, or whether they realize it or not.

Gee, I wonder if this is why in the Days of Noah when they were first doing this hybridization of humanity that the same text in the Book of Genesis that mentioned the hybridization also stated that mankind was continually wicked all the time.

Genesis 6:5,11-12 "The LORD saw how great man's wickedness on the earth had become, and that every inclination of the thoughts of his heart was only evil all the time. Now the earth was corrupt in God's sight and was full of violence. God saw how corrupt the earth had become, for all the people on earth had corrupted their ways."

Now, certainly the entrance of sin is what's responsible for man's wicked rebellious behavior throughout all time, period. But it makes you wonder if some of the "continual" wicked behavior mentioned here in the Genesis account was due to a manipulated side effect of hybridization, you know, like the vaccines people are receiving today. Again, people are responsible for their sinful wicked behavior, but how did it get so wicked to the point that it was literally "only evil all the time." Makes you wonder, doesn't it?

But the greater point is, as you can see, even in our own country that's supposed to have our own best interests at heart and regulations in place to prevent and protect us from this kind of genetic abuse, genetic modifications of people against their own will for nefarious purposes is already occurring. And now that CRISPR has come along, making all this genetic modification so much easier, faster, and much more precise, do you really think the so called regulations which "they themselves" have put in place are going to stop them from abusing this kind of technology? You know, like the other countries around the world are already doing themselves? If you'll do it with vaccines and chemicals and who knows what else, CRISPR is your dream come true!

But speaking of changing things, there's yet another danger on the scene with this CRISPR genetic altering technology. Could it also change society into a Gattaca-type world where we have the genetically modified superior people ruling over the genetically inferior people, you know, the ones who couldn't afford the upgrades? Let's remind ourselves of that movie premise for those of you who aren't aware of it.

"Genetics, what could it mean? The ability to perfect the physical and mental characteristics of every unborn child. In the not too distant future,

our DNA will determine everything about us. A minute drop of blood, saliva, or a single hair determines where you can work, who you should marry, what you are capable of achieving. In a society where success is determined by science. Divided by the standards of perfection. One man's only chance...

'How do you expect to pull this off?' 'I don't know exactly.'

Is to hide his own identity...

'This is the last day that you are going to be you and I am going to be me.'

By borrowing someone else's...

'Congratulations.' 'What about the interview?' 'That was it.'

'Do you think you would be doing what you are doing if it wasn't for who you are? What you are?'

'I have a feeling that it might be under false pretenses, you're playing somebody else's hand.'

'They have my picture plastered up all over the place, they will recognize me. They will recognize me!'

'I don't recognize you. They won't believe that one of their elite could have suckered them all this time.'

'They are going to find me.'

But in a place where any cell of any part of your body can betray you, how do you hide, when we all shed 500 million cells a day? Welcome to Gattaca. There is no Gene for the Human Spirit."[8]

Yeah, real funny. But folks, I'm here to tell you, even that science fiction movie is about to become our nightmarish reality! Believe it or not, these same scientists and geneticists who are on the forefronts of utilizing CRISPR technology, even they are saying this is exactly the kind of horrible society we are headed for!

"But there is a bigger obstacle with CRISPR, the emergence of 'designer babies.' People could use gene editing for 'non-therapeutic genetic enhancement' – making designer babies with blue eyes and high IQs and Gattaca-type dystopian futures.

This research rings ethical alarms bells. Human embryo editing research may not be adequately controlled, leaving it open to a lab somewhere to create the first gene-edited babies.

You could find wealthy parents buying the latest offspring upgrades for their children. We could see the emergence of genetic haves and have nots, leading to even greater inequality than we already live with.

Some of the key scientists in this field have concerns about the potential misuse of a technology that could be used for eugenics, to create genetic discrimination."

In other words, we're headed for Gattaca. Folks, this is not good! Again, you wonder why God says, "Don't do this!" I mean, when will we ever learn? How many times does He have to warn us before we'll get it? This genetic modification is to be off limits!

In fact, speaking of not learning a lesson, if any of this is starting to sound familiar to Hitler's evil eugenics program and the horrible atrocities he committed during WWII seeking to create his "superior master race," you're exactly right. And wonder of wonders, the scientific genetic community today is also saying this is exactly what we're doing, that is, a repeat of Hitler's nightmarish eugenics behavior.

"In a recent Washington Post article, writer Robert Gebelhoff was asked, 'What's the difference between genetic engineering and eugenics?' His answer: 'not much, really.' After all, technology like CRISPR holds forth

the promise of one day being able to 'eliminate genetic disorders in humans.'

While we can all get behind eradicating terrible genetic disorders like Tay-Sachs and Cystic Fibrosis, the fact remains that 'editing out inheritable traits from the human population' is in fact what the eugenics movement was all about.

As Gebelhoff points out, 'The field of genetics has always had an uncomfortable link to eugenics,' which he defines as 'the science of improving people through controlled breeding.'

As Edwin Black chronicles in his definitive history of the eugenics movement, 'War Against the Weak,' after the horrors of the Third Reich, eugenics was re-named 'genetics' to rid itself of the taint of things like mass involuntary sterilization.

But scientists have never given up the idea of using 'genetic engineering as a means of perfecting the human species.' And the only restraint on what Black has dubbed 'newgenics' seems to be 'Well, just don't be a Nazi about it.'

And that's not a joke. Scientists like the Nobel Laureate Joshua Lederberg and evolutionary biologist J.B.S. Haldane maintain that what Haldane called 'positive eugenics' was different because 'No living person would be eliminated from the gene pool.' Instead, 'society could guide human development by eliminating negative traits and encouraging desirable ones through genetic engineering.'

Phrases like 'no living person,' 'negative traits,' and 'desirable traits' strongly suggest that the sanctity and dignity of all human life doesn't play much of a role in 'newgenics.' 'Positive eugenics' is at odds with the idea that there's 'a moral, social and physical advantage in allowing diversity to flourish within the human gene pool.'

Instead, what's 'negative' and what's 'desirable' will be determined by a worldview that prizes physical perfection above all, only considers temporal criteria of value, and uses some image bearers as tools and eliminates others – much as we saw in the 1997 film, 'Gattaca.'

This war on the weak, like the original one, will be waged by people claiming to act in the name of the public good under the mantle of scientific objectivity. What could possibly go wrong? "

Gee, I wonder if that was the same rationale Hitler's scientists had as well? "What could go wrong? It's for everyone's good." But I need to clue you in on something here. Most people think it was just Hitler and his evil Nazi regime that was involved in this horrible Eugenics program. You know, creating a super Gattaca type race of people. Unfortunately, that's not true. Believe it or not, even here in America, Eugenics was in high gear long before Hitler got the credit for it.

American Experience: *"On August 18th, 1934, 20-year-old Anne Cooper Hewitt, heiress to one of the largest fortunes in the United States was admitted to a San Francisco Hospital for an emergency appendectomy. She later learned that the surgeons not only had removed her appendix but also a length of her fallopian tube rendering her incapable of ever becoming pregnant. The story of the sterilized heiress hit the papers just after the new year in 1936 when Anne filed a half-million-dollar damage claim against the surgeons and her own mother for sterilizing her without her knowledge or consent.*

Anne's mother denied any wrongdoing. She done what she done for society sake, she insisted, because her daughter was feeble minded. It was the sort of bazaar high society scandal that would have captured the national imagination under any circumstances. But that one word, feeble minded, struck a familiar chord for Americans and linked Anne's plight to a decades old campaign to control human reproduction known as eugenics."

What is the bearing of the laws of heredity upon human affairs? Eugenics provides the answer. Eugenics was proposed as the scientific solution of social problems. It was a combination of hope and aspiration on one side and on the other side it was about fear and in some cases, about hate. They are identified early, categorized feeble minded, imbecile, idiot. It would have been better by far if they had never been born.

People tend to think that eugenics was about and originated with the Nazi's, that it was grounded in wild claims that were far outside the scientific mainstream. Both of those impressions were fundamentally not true. It was almost a mania that swept through the country and there was that kind of that naive optimistic vision of eugenics like hey let's all get together and make better people.

The eugenics movement was about having healthy children, about having a stronger society. There is nothing wrong with that. You have to look at the under belly of what was implemented in the name of eugenics to see what was so problematic about it.

In the fall of 1902, an American Biologist named Charles Benedict Davenport arrived in London on a pilgrimage. He was 36, Harvard educated and like many biologists of his generation absorbed with the study of evolution. He had been traveling in Europe with his wife collecting seashells for research on species variation, but this was to be the highlight of the trip. A meeting with the world renown gentlemen's scientist, Sir Francis Galton.

A pioneering statistician Galton had lived his 80 years by a single motto. 'Whenever you can, count.' His obsession with measurements and patterns had led him to create the world's first weather maps, establish finger printing as a means of identification and set data back parameters for the perfect cup of tea. Charles Davenport had come to discuss another matter, Galton's work on heredity."

Dr. Siddhartha Mukherjee, writer: *"Francis Galton was a great quantifier. He liked to quantify height, hair color, you know, what is the* *chest size of an average man. What is the thigh length of an average man? Even things like intelligence."*

Jonathan Spiro, Historian: *Galton had a theory that talent, what we would call intelligence, seemed to run in families and so it quickly occurred to him, if we can get people with high talent to mate with each other, prevent people with low talent from mating with each other, we will within a few generations create this race of super men."*

Nathaniel Comfort, Historian: *"Francis Galton was borrowing ideas and kind of riffing off of the work of his half-cousin Charles Darwin."*

Keith Wailoo, Historian: *"Darwin believed that evolution was just this natural process that was inevitably leading towards what they called the survival of the fittest. Galton really turns that idea on its head and says, 'You know natural selection isn't working very well. We need to do a form of selection; we need to intervene."*

To name the effort Galton had coined the term Eugenics, a hybrid derived from two Greek words meaning well and born. Charles Davenport believed as Galton did. That selective breeding could transform the human race. What was needed was a scientific understanding of how heredity really worked. Over dinner at Galton's home Davenport declared his intention to get to the bottom of it.

Nathaniel Comfort: *"Davenport said, 'I'm going to create a new kind of institution, a station for experimental evolution. Not Darwinian natural selection that you just go out and observe, but can we figure out how inheritance works. Can we do experiments and find the patterns of heredity."*

Thomas C. Leonard, Historian: *"When Davenport sailed for home in December 1902, he carried with him not only a letter of recommendation signed by Galton, but also, he later wrote of a renewed courage for the study of evolution. Davenport and Galton really did imagine that the idea of improving human heredity was of almost religious significance, of* *profound moral importance. They also believed they were qualified to breed a better race because they believed that they were the best and the brightest."*

Scarcely more than a year later, with funding from the Carnegie Institution, Davenport opened his research station on the north shore of Long Island, at Cold Spring Harbor.

Wouldn't it be a better world if we could wipe out poverty, wouldn't it be a better world if we didn't have criminals, wouldn't it be a better world if everyone behaved themselves and if the reason we have poverty and crime is something that is determined by our genes? If we can change that and make it so the people who have those bad traits don't pass them down, wouldn't that make a better world?

Davenport investigated any and all traits, eye color, weight, mood, habit, temperament, diseases, anything. And then he finds this psychologist in New Jersey and he begins to zero in on low intelligence, something known as feeble mindedness.

Henry Goddard was 42 and a one-time teacher in Quaker Schools. It was in part an interest in education that brought him to Vineland in 1906. He had spent the 3 years since trying to parse the many varieties of feeble mindedness. An all too common state of mental deficiency associated with anti-social behavior. Some of Vineland's 300 inmates were violent or deranged, others unruly, still others merely slow. Hoping to improve their individual care and training, Goddard had pioneered the use of an intelligence test which purported to measure a person's mental abilities in relation to that of so-called normal people of the same age.

The scores enabled him to sort his charges into categories to the existing classifications of idiot and imbecile which long had been used to describe debilitating mental impairment. Goddard had added a third, a higher functioning group he called morons.

Wendy Kline, Historian: *"That was actually a diagnostic term not just an insult. Henry Godard argued that the high-grade moron was high functioning enough to act normal, but they are kind of stuck in this evolutionary phase and they don't emerge as true adults. What is missing is moral judgement, so Godard constructs that word moron and mental deficiency and immorality become basically interchangeable."*

Now with Davenport's tutoring, Godard began to survey the family history of 35 of his students at Vineland. What he found made him an instant believer in eugenics. Not only did morons seem clearly to pass on their feeble mindedness to their offspring, their family trees often were rife with alcoholics, prostitutes, criminals, and paupers. As Godard put it to the New Jersey state conference of charities and corrections of 1910, feeble mindedness is at the root of probably two-thirds of the problems that you have before you. The cause was defective ancestry.

Nathaniel Comfort: *"Henry Godard puts forward this idea that if you got rid of feeble mindedness you would get rid of all these problems or greatly reduce them, and we love explanations like that. Oh, it's so simple, it's just simple mindedness so that's the fix."*

Godard reasoned that if the test he devised to better care for the feeble minded instead was used to identify them, the contagion could be halted, and future generations could be spared the scourges of mental deficiency.

Henry Godard said, 'You know it takes an expert to identify the true menace of simple mindedness, so someone you are sitting next to in a restaurant or a theater could look perfectly normal to you and it only takes one feeble minded person to marry another one, even one that's not feeble minded to create generations of feeble mindedness. What it did is up the stakes of feeble mindedness by claiming it was a hidden menace that was difficult to pinpoint than people might think."

By early 1910 Charles Davenport was convinced that certain human traits were passed down in a predictable way and that American society could be dramatically improved if only reproduction were controlled. Anxious to spread the word he began to lay plans for a new institution dedicated to eugenic research and education.

Keith Wailoo, Historian: *"By limiting the birth of people who are deemed to be unfit you were by definition enhancing the stock of human society. And so, there was a social mission of really fighting dependency, fighting crime, through eugenics. The idea was that eugenics would solve all of these broader social problems if enacted in a robust way."*

Sterilization was a radical procedure. Between 1915 and the mid 1920's you have a dozen or more states that passed laws that allowed for mandatory sterilization of people in institutions. If you look back at all the sterilization laws passed the easiest way to sum up who their targets were, is round up the usual suspects. You are generally going to be dealing with the poor people, people who are part of a disfavored minority, people who are on a private charity or public welfare, people who have disabilities, mental or physical, and people who are generally considered on the margins of society.

In July 1933, in Germany, Adolph Hitler came to power and immediately enshrined eugenics in state policy with a law that mandated the sterilization of men and women suffering from any one of nine presumably heritable conditions. It had been based on a model law written by Harry Laughlin. For a time, the enemies within America's society were eclipsed by those without and the nation's attention diverted by a conflict that consumed much of the world. Then came the liberation of Buchenwald and Dachau and the chilling evidence of eugenic policies carried to a monstrous extreme.

Dr. Siddhartha Mukherjee, Writer: *"In the 1940's the full horror of what had happened in Nazi Germany had become apparent. The movement from sterilization to extermination, the killing of several millions based on this kind of idea, for the betterment of the human race. It creates a vast embarrassment for the American eugenics movement."*

Daniel Kevles, Historian: *"People were repelled and began to turn away from eugenics and eugenics became a dirty word."*

The Holocaust being tied to a wide range of eugenic practices is a blemish on humans as a species and it undercuts any notion that eugenics was any positive force in American society.

Sterilization was thought to be too slow and too expensive to be used on a mass scale. After the war when the allies put the Nazi's on trial in Nuremburg, one of the charges were eugenic sterilization and the lawyer for the Nazi who was charged said, 'How can you charge my client with the crime of eugenic sterilization when your own U.S. Supreme court said this was okay?"[9]

In other words, Hitler wasn't the one who started this. The Eugenics movement in America was the one who kick started this evil genetic modification behavior! And do you think this has all just magically disappeared? I don't think so. As we already saw, they just changed the terminology to "newgenics."

But speaking of Hitler and Eugenics, what's totally ironic, is that Professor Doudna, the co-developer of the CRISPR gene editing tool, actually stated in a recent interview that she had a dream where she saw Hitler to whom she was to explain this new technology to, and upon seeing him she then remarks about her invention, "What have I done!"

Is Gene editing a dream or a nightmare?

Jennifer Doudna: *"Well CRISPR is an acronym that actually represents a sequence of DNA letters in the genomes cells, it is found in bacteria and it was interesting to scientists originally because it is a bacterial immune system, the way that bacteria can fight viral infection. The CRISPR acronym has now become widespread in the media as an indication of a new technology for gene editing. So, the CRISPR gene editing technology is a tool that scientists can use to change the letters of DNA in cells in precise ways.*

I like to use the analogy of the word processor on our computer. So you have a document, you can think about the DNA in a cell like the text of a document that has the instructions to tell the cell how to grow and divide and become a brain cell or a liver cell or develop into an entire organism. Just like in a document the CRISPR technology gives scientists a way to go in and edit the letters of DNA, just like we might cut and paste the text in our document to replace whole sentences, even whole paragraphs or chapters. We can do that by using the CRISPR technology in the DNA itself.

Over the last few years as this technology has begun to be deployed globally for different applications I have found that I have gone from thinking about it initially just with almost wide eyed excitement and thinking about all the opportunities that this offers to realizing that there was real risk and we really needed the scientific community and frankly the human community. They needed to be aware of this and to discuss this.

One of the things brought that to the forefront of my mind was a dream that I had fairly early on in which I walked into a room and a colleague said to me, 'Jennifer, I would like for you to explain the CRISPR technology to a friend.' He brought me into a room and the person was sitting with his back to me and as they turned around, I realized with a sort of horror that it was Hitler. It was actually Hitler with a pig nose, it was almost a chimeric pig-human sort of creature. It sounds funny in a way to relay that image but in the dream it was a terrifying thing and I felt really stone cold fear in the dream and woke up from that dream with a start and realized, I had this initial feeling of 'What have I done?'"[10]

Yeah, real funny! Maybe somebody was trying to warn you! In fact, it gets even worse. Professor Doudna not only dreams of Hitler and his nightmarish behavior with the eugenics program, acknowledging that CRISPR would have made his wicked aspirations super easy to do and in essence that he would be proud of her work, but she also admits in other interviews that there's yet another danger involved here with this invention called CRISPR. Not just the ability to make eugenic type changes into the human species, but to make permanent irreversible genetic changes to any species, human or animal, including plants and bacteria. Permanent changes mean that if you made a mistake, you could never reverse it! It's too late! You've gone too far!

Again, this is the danger of the other recent development we saw earlier in the history section of Genetic Engineering that of the device called Gene Drives. These Gene Drives literally "force" genetic modifications throughout and "entire" species that can never be reversed again.

Bloomberg Reports: *"Consider our mosquito. Scientists have successfully used CRISPR to deliver a genetic tweet to make mosquitoes immune to the malaria parasite so they can't spread it to humans. But there was still a problem. How to get this gene to spread through an entire population of mosquitoes. Genetic changes are usually only inherited by half an organism's offspring and by a quarter of those offspring's offspring. It is quickly swallowed up by a large gene pool.*

But last year scientists unveiled another CRISPR breakthrough, a gene-drive that pushes the genetic changes to almost 100 percent of offspring. Mosquitoes reproduce so quickly that immunity could flash through an entire population of mosquitoes in a single season."

BBC Reports: *"Just because we can do something doesn't say that we should. What to you are the red lines which we shouldn't cross?"*

Jennifer Doudna: *"There's a couple of areas where it is very important to have a global conversation about application, one of them is something that has been discussed quite a lot in the media which is the idea of making heritable changes to human beings. In other words, making changes to a human embryo, for example, at a very early stage such that those changes could be inheritable by future generations.*

The other application that I think is one that I think that deserves careful thought before forging ahead is the idea of gene drives. The idea of gene drive is the technology that can introduce a change so rapidly in a cell that it can be used to drive a trait through a population very quickly. And so, people have been considering using this idea of getting rid of mosquitoes for example. On the one hand that might be an attractive option as opposed to using chemicals to eradicate mosquitoes. On the other hand, there could be some very serious environmental risks. [11]

Which includes, you can't go back. You literally just changed an entire species with a rapid genetic altering process and gee, I sure hope you got it right! That's not just risky, that's dumb! I mean, it's one thing to manipulate one organism, and if you got it wrong, oh well, there's plenty of other "originals" still out there you could go back to. But to build a Gene Drive genetic altering system that forces these genetic changes to go throughout an entire species with irreversible side effects is another thing. A dumb and dangerous thing. Yet, this so-called scientific community still persists. It starts to make you wonder if this why they're storing all those "master seeds" in the Arctic, as well as why Russia, for some unknown reason is storing the "DNA of all living things" in a "Noah's Ark" type of endeavor? Do you know something we don't know? Makes you wonder, doesn't it.

In fact, Professor Doudna is not the only one warning about these Gene Drives and their irreversible side effects. So are many other scientists in the genetic community. Not so surprisingly, they too have been warning about its dangers for a long time, as this article shares.

"The advantage of altering genes may also come with a tradeoff of removing genes that are 'hitchhiking' nearby and dispose an associated risk for cancer or neuropsychiatric disorders. Losing the bad can mean losing the good, too. One reason we should not be so quick to clip snippets of code out of our genomes.

Yet, a decade ago, an evolutionary geneticist named Austin Burt proposed a sneaky way to tether one gene to a separate gene – one that you wanted to propagate through an entire population. If it worked, you'd be able to drive the gene into every individual in a given area.

Your gene of interest graduates from public transit to a limousine in a motorcade, speeding through a population in flagrant disregard of heredity's traffic laws. Burt suggested using this 'gene drive' to alter mosquitoes that spread malaria, which kills around a million people every year. It's a good idea.

In fact, other researchers are already using other methods to modify mosquitoes to resist the Plasmodium parasite that causes malaria and to be less fertile, reducing their numbers in the wild. But engineered mosquitoes are expensive. If researchers don't keep topping up the mutants, the normals soon recapture control of the ecosystem.

But if you push those modifications through with a gene drive the normal mosquitoes wouldn't stand a chance. The problem is, inserting the gene drive into the mosquitoes was impossible. Until Crispr-Cas9 came along.

Today, behind a set of four locked and sealed doors in a lab at the Harvard School of Public Health, a special set of mosquito larvae of the African species Anopheles gambiae wriggle near the surface of shallow tubs of water. These aren't normal Anopheles, though. The lab is working on using Crispr to insert malaria-resistant gene drives into their genomes.

Consider this from the mosquitoes' point of view. This project isn't about reengineering one of them. It's about reengineering them all.

Kevin Esvelt, the evolutionary engineer who initiated the project, knows how serious this work is. The basic process could wipe out any species. Scientists will have to study the mosquitoes for years to make sure that the gene drives can't be passed on to other species of mosquitoes. And they want to know what happens to bats and other insect-eating predators if the drives make mosquitoes extinct. 'I am responsible for opening a can of worms when it comes to gene drives,' Esvelt says.

Within a year, and without seeing Esvelt's papers, biologists at UC San Diego had used Crispr to insert gene drives into fruit flies – they called them 'mutagenic chain reactions.'

*Some scientists said the San Diego researchers had gone 'a step too far' –
big talk from those same scientists who say they plan to use Crispr to
bring back an extinct woolly mammoth by deriving genes from frozen
corpses and injecting them into elephant embryos.*

*Ethan Bier, who worked on the San Diego fly study, agrees that gene
drives come with risks. 'If a pregnant female got out, she and her progeny
could reproduce in a puddle, fly to ships in the Boston Harbor, and get on
a boat to Brazil.'*

*These problems don't end with mosquitoes. One of Crispr's strengths is
that it works on every living thing. That kind of power makes Doudna feel
like she opened Pandora's Box.*

*Use Crispr to treat, say, Huntington's disease – a debilitating
neurological disorder – in the womb, when an embryo is just a ball of
cells? Perhaps. But the same method could also possibly alter less
medically relevant genes, like the ones that make skin wrinkle. 'We
haven't had the time, as a community, to discuss the ethics and safety,'
Doudna says."*

In other words, this is dangerous, it's irreversible, we need to talk
about it, but hey, we're marching ahead with it anyway without thinking
much about the consequences. Yes, you did open up Pandora's Box and in
direct rebellion to God's warnings you refuse to put the genetic genie back
into the bottle and the consequences are going to be simply horrible. Our
future is not looking bright.

Tech Insider Reports: *"In 2011 scientists created glow in the dark cats.
The researchers took a gene from glowing jelly fish and inserted it into the
unfertilized eggs of housecats. It was a neat trick, but they had a bigger
goal in mind. They also made cats more likely to be resistant to a feline
form of AIDS by again manipulating their DNA. So why can't we engineer
humans in the same way? Well we can engineer ourselves to be resistant
to life threatening illnesses. In fact, one scientist claims he has genetically
engineered two babies using the revolutionary tool called CRISPR.*

But what exactly is a CRISPR baby anyway? Would you like to be 6 ft tall, or never bald, the secret to traits like these lies in the six billion letters of your genetic code. Just like that, you can edit the human genome. But while the edits may be quick, it's changes can last for centuries. Especially if you are editing the DNA in an embryo. Embryos start out with a single cell and eventually replicates into millions and then trillions more.

So, if you alter that initial cell first, you are manipulating the ingredients of every cell that follows later in life. And the same altered cells can be passed on from generation to generation. That is one reason that most experiments on human embryos haven't left the lab.

That is, except for the work of Dr. He Jiankui, he claims to have used CRISPR to target and knock out the CCR5 gene in human embryos linked to HIV infection. Then he did something that shocked the scientific community. He implanted the embryos into several women. One of whom gave birth to genetically modified twins. Resistance to HIV aside most scientists say the procedure was too risky. At least two studies suggest that edited cells might actually trigger cancer. Another found that CRISPR could accidentally take aim at healthy DNA. So, while CRISPR could make us immune to disease who knows what else we might get on the side."[12]

You know, like some sort of weird Nephilim like creature that's huge, massive, scary and freaky. Gee, where have I heard that before? It's almost like history is repeating itself, just in time for the Second Coming of Jesus Christ and God's next judgement upon the whole planet. Gee, I wonder why?

And yet, even with all these warnings from God and even dangers admitted by the scientists in the genetic community themselves, they still persist and there still seems no stopping this hybrid experimentation with genetic modifications any time soon.

So now let's move on to the actual outcome of all this Historical evidence and Dangers of Genetic Engineering. As you saw it speeds up with each succeeding year. The trends, behavior, and risks get worse and worse as the weeks go by. But the question is, "Is genetic manipulation really being put into play as we speak on a massive scale around the world? Are there actual hybrids of creatures including human beings created today similar to what it was like in Noah's day?" Unfortunately, the answer is yes.

Chapter Four

Animal Enhancement

The Book of Romans in the Bible clearly reveals that we are in the final unfortunate stages of a society that is on the brink of disaster. It also tells us the reasons why.

Romans 1:18-32 "The wrath of God is being revealed from heaven against all the godlessness and wickedness of men who suppress the truth by their wickedness, since what may be known about God is plain to them, because God has made it plain to them. For since the creation of the world God's invisible qualities – His eternal power and divine nature – have been clearly seen, being understood from what has been made, so that men are without excuse. For although they knew God, they neither glorified Him as God nor gave thanks to Him, but their thinking became futile and their foolish hearts were darkened. Although they claimed to be wise, they became fools and exchanged the glory of the immortal God for images made to look like mortal man and birds and animals and reptiles. Therefore, God gave them over in the sinful desires of their hearts to sexual impurity for the degrading of their bodies with one another. They exchanged the truth of God for a lie and worshiped and served created things rather than the Creator – Who is forever praised. Amen. Because of this, God gave them over to shameful lusts. Even their women exchanged natural relations for unnatural ones. In the same way the men also abandoned natural relations with women and were inflamed with lust for one another. Men committed indecent acts with other men and received in themselves the due penalty for their perversion. Furthermore, since they did not think it worthwhile to retain the knowledge of God, He gave them over to a depraved mind, to do what ought not to be done. They have become filled with every kind of wickedness, evil, greed and depravity. They are full of envy, murder, strife, deceit and malice. They are gossips, slanderers, God-haters, insolent, arrogant and boastful; they invent ways of doing evil; they disobey their parents; they are senseless, faithless, heartless, ruthless. Although they know God's righteous decree that those who do such things deserve death, they not only continue to do these very things but also approve of those who practice them."

So how does a society completely fall apart and unravel to the point of total destruction headed for the wrath of God? Simple. Follow the order. It starts with ignoring God's existence and the plethora of proofs that He gives us to show us that He really is real. That evidence being His design or handiwork seen throughout all His creation, the things that He made. Man not only deliberately exchanges this truth for a lie, but they also suppress this truth of God's existence with the lie. That lie is called evolution. Even though they know God is real, they would rather choose to believe a lie and instead worship created things, even animals, instead of the Creator Who is to forever be praised. So, because of this, God gives them over to their sinful desires and thinking and they immediately began to act like immoral animals.

Then because they refuse to stop that evil behavior, God gives them over to the next stage. They indulge in shameful lusts. Now they pervert God's design for human intercourse and propagation and indulge in same-sex relations including lesbianism and homosexuality.

Then because they refuse to turn away from these atrocities and acknowledge God, He them gives them over to a depraved mind and in no time, they start doing things that ought not to be done. This stage of judgment is then followed by a whole list of evil, wicked, destructive behaviors, of which every single one of them we are engaged in today in our world.

Yet, even though God warns that those who live like this deserve His righteous judgment, and even deserve to die, they not only ignore this warning and continue to engage in these sinful behaviors, but they even "approve" of those who "practice" these wicked deeds. In fact, it says that this society is at the last stages of destruction, they even start to "invent ways of doing evil."

Can I tell you something? We're even doing that today with genetic engineering. We already saw that God forbids modifying lifeforms, but now with these new genetic manipulation "inventions" including CRISPR, we are now using them to rebel against God and break His commands, starting with animals. We just can't seem to leave well enough alone.

If you look at the genetic altering community, one of the biggest areas they are violating God's commands is in the area called, **Animal Enhancements**. Call them what you will, but these so-called "enhancements" to the animal kingdom are leading us down a path of destruction. Let me share with you just a few of the current ways the scientific community is inviting the "wrath of God" with genetically altering animals.

First, they are "modifying" the animal kingdom. Second, they are "cloning" the animal kingdom. And third, they are even "resurrecting" if you will the animal kingdom. Let's start off with the first one, modifying the animal kingdom. Here's just a few examples.

INSECTS: Insects have been a long-established category for genetic modification experiments. Over the years, some of their favorite targets have been fruit flies due to their short life cycle, rapid reproduction rate, and low maintenance requirements. They also have a fairly simple genome compared to other insects.

However, another popular insect that has long been desired to be modified is the **mosquito**. Not only are genetic scientists looking to making them sterile so as to reduce their populations, but as we've already seen a couple times before, another one of their illusive goals with these pesky insects is to make them resistant of dengue fever, the Zika virus, or even malaria.[1]

X-talks Vitals Reports: *"Thanks to the research performed in the University of California we may be one step closer to stopping the transmission of malaria by mosquito vectors using a gene editing technique called CRISPR. The researchers generated a new strain of mosquito which is capable of transmitting malaria resistant genes to their offspring. The gene encoding anti-malaria antibodies was inserted into the specific site in the mosquito's embryo germ cell DNA. The hope is that the genes will rapidly be disseminated throughout the mosquito population in any given area, effectively eliminating the spread of the disease.*

Nearly half of the world's population is at risk of contracting malaria, a blood born parasite that is transmitted through bites from female mosquitoes. The team at the university performed their research using a species of mosquito which is the primary carrier of malaria in Asia. After inserting a DNA element into the reproductive cells of the mosquito using CRISPR, 99.5% of the resulting offspring were confirmed to be unable to transmit malaria.

The researchers admit they face a long road ahead before being able to test the method in the field. The antibodies need to be confirmed to be effective against malaria and the researchers must overcome regulatory hurdles in order to release the mosquitoes into the wild."[2]

But apparently, they're not waiting for those "regulatory hurdles" to be overcome, because as we will see in a second, they're already releasing them in the environment. Gee, I hope it works out. Yeah, you and me both, as well as the scientific community. They even stated to their own fellow colleagues, "Caution is urged over unpredictable ecological consequences." And as we saw before, if they combine this genetic modification to mosquitoes with the Gene Drive system, then whatever genetic changes that are made will be "forced" through the entire species making the changes irreversible. I hope you get it right! Caution is right! In fact, they even warn their own community with these next words.

"We call on scientists to ensure that experimental organisms cannot escape from their labs, be released on purpose, or even find their way out accidentally in the event of a natural disaster. Researchers must use multiple safeguards that are robust to human error and nefarious actions."

Doesn't sound to me like modifying mosquito genes is guaranteed to have positive results and that somebody's playing with fire here! But too late, as I mentioned earlier, they're already releasing them into the environment. In January 2016 it was announced that in response to the Zika virus outbreak that Brazil approved the release of even more genetically modified mosquitos throughout their country. Hope it works out for you!

But, be that as it may, this doesn't stop them from altering the genes of many other insects as well, like **moths** for instance. This is due to the fact that moths, like mosquitoes, come with pesky ramifications. Moths alone cause anywhere from 4 to 5 billion dollars' worth of damage each year worldwide. So again, scientists are looking at genetically modifying the moths, just like with the mosquitoes, to make them sterile and reduce their populations as well. And like the mosquitoes, these genetically modified moths have already been released into the environment and even one strain they created were genetically engineered to express a red fluorescent protein making it easier for researchers to spot them.

Then there is the **silkworm**. Believe it or not, researchers are not looking so much to sterilize and eradicate the silkworm, so much as they are looking to "enhance" their silk quality and quantity. For instance, they actually want to modify the silkworms so they will make "valuable" proteins for humans, such as a human protein serum for blood, human collagens, and even human antibodies. Then they have even genetically modified silkworms to produce "spider silk."

UncoTV Reports: *"In a non-descript metal framed building in an industrial park in Charlotte, the ultimate textile target may finally be reached."*

David Brigham, Founder/CEO, Entogenetics: *"These are all cocoons from silkworms. They are ordinary standard silk that we keep here for testing. So, this fiber is a lot thinner than the hair on your head, but this is a mile long inside this cocoon. A mile long of continuous fiber."*

UncoTV: *"The target is silk. It has been collected like this from cocoons of the silkworm for thousands of years and the material is prized for its beauty and its texture. But these are not typical silkworms."*

David Brigham: *"This one right here, one of the parents tested out at full strength spider silk. So, I have great hopes and they just hatched this morning."*

UncoTV: *"Did you catch that, spider silk?"*

David Brigham: *"We are taking the black widow gene and putting it in place of the silkworm silk gene. So, when they go to make the cocoons, they read the gene and they just make it and instead of making regular silk they make spider silk."*

UncoTV: *"You heard correctly; David Brigham is producing spider silk from silkworms. But the Black Widow produces a silk that is much stronger and stiffer than most spiders. Brigham implants the gene that controls the production of spider silk into the silkworm."*

David Brigham: *"That's right, they eat mulberry leaves grow big and fat, they spin a cocoon and then they start turning into a moth. They would come out as a moth, but we interrupt the process. We pull all the silk off the cocoon for yarn and fabric."*

UncoTV: *"You could call it agricultural alchemic since silk is a natural protein fiber, putting the spider gene into the silkworm transforms the worm into a kind of protein factory for spider silk. The silkworm doesn't change but thanks to genetic engineering it's just making a different silk."*

David Brigham: *"The engineered silkworms, which we tested to see if they had the spider silk gene, and they did, one copy. So now we are breeding transformed silkworms together, so we have offspring that have two copies of the spider silk gene and are full strength."*

UncoTV: *"By now you are probably asking why exactly make spider silk?"*

David Brigham*: "Spider silk is five times tougher than Kevlar. It doesn't have as much strength, but it has stretch, it is very, very tough. My favorite analogy is a plate glass window and a trampoline. You put Nolan Ryan in front of a plate glass window and you are pretty safe for a while but eventually he is going to throw a fast ball hard enough that it's going to break that window and you have no protection. But nobody throws a fast ball through a trampoline. Kevlar, Spectra, those are plate glass windows, spider silk is the trampoline."*

UncoTV: *"The military is searching for a material that is not only strong but also more elastic and light weight. This creation has already under gone ballistic testing."*

David Brigham*: "I am seeing a soldier writing me a letter saying, 'I'm home because I was wearing your spider silk vest', and that is why this business is here."*

UncoTV*: "The fabric can also be used in a host of medical applications such as sutures, implant coatings, or even artificial pendants because the human body doesn't reject spider silk."[3]*
    But then again, this isn't just spider silk, is it? It's genetically modified spider silk that's been combined with a silkworm. So, I'm sure...it...will... be...okay...yeah, right!

Other insects they're also modifying are **fruit flies, beetles, butterflies, wasps,** and again for so-called "pest management" reasons. And again, not so surprisingly, these other insect modifications also come with major concerns. For instance, one article shared this danger.

"The Mediterranean fruit fly is a global agricultural pest. They infest a wide range of crops (over 300) including wild fruit, vegetables and nuts, and in the process, cause substantial damage.

The company Oxitec has developed GM-males which have a lethal gene that interrupts female development and kills them in a process called 'pre-pupal female lethality.' After several generations, the fly population diminishes as the males can no longer find mates.

Opponents argue that the long-term effects of releasing millions of GM-flies are impossible to predict. Dead fly larvae could be left inside crops. Helen Wallace from Genewatch, an organization that monitors the use of genetic technology, stated, 'Fruit grown using Oxitec's GM flies will be contaminated with GM maggots which are genetically programmed to die inside the fruit they are supposed to be protecting."

Mmm mmm. Yummy. Doesn't that sound delicious? A genetically modified maggot in your next apple? What's there to worry about? Actually, a lot. It gets even worse. There's also a danger of what's called (RIDL) or Release of Insects carrying Dominant Lethals. Yes, riddle me this Batman! Here's what this term means as well as its concerns.

"RIDL is a control strategy using genetically engineered insects that have (carry) a lethal gene in their genome (an organism's DNA). Lethal genes cause death in an organism. This lethal gene is dominant so that all offspring of the RIDL insect will also inherit the lethal gene.

This lethal gene has a molecular on and off switch, allowing these RIDL insects to be reared. The lethal gene is turned off when the RIDL insects are mass reared in an insectary and turned on when they are released into the environment.

It has been used in the Grand Cayman Islands, Panama, and Brazil to control the mosquito vector of dengue. It is being developed for use in diamondback moth, medfly and olive fly.

There are concerns about controlling the expression of lethal genes. Resistant genes could develop in the bacteria within the guts of GM-insects and from there, to circulate widely in the environment. For example, antibiotic resistant genes could be spread to E. coli bacteria and into fruit by GM-Mediterranean fruit flies."

Wow! First it was a maggot in my apple, now it's E. coli! Thanks GM companies! What could go wrong? Actually, everything! Are you starting to wonder why God said NOT to mess with this kind of modifying behavior? No wonder He had to destroy the whole planet with a worldwide flood and in effect hit the restart button. Man really messed it up!

Unfortunately, in our persistent rebellion today, we just can't seem to leave well enough alone. And I quote, "Scientists create world's first mutant ants with gene editing technology." Here's what they did.

"It may sound like a script for a science fiction movie, but scientists have created the world's first mutant ants.

Two independent research teams have harnessed the gene editing technology CRISPR to genetically alter the ants. In one study, researchers at Rockefeller University modified a gene essential for sensing the pheromones that ants use to communicate.

Ants use porous hairs on their antennae to detect pheromones. Scientists developed mutant ants lacking this ability.

'Once the ants successfully made it to the adult phase, we noticed a shift in their behavior almost immediately.' While ants typically travel single file, researchers noticed that the mutant ants couldn't fall in line, along with other behavioral abnormalities.

In another related study, scientists injected the brain chemical corazonin into ants transitioning to become a pseudo-queen, which simulated worker-like hunting behaviors, while inhibiting 'pseudo-queen' behavior, such as dueling and laying eggs."

Purposely creating "behavioral abnormalities" in ants and injecting chemicals into their brains that "stimulate worker-like hunting behaviors." Gee, what could go wrong with that scenario? Oh, just everything, like this.

"There are more than a hundred billion fire ants on earth. They swarm in seconds, attack in the thousands and kill within minutes. It used to be if you killed the queen the rest of the ants would die but that isn't happening anymore. Now they are coming for you. Climbing on your while you are asleep, standing in your yard, driving in your car. They bite, they burn, they leave big welts where they have bitten you. And if enough get to you, you die. This is the attack of the ants."[4]

But hey, that'll never happen! Yeah, right! And I quote from *Genewatch*, "There are no specific regulations for Genetically Modified insects in any country." Sounds to me like we're headed for a scary movie scenario like the one you just saw! In fact, it's almost like we refuse to learn from our history. Remember what happened with these modified insects?

"Killer bees, what could go wrong when humans meddle with nature? For an answer, look to the 1950's when the European honeybee was cross bred with its African counterpart with the intention of increasing the production of honey, the insects were released into Brazil. But these Africanized honeybees turned out to be highly aggressive and two swarms of them managed to escape quarantine in 1957.

After spreading throughout the Americas, they became known as killer bees due to their nature. They can deliver more than ten times the sting of the European honeybee. In addition to amassing to more than 800,000 individuals they are known to have killed about 1,000 humans and since these tiny terrors can survive in habitats ranging from jungles to deserts there is no escaping them."[5]

In other words, you can run but you can't hide! When will we ever learn? It reminds me of the classic axiom, "Those who don't learn their history are doomed to repeat it." Boy are we doomed when it comes to repeating these genetic modification mistakes! The killer bees was a total modifying debacle back then, turning them into literal killers, and they got out and spread, but somehow, these people want us to believe that all these insect modifications today will work out just fine. Yeah, right! Who knows what we're going to be running for our lives from in the very near future!

RODENTS: Speaking of pesky organisms, another "vermin" that the genetic altering community wants to mess with is in the area of rodents, starting with **mice**. Mice have long been the standard of choice for organisms that scientists want to do experiments on.

"Some examples of human disorders and diseases for which mice and rats are used as models include:

- *Hypertension*
- *Diabetes*
- *Cataracts*
- *Obesity*
- *Seizures*
- *Respiratory Problems*
- *Deafness*
- *Parkinson's Disease*
- *Alzheimer's disease*
- *Cancer*
- *Cystic fibrosis*
- *HIV and AIDs*
- *Heart Disease*
- *Muscular dystrophy*
- *Spinal cord injuries*

Mice are also used in behavioral, sensory, aging, nutrition and genetic studies, as well as testing anti-craving medication that could potentially end drug addiction."

So, as you can see, mice are a very popular choice to modify for scientific purposes. And that's why it's not overly surprising that mice have also become a target for genetic modifications within the animal kingdom. In fact, one of the latest attempts made by the scientific community was to try to make baby mice without using a female egg.

TOMO News Reports: *"Researchers produce mice embryos from non-egg cells. Scientists at the University of Bath in the UK have made a discovery that they say challenges almost two centuries of knowledge on fertilization. It was widely thought that mammals could only be born from an egg fertilized with sperm. But this research bypasses that entirely. The researchers used chemicals to trick mouse eggs into developing as if they had been fertilized.*

This produced parthenogenodes, a peculiar type of embryo that dies after a few days. At this point the embryos had a half set of chromosomes and were in the stages of cell division. It's here that researchers injected them with sperm. These embryos were then inserted into female mice. The process produced thirty mouse pups with a success rate of around one in four."[6]

Gee, what could go wrong with that? Nothing, absolutely nothing.

"The mice in the cages in the lab are going crazy. They are trying to get out. The cages are bouncing around on the table getting ready to fall on the floor. The researcher is trying to get out the door before they escape the cages, but the door is stuck. He can't get out. Now the mice are out of the cages, they are coming out of the walls. He sees them coming at him and he can't get out. He trips and falls on the floor. It seems like hundreds of mice are coming at him. He screams but no one hears him. They are eating at his flesh as he is trying to get up off the floor, but it is too late. There are too many of them. His screams are silenced."[7]

Oh yeah, nothing could go wrong.... nothing at all. In fact, the report goes on to say that the reason why they are trying to create baby mice without an egg is, "This could have potential applications for future treatment of infertility. It may help us understand more about how human life begins and what controls the viability of embryos."

So, what's next? Are you going to be doing this on humans? Actually, we'll get into that in the next section, but the answer is yes. However, speaking of mice, trying to create them without an egg for supposed infertility purposes is just the tip of the iceberg. Japanese geneticists are also modifying mice so they could become transparent or literally see-through.

"The Japanese create invisible mice? Well mouse traps are practically going to be useless. That's right guys, Japan has done it again. Really giving us amazing science, technology stuff and I'm not talking about singing toilets. This time it's mice that are transparent. So, what does a see-through mouse look like? So, let's take a look at it, but be prepared, it is disgusting. Oh man, what the heck is that thing. It looks like a giant blob of Vaseline. So, the scientists at the Brighten Quantum Biology Center in Osaka University have made mice practically see-through by changing the pigment of their tissues. I'm talking tissue like this sort of stuff (he pinches his stomach).

Now originally, they actually had problems trying to change the mice's color of their hemoglobin. That pretty much puts the red in the red blood cells, but they actually discovered that the same process that they used to make the brain transparent for an imaging works the same way for hemoglobin. This has been a challenge they have been working on for years. They actually do this process so they can see what is on the inside of the mouse without cutting it up. Like the invisible man, you inject yourself with a needle and all of a sudden it's like you completely disappear."[8]

Nah, they wouldn't be working on something like that, would they?

Movie clip from The Invisible Man: *The cop and several other men are standing in the doorway. The cop says, "Come along here, quietly, unless you want me to put the handcuffs on." The camera sweeps over to a man wrapped in bandages with sunglasses on.*

The invisible man says, "Stop, you don't know what you are doing."

The cop says, "I know what I am doing, alright, come on." The men behind him are encouraging him to put handcuffs on him and take him in. Lock him up!

The invisible man says, "All right, you fools, you brought it on yourselves. Everything would have been all right if you had just left me alone. You have been peering through the keyholes and peeking through the curtains and now you will suffer for it. You are craving to know who I am, aren't you? All right, I'll show you!" He pulls off his nose and throws it at them.

"Here is a souvenir for you!" There is a hole in his face where his nose was. As he is unwrapping the bandages from around his head, he proceeds to throw his eyes at the men. "And one for you" he yells at them. They step back in horror. "I'll show you who I am and what I am," he yells and then starts to laugh as he sees the shock on their faces. He throws the bandages at them and asks, "how do you like that?" As he continues to laugh at them, they run out the door and down the stairs."[9]

Yeah, real funny is right! That was back in 1933. What did H.G Wells know that we didn't know?

But they're not going to do this on humans are they? And I quote, "In the future, the group plans to make improvements to the method to allow for the rapid imaging of whole bodies of adult mice or larger samples such as human brains." Okay, let's just hope they're not alive when they do that to those human brains!

But be that as it may, if you thought we had a problem with an overabundant supply of mice multiplying endlessly as we all know, you ain't seen nothing yet. Check out this story:

"Chinese scientists edit genes to produce artificial sperm capable of creating 'army of half-cloned mice.' A powerful gene-editing tool called CRISPR-Cas9 has allowed the researchers to add, disrupt or change the sequence of specific genes in the sperm. 'We thought it would be great if the sperm could be cultured to multiply endlessly like normal cells.' It was the first mass production of man-made sperm with this technology. These half-cloned mice will fight on the frontline in battles against cancer and other genetic health issues."

Then they go on to say that, "This procedure can be used to generate an army of half-cloned mice with ease and efficiency." Now you can REALLY crank out those mice! But gee, I hope they don't escape from the lab! That would never happen, would it?

Animal Planet: *"The plague is spreading beyond the farmers' fields and into the surrounding homes."*

Kelly Lake: *"The mice are getting into everything they could. In your wardrobes, your drawers."*

Animal Planet: *"The desperate homeowners can't hold back the tide of mice with traps."*

Kelly Lake: *"If you set them up before you go to bed, if you heard any go off while you are awake you get up and change them again. We have 30 in the house, trap after trap."*

Animal Planet: *"The farmers use water troughs to trap the mice. The sea is the only place around Streaky Bay not infested with rodents. This is a plague of Biblical proportions"*

Being in the middle of this mass plague is a surreal experience. They are everywhere. The ground is moving. They are going in all directions. "

Kelly Lake: *"You could see at the front of our house; the ground was moving. It was just mice.*

Animal Planet: *"The locals can't leave their homes. If they drive, they risk skidding off the road. Farmers don't want to go into their barns. "*

The ground is moving, the walls are moving, things are running on rafters, they are going in all directions. I've had a few go up my trouser leg, it's not a good feeling. "

Animal Planet: *"There is no refuge from the plague. Anywhere. "[10]*

But don't worry…that…would…never…happen…with this…. army of… cloned…mice…would they? Well, we hope not, but let's upgrade our discussion from mice to **rats**. Even they can't be left alone by this genetic altering community. Believe it or not, scientists are already using rat parts to create "artificial animals." They're calling them "Bio-Hybrid Beings" and one of them they recently produced was something that functioned like a stingray.

RT News: *"On a quest to create the first biomechanically engineered human heart, Dr. Kit Parker of Harvard University designed one of the first successfully functioning robots made partially of machine and living cellular tissue, a robot stingray, although about $1/10^{th}$ the size of an actual stingray.*

This is an artificial creature, not quite robot, not quite living organism. It has an elastomer body. The small elastic body is built to resemble a ray. It has a stiff gold skeleton that gives it a way to store elastic energy. The body is coated in living heart cells genetically engineered to respond to light. When exposed to light the cardiomyocytes contract and the ray's wings flap. The cells are printed on in a serpentine pattern. This dictates the motion of the wing as the cells contract one after the other. Each wing is tuned to a different light pattern, allowing the raybot to turn.

Why make a hybrid ray? On the tissue-engineering side... Learning to structure and control heart cells like this could lead to creating artificial hearts. On the artificial animal side... hybrids like these pave the way for artificial creatures that can use many sensory inputs and respond with complex behaviors. A small step towards synthetic cognition.

Scientists are calling this the first robot designed that doesn't run on electricity. So, for non-science people like myself, how does it get its power to move?"

Dr. Kit Parker: *"Well there are some cells that live on a layer of selastic and a layer of gold so we have a pinch of rat heart cells, a pinch of breast implant, that's the same as silicone, and a pinch of gold, then we genetically engineer the cell so they can see light, only one wave-length. So, you can point a light at it, the stingray, and it will swim towards the light."[11]*

Well gee, what could go wrong with that scenario? Let me get this straight. You created an artificial animal with rat parts, breast implants, and gold. I sure hope it doesn't swim out of the lab and reproduce! But hey, that would never happen would it?

Movie Clip from Attack of the Leeches: *An old hunter is standing in the shallow part of the bayou. He has seen something in the water, and he tells his friend. "I seen these thangs. Huge black thangs."*

THEY CAME FROM THE MURKY DEPTHS

Some girls are playing in the water and one notices that something has just brushed her leg. She looks around to see just what that was. She says, "Somethings in here!"

Then another hunter is standing on the edge of the water, he is pointing his gun at something but not sure what as his friend is being pulled down into the water by something. His friend is screaming in pain. He goes to save him, but his buddy is dead and is floating up to the girls playing in the water. One of them screams. By now the sheriff has been called and he is standing on the bank pointing his gun but still not sure just what is in the water. Then another onlooker, standing on the edge of the water, is attacked and taken out into the water. Now the sheriff and the lady with him see this huge black thing that just pulled him down. She yells, "did you see the size of that thing?" By now one of the girls that was playing in the water is also dead and being devoured by the big black leech. [12]

YOU BLEED ... THEY FEED

Yeah, coming soon is right! Thanks to genetic modifications! But that's not all. Speaking of rat parts being used to create new creatures, apparently, we don't have enough of them, that is, rat parts. Now they're actually making their own rat parts in the laboratory, starting with their limbs.

New Scientist/Ott Laboratory: *"Imagine you can grow back the limbs that people lose, it's not insane. About 185,000 Americans become amputees every year. Hands, feet, legs, and arms and that works up to roughly 2 million people in the US living with an artificial limb. Scientists from Massachusetts are growing replacement limbs and they are starting with rat legs. They are calling them biolimbs. They have blood cells, tendons, muscles, everything. An electric current can even make them flex, so how do they do all that?*

They flush out the cells of one rat, so it is just bone and they dump cells from a second rat into that hollow leg and the cells begin to grow. Now get this... the leg is made up of the second rat's cells, so the organ doesn't get rejected. When you flush out the organ it looks clear.

They have done the same thing in cow and pig hearts. The donor cells of this heart were flushed out and replaced with the cells of another animal.

So, we started putting human cells into empty monkey arms. Getting human cells to grow in there would surpass any prosthetic we have ever made.

Before the 20ᵗʰ century fake limbs were made of wood or steel and they only looked real. Now we focus on function rather than appearance. We can control prosthetics with our minds. But growing replacement limbs will be a huge leg up."[13]

Oh, did you get it? Leg up. Real funny, starting with a rat leg. And did you notice they're already doing this with other animals such as pigs, cows, and monkeys? Yeah, we'll get to that in another section. But don't forget, it's all designed to be combined with humans. They go on to say this:

"We're focusing on the forearm and hand to use it as a model system and proof of principle. But the techniques would apply equally to legs, arms and other extremities. This is the first step towards human-scale bio-limb development, and we have started experiments using human muscle cells in rats instead of the mice ones."

In other words, it's already begun! And of course, the article concludes with, "You've got to hand it to them." Yeah, real funny, you got to hand it to them because we all know nothing could go wrong with this genetic modification scenario of combining rat parts and human parts, right? Well, you might want to ask this guy.

Biological Research Facility, Chatsworth, NH

Two men walking down the hall talking business. One says to the other, "What we are going to do is inventory the place. The tenant just got evicted, so we're just going in there to get a record of what they left." They walked through the door but as they went in without noticing there was a shadow of something that ran across the room. They looked around and then one guy says, "Oh great, this is the animal place." The other man said, "Looks like there was some animal testing going on here." The other replied, "Using animal DNA and mixing it with human DNA. Sick stuff man."

There were cages that had been left with rats in all of them. The partner says, "There is such bad energy in here." His boss replies, "Yes I know. Are you sympathetic towards animals or something?" "Yes," he replied. "I'm about ready to bust into tears actually. What was that?" Something big ran behind the table. "What was that???" He saw it again and jumped. "I heard something, I saw something, I gotta get out of here!!! What was that dude?" As the door slammed. "I'm really scared!" Just at that moment something came out of the closet and jumped at him. He started screaming and then he saw an animal looking creature with a man's face and arms but had the body of a rat with hind legs like a rat with long hair and tail. As the creature turned around to look directly at the two men, he starts screaming along with the guy trying to get the door open to run to safety."[14]

Yeah, what could go wrong? What could go wrong? But hey, that was just a prank, right? Well, maybe not, in the not so distant future! You keep combining rat parts with human parts, and by the way, who knows what else you're combining it with, and we have no idea what they're going to come up with! Who knows what kind of nightmarish creatures they are going to unleash on us? In fact, it makes you wonder if this was some of the same kind of problems they experienced back in Noah's Day.

DOGS: They've been called man's best friend, but when man gets done modifying dogs, maybe they won't want to be friends with us anymore. And if you think I'm kidding, I'm not. It seems that no relationship in the animal kingdom is sacred to these genetic modification scientists. Let me show you just a few of the ways they are already modifying our dogs.

First of all, they are creating glow in the dark dogs. And I quote, "Fluorescent puppy is world's first transgenic dog." Yeah, apparently the GloFish wasn't enough. Here's just one article revealing this "illuminating" experiment on dogs.

"A cloned beagle named Ruppy – short for Ruby Puppy – is the world's first transgenic dog. She and four other beagles all produce a fluorescent protein that glows red under ultraviolet light.

A team from Seoul National University in South Korea created the dogs by cloning fibroblast cells that express a red fluorescent gene produced by sea anemones.

After a few hours dividing in a Petri dish, researchers implanted the cloned embryo into a surrogate mother. The team ended up with seven pregnancies. Five of the dogs are alive, healthy and starting to spawn their own fluorescent puppies."

And here they are in action.

AP Seoul South Korea: *"They look like your average Beagles all frisky and rambunctious, but they have a special feature. Once you turn off the lights and shine an ultraviolet light on them, they glow. Scientists in South Korea have engineered these dogs with fluorescent genes. You can actually see some of the redness in the daylight. He says they are not playing mad scientist. He said this has a unique medical purpose. He said it shows that it is possible to successfully insert genes with a specific trait into a living animal and that could lead to other non-fluorescent genes that could help treat specific diseases.*[15]

So, in other words, we first messed with the genes of dogs so we can feel more comfortable later about doing it in humans. If the dogs survived, then surely the humans will too. And that's exactly where it's headed. But it isn't just modifying dogs so they will glow in the dark. It's also modifying them so they will become huge and massive. Or to use their term, "muscly." Here's just one dog named Wendy; whose owner is apparently a huge fan of Arnold Schwarzenegger.

Animal Planet: *"Rock hard abs, buns of pure steel, tight killer thighs, no this isn't Mr. Universe. This is the Conan of Canines. Meet Wendy, one brawny, bully, Whippet. No, she's not on steroids, in fact Wendy is* perfectly healthy. Her booming body is all due to a rare genetic mutation that has actually given her double muscles. It's so rare that the only breed to suffer from it are Whippets like Wendy.

Owner: *"Wendy is referred to as a Bully Whippet, the term they have applied to Whippets that are born with a genetic mutation and it causes double muscling. So, there is Wendy's stomach. You can see all the muscles; her hind end muscles are very large. They almost look like hams."*

Animal Planet: *"At 65 lbs. Wendy is nearly twice the size of a normal Whippet and three times the size of non-racing Whippets."*

Owner: *"I have a little non-racing Whippet and she weighs only 20 lbs. Whereas Wendy weighs 65 lbs."*

Animal Planet: *"And though this muscular mutt was jacked from day one, Wendy's owner Ingrid saw the beauty behind her brawn."*[16]

And apparently, so has the scientific genetic altering community. Believe it or not, they are not waiting for some random genetic mutation to arrive on the scene to produce a freakishly large dog like Wendy there. They're already creating them in the laboratory. Here's just one article admitting it.

"Chinese scientists just made the world's first genetically edited, super muscly dogs – and they named one Hercules.

Researchers in China have created the first dogs whose DNA was modified by gene editing.

By tweaking a dog's DNA to cut out a gene for the muscle-limiting protein myostatin, they created a beagle with twice the normal amount of muscle. A team of researchers led by Liangxue Lai of the Guangzhou Institutes of Biomedicine and Health used an increasingly popular technique known as

CRISPR/Cas9, which makes it relatively cheap and easy to cut and paste bits of the natural DNA of any organism.

They edited the DNA of dog embryos to cut out the myostatin gene, which produces a protein (myostatin) that limits muscle formation.

This isn't the first-time scientists have tinkered with an animal's DNA to give it more muscle. In June, researchers from South Korea and China created 'double-muscled pigs' by tweaking the same gene.

Mutations in the myostatin gene can also happen naturally. A breed of cattle called Belgian Blues normally lack this gene and grow to massive proportions. The only dogs known to have this mutation naturally are Whippets."

So, they admit that they are taking Wendy's genetic muscle aberration and are recreating it in the laboratory. In fact, they're doing it to the same kind of dogs that they were already making glow in the dark.

"Scientists in China are engaged in a controversial research, genetically modifying Beagles to be more muscular. They say for medical reasons, but they have been accused of animal cruelty."

"Of the 2,000 Beagles in this laboratory in Southern China, two are making headlines."

"These are the ones you are caring about most. Scientists lead by Mr. Lei Young at the Institute of Biomedicine and Health claim they are the first to successfully alter the genetic makeup of dogs. They doubled the muscle mass of these Beagles through the process of gene editing. He said they knocked out a gene that would ordinarily stop muscles from growing, so these dogs became much more muscular."[17]

So, first, you modify dogs, so they'll glow in this popping bright color, and now you're messing with their genes to make them super-duper muscular. I mean, what's next…humans? Well, funny you should ask, an article goes on to share this.

"The beagles, who will be kept at the Guangzhou General Pharmaceutical Research Institute, are from the first dogs to be seen with the genetic quirk. Losing the myostatin gene happens naturally in whippets and leads to the creation of double-muscled "bully whippets" who are much more strong than standard animals.

The change can also happen very rarely for humans. Doctors reported around ten years ago that a child had been born with extra muscles and unusually strong, as a result of being born without the gene. "

So, is this why you're recreating this genetic mutation in dogs? It can also happen in people, but rarely, just like Whippets. So how about we no longer wait to let it happen randomly, let's first perfect it in dogs, then we'll use it on humans. If I didn't know better, this is all starting to sound like this scenario.

Clip from the Incredible Hulk: *"I've been alone for a long time. Not because I want to be, but because until I solve this problem I have to be. "*

As the helicopters are flying, they are getting the order, "The target is a fugitive from the U.S. government who stole military secrets. "

"This is the location. Snatch and grab only. Live capture. "

As he is laying in his bed, he hears them coming. The general says, "Take him!" He gets away but they start a chase to catch him that will take him around the world.

"As far as I'm concerned that man's whole body is government property. "

Hulk: *"You need to get as far away from me as you can. Go!" He tells his girlfriend. "There are aspects of my personality that I can't control. When I lose control, it is very dangerous to be around me. "*

As the army is closing in on him, cornering him on an overpass, shooting at him with high powered weapons. Suddenly something comes over him that is completely out of his control. He turns into a giant green hulk. Now no one can control him.

But when the military realizes that they cannot defeat him a man comes forward and volunteers to become an equal to the hulk and be injected with the serum to make him the same. They might have a fighting chance if one can meet him on common ground.

Hulk: *"They want it as a weapon and if we let it go, we will never get it back!"*

They inject the serum into the soldier, and he becomes like a large lizard with fins and scales. Unfortunately, this one goes haywire. He is going through the streets tearing up everything in his way. He becomes the bad guy. The only hope is to get the Hulk to rescue the city.[18]

But hey, that's just a fictional movie, right? I mean, they wouldn't really be planning on making freakishly hulkish people for the military or other purposes, would they? Actually, yes, and I haven't even gotten to the Super Soldier section of the book yet.

But be that as it may, we've already seen that these genetic scientists admit that these experiments on dogs are paving the way for human experimentation. That's why they're doing it on dogs first.

Second, they also admit in the previous article that, "The technique is now used in a wide variety of animals, and has even been used on human embryos" which is why some in the media are saying these scientists are playing with genetic fire.

"Another lab has drawn worldwide condemnation for carrying out genetic editing tests on human embryos. Some major scientific journals would not even publish the work.

Critics have called China the wild west of gene editing, is that fair?

'I don't think it's fair. What we do in our lab is for the betterment of humankind.' He added."[19]

Yeah, sure it is. The same scientists doing these genetic modifications on dogs, glow in the dark and super muscles, and who knows what else, are admitting it's ultimately for mankind and for our so-called betterment. Really? Well maybe I don't want to be popping green or have huge massive muscles like the Incredible Hulk. But then again, I'm not in the military for whom much of this technology is being developed for. Don't believe me? Here's what these two recent articles shared.

"Scientists have created a new breed of stronger, faster dogs using DNA manipulation.

If you've ever read recent dystopian sci-fi books such as Margaret Atwood's Oryx and Crake or Paolo Bacigalupi's The Windup Girl, you'd know that one of their common predictions is that in the future genetically mutated super animals will run amok and make day-to-day life very dangerous for the world's remaining humans.

Now Technology Review brings us word that scientists in China claim to have used DNA manipulation to create a stronger, faster breed of dogs that will ominously be used for various police and military operations.

Gulp.

'The dogs have more muscles and are expected to have stronger running ability, which is good for hunting, police (military) applications,' Liangxue Lai, a researcher with the Key Laboratory of Regenerative Biology at the Guangzhou Institutes of Biomedicine and Health, explained in an email to Technology Review."

"China unveils gene technology to create SUPERHUMANS with hyper-muscular test-tube dogs.

ARMIES of SUPER-SOLDIERS were a step closer to reality today after China announced it was genetically engineering hyper-muscular SUPER-DOGS.

The dogs, which are test tube bred in a lab, have twice the muscle mass of their natural counterparts and are considerably stronger and faster. The canine genome has been especially difficult to engineer and replicate – but its close similarity to the human genome means it has long been the prize of geneticists.

Now the Chinese success has led to fears the same technology could be used to create weaponized super-humans – typified in Marvel Comics by Captain America and his foes.

David King, director of Human Genetics Alert (HGA), voiced his fears over what is widely viewed as the first step on a slippery slope.

He told Express.co.uk: 'It's true that the more and more animals that are genetically engineered using these techniques brings us closer to the possibility of genetic engineering of humans. Scientists are interested in being the first person in the world to create a genetically engineered child.

That does set us on the road to eugenics. I am very concerned with what I'm seeing. An army of super-humans has been a staple of science fiction and superhero comics for decades – but the super-dog technology brings it closer to reality.

In terms of genetic engineering we will be seeing this more and more. I'm seeing the beginning of a campaign within the scientific community to legalize human genetic engineering.'"

In other words, Incredible Hulk, Captain America, and all those other Marvel movies are about to become our reality.

CATS: Hey, if you're going to modify dogs, then why not mess with the other favorite choice of pets, that of cats? Well, wait no more! It's already being done! They too are being made to glow in the dark!

CNN Reports: *"You know some people think that cloned cats are creepy, but what about a cloned cat that also glows in the dark. It's an incredible story, but not everybody is happy to hear this though. A scientist in South Korea cloned a pair of kitties who light up with a fluorescent glow when exposed to ultraviolet light. Glow kitties. All right, now the question is, what was all this for? Apparently, there is a good reason for it. Christie Rostell has the story.*

Christine Rostell*: "At first glance these cats look like any normal cat, but there are two big things that make them very different. One, the cats are clones, two they glow in the dark. You heard right, when they are put underneath ultraviolet light, they glow a dull red, and it's no accident. Scientists have manipulated the donor cat's genetic codes and passed those changes onto the clone."*

Ong Il-Keun: Professor, Gyeongsang University: *"It's meaningful as we introduce outside genes to transgenic cloned cats for the first time and as they have their red fluorescent protein gene in their organs, they give off a red color."*

Christine Rostell: *"Here's how they do it. Scientists took skin cells from a Turkish Angora female cat and used a virus to insert the genetic instructions for making red fluorescent protein, Then, they put in the gene altered nuclei eggs for cloning. After that they implanted the eggs back into the donor cat which effectively became the surrogate mother. Now, these glow in the dark cats shine a light on what may be possible down the road. Scientists say if you can pass along coding for fluorescent markers through cloning you can eventually pass along more complex genetic coding. That means cats can help develop treatments for diseases for animals and for humans."[20]*

Oh, there you go again! You admitted this was going to lead to human usage as well. First get this genetic altering perfected in pets, dogs and now cats, and then it's off to humans. And just like dogs, cats too are also modified to come out super huge and freaky! Here's a new breed of cat they created called the Liger. It's a cross between a Lion and a Tiger and when you put those two together, man you get some freakishly large felines!

Barcroft.TV reports: *"Hercules is a Liger. That means that his father is a lion and his mother is a tiger. This makes him a giant. He is almost 900 lbs. and 12 feet tall."[21]*

Yeah, Hercules is right! Have fun trying to run away from that! But this is just one of many hybrid cats that scientists are making nowadays. Not only are there Ligers as you just saw, but Tigons. A cross between a tiger and a lion. Lions and tigers have also been bred with other big cat species, such as jaguars and leopards. Leopards and lions have been bred together to create leopons and lipards. A tiger-leopard pairing is called a tigard. And on and on it goes, this never-ending mixing, seeing what we come up with. But Ligers are considered the biggest cat on earth because tigers weigh about 500 pounds and lions max out at about 600 pounds. But the heaviest liger on record was 1,600 pounds. They're huge and massive!

But wait a second here, I'm starting to see a pattern. Making animals glow in the dark and making them super huge. First it was dogs, now its cats. And if you already admitted that that these genetic modifications you're making on dogs was ultimately for human purposes, then does that mean these genetic modifications you're making on cats will likewise be for human purposes? Well, wonder no more. They actually admit it when it comes to the new and improved Super Soldier. Again, let me give you a little teaser of what's to come.

"Tomorrow's Super-Soldiers Will Wear Night Vision Contact Lenses. As the Pentagon continues to build a lighter, faster and stronger soldier of

180

the future, new technology that could provide night vision without bulky goggles has caught the Army's eye.

Researchers at the University of Michigan, Ted Norris and Zhaohui Zhong, have created a super-thin infrared light sensor using graphene – an atom-thin material related to graphite – that could be layered onto contact lenses.

'If we integrate it with a contact lens, or other wearable electronics, it expands your vision,' said Zhong.

In 2011, some speculated that 'cat vision' contact lenses were used by the Navy Seals in the Osama bin Laden raid."

But wait a second. That's cool and all, but that's just contact lenses giving soldiers cat-like vision. That's not genetically altering human vision with literal cat DNA to give them cat vision. Well, keep reading. Step by step. We get there.

"Some feline organs, such as the eye, are much more similar to humans than the same organs in mice. The cat brain, particularly the cerebral cortex and vision-processing parts, is the best understood of any species.

As such, transgenic cats might be of help in understanding the workings of the brain and neurological diseases such as Alzheimer's, or with genetic illnesses and major eye diseases such as glaucoma or macular degeneration."

In other words, our cat experiments should transfer very easily over into our human experiments, due to the similarities, including improved eyesight. And that's exactly what the military is talking about doing.

"Human augmentation. There are many ways to improve a person, from vaccines to corrective eye surgery. The question becomes when such efforts cross the line into 'human enhancement.'

As scientists learn more about how to hack the human body the more enhancements become possible. This is most evident in genetic therapy when doctors add DNA containing a functional version of a lost or defective gene back into a cell.

Medical researchers are getting good at this: Just this month, medical researchers for the first time cured an inherited disease that blinds its victims. 'This restored vision to treated children and adults,' the news release claimed, 'and in turn their success enabled the entire field of gene therapy for human disease.'

Just as prosthetics for amputees can lead to exoskeletons, gene-based cures can be adapted to become enhancements. If scientists can discover a way to circumvent a genetic limitation – say, adding cat DNA to human eyes cells to see better in the dark – such therapies can become tools in the enhancement chest.

The coming issues with human enhancement will ripple across the military and society."

In other words, the military really is pushing this, and this kind of human modification is coming whether you like it or not. First dogs, then cats, then who knows, the Incredible Hulk, Captain America, Batman, Catwoman, it's not sounding so science fiction anymore is it?

But once again, mankind can't leave well enough alone. First it was insects, then it was rodents, then it was our pets, now they're moving on to our livestock, starting with this next category.

PIGS: Most people don't realize that pigs have been modified for quite some time now. In fact, if you do the research, you'll even see here in America that in just the last few decades, pigs were much smaller and fatter than today's pigs. This is because we were told fat was bad for us and we needed to "breed" that right out of them.

"This is the payoff of in the hog business, the market. Here the hog man gets paid for his months of labor, his management, his judgement and his capital. The market is the end of the line for the hog raiser. Frank Farmer seems happy as he pockets his check and heads back home. He has reason to be happy. He sold what the market is looking for, meat type hogs.

There are thousands of hog raisers in Illinois and many of them are on the market today. But not all will be as happy as Frank Farmer. Some hogs are simply not worth as much pound for pound as others. This is the story of the hogs that are worth more money. The story of meat type hogs.

Here's another load of hogs that will make the farmer happy and these are hogs that the buyers like to see too. They are not over fat, but they are long and meaty with a well-rounded turn over the loin. This type of hog gives a high percentage of the lean cuts.

Here is another familiar everyday scene. The American housewife shopping. She is the person everyone in the meat industry, producer, packer, retailer, is trying to please. Let's follow this determined young lady past the meat counter where there are all kinds of meats competing for her attention. What does she buy? Not the ham slice with all the fat that will fry away in drippings. She doesn't want these pork chops, not enough lean meat. And she is passing up the pork roast with too much fat.

But here is something she likes. And the pork industry has lost another sale. Fat pork has been losing in popularity. Quality today means lean pork. Pork with only enough fat for flavor and tenderness. Now the ham slices. Notice the grease on the right that came from another similar fat ham slice. Can you blame the alert shopper for picking up another type of meat if she can't find good lean pork? Other meats are good, and pork must meet the competition. It will take cooperation all along the line from feed lot to supermarket. The housewife will buy pork when she can get what she wants. When she can find lean ham in the meat markets, she will buy ham, she'll buy pork chops too. But she wants the good lean pork chops. The solution to this problem lies in producing a meat type hog, a hog that will yield a lot of lean meat and relatively little fat."[22]

And that's literally what they did. They bred the bulk of the fat out of the hogs and made them meatier, i.e. the meat type hog. In fact, if you look at the hogs today versus even the meat-type hogs you just saw depicted in 1956, our hogs today are way longer, not as short and stout as they were back then, and today's hogs have much more meat on them. Now, it all sounds great, but unfortunately, we've been sold a bill of goods. Current research has shown that maybe we should have left the hogs alone and maybe God knew what He was doing all along. Go figure! One researcher shared this:

"We engineered pigs for consumers who wanted leaner meat, and now we have a tasteless product that many don't want to buy."

And it's not just made them tasteless, but it turns out, shocker, that we need fat in our diet for some very important functions.

"Fat is as essential to your diet as protein and carbohydrates are in fueling your body with energy. Certain bodily functions also rely on the presence of fat. For example, some vitamins require fat in order to dissolve into your bloodstream and provide nutrients."

So, it not only turns out we need fat, but we also benefit from even animal fat, as this recent article exposed:

"Sorry, vegetarians: Animal fat may actually lower cholesterol, newly discovered study finds.

There's an age-old assumption almost cemented as fact in the public consciousness: vegetable fat is healthy fat, while animal fat is just plain old bad for you. It's the reason why some vegetarians quit meat altogether, while many dietitians say avocados are better than beef.

But thanks to a scientist, everything we seem to know about the juxtaposition between fat found in vegetables and animals may actually be a lie.

The raw findings of a study conducted nearly 50 years ago and revealed in Tuesday's edition of the medical research journal BMJ shows 'the benefits of choosing polyunsaturated fat over saturated fat seem a little less certain than we thought.'

The previously unreported findings come from the largest study of its kind to dispute the idea that polyunsaturated fat, typically found in vegetable products, is healthier in the long term than saturated fats, found in meats, creams and butter.

The report addressed vegetable oils not reducing the risk of coronary heart disease and directly contradicts the diet-heart theory; that eating vegetable oils loaded with linoleic acid like corn are less likely to clog the arteries and cause heart attacks than saturated fats from red meat."

In other words, we were lied to and sold a bill of goods, and they literally forever changed the genetic makeup of hogs to meet (no pun intended) the lie they made up. I mean, how many times have you heard older generations say today in regards to the meat being sold in stores today, "The meat just doesn't taste the same as it was when I was growing up." They're not crazy, they're absolutely right.

In fact, recently, geneticists have taken the term "meat-type hog" to a whole new level. No longer is it just good enough to breed out certain traits, apparently that takes too long. Now with modern technology you have to speed up the process and genetically modify the traits in pigs you desire. Watch what these people are doing to them.

Did You Know? *"Photos of extremely muscular pigs bred by a farm in Cambodia have been doing the rounds online, sparking controversy about genetically modified animals. The hulk like pigs are apparently bred by Dirac Cambodia, a pig farm in the Asian country's Bantimenshe Province. The company's Facebook page is littered with photos and videos of these freakishly muscular animals that appear to be the results of some extreme genetic tampering. Some have accused the breeder of using hormones and steroids to turn the pigs into nightmarish monsters.*

But seeing as Dirac Cambodia is also selling insemination kits to people wanting to grow their own, their unnatural physique is most likely caused by genetic modifications. Dirac Cambodia has been sharing updates on the incredibly muscular pigs since December of last year including videos of the animals struggling to walk under the weight of all that muscle mass and trying to keep their heads up. Photos of the mutant pigs recently went viral online, leaving most social media users furious.

'This breaks my heart how many people don't give a flying blank about animals and how they are treated.' One person wrote on Facebook. 'This is disgusting. Those poor pigs can't even hold their heads up. It looks painful, if you ask me. This is horrible!' Another commented.

Hulk like pigs are the stuff of nightmares, not meals. And those that are genetically engineered are also likely to be born with painful health issues. "[23]

But don't worry! It's healthy for you! Yeah right! You lied before; I think you're lying again! And you wonder why they've given those hogs the name Frankenswine! Yeah, very appropriate! But speaking of horror stories, the modification of pigs doesn't end there for supposed "health" reasons. China has just used the genetic modification tool, CRISPER, to make low fat pigs.

Time Health Reports: *"Chinese researchers have used CRISPR gene editing to create healthy pigs with less body fat. They inserted a gene into the pigs that helps them burn fat to stay warm. Pigs don't naturally have this gene, which other mammals use to regulate body temperature. The genetically modified pigs contained about 24% less body fat than pigs without the gene. If the results are replicated, the pigs could represent new agricultural potential. Leaner pigs that don't get cold, don't cost as much to raise and make potentially healthier bacon. It is not yet clear whether the genetic change affected the taste or quality of the pig's meat.* "[24]

But don't worry. It's healthy for you. Isn't that great! Low fat pigs. Low fat bacon even! I mean, surely that's good for us, right? Well, first of all, they didn't tell you the reason why they have to spend so much money on keeping the pigs warm now is because they bred out almost all of their fat that would naturally keep them warm. Mistake number one.

Secondly, I personally wouldn't eat any of these modified pigs, because what they carefully "edited out" (no pun intended) of that story is that the gene they inserted into these pigs to make them so-called low fat, was actually a gene from a mouse! That's right! Now we have rat pigs so to speak running around! Gee thanks! I think I'll pass. I like my bacon without rat genes thank you very much!

But it gets even worse than that! Now scientists are even creating what's called "Enviropigs" to supposedly help protect even the so-called "health" of the planet, if you can believe that.

"Pigs are an important part of human culture, mainly in terms of food. However, inside them they have a potentially very dangerous byproduct, phosphorus. They have it in their bodies and they emit it into the general environment with their bowel movements. If you take all the pigs that are on the planet that leads to a lot of phosphorus being put into the atmosphere which is not a good thing.

Therefore, scientists have experimented on pigs to try and limit the amount of phosphorus they emit via their waste. So, enviro pigs were born. They are genetically modified Yorkshire pigs that have been approved for limited production in controlled research settings in Canada and the U.S. Of course, there are many ethical concerns related to these animals and testing is still being done to see if they are safe for human consumption.

You have to decide for yourselves. But it is good to know what is going on. Clever names aside, their experiments were both simple yet effective. They were able to make it so that these pigs would absorb the phosphorus that was being produced in their bodies, drastically limiting the amount that was put into the air. While phosphorus is a necessary part of the natural life cycle, having too much of it can cause overgrowth in plants. While this may sound like a good thing, an imbalance can cause a lot of problems, especially in oceans, lakes and rivers with algae.

As of right now the state of Florida has declared a state of emergency because of a large spread of red tide which is toxic that kills everything in its path. With these enviro pigs, the balance will likely be maintained if done on a large scale. Furthermore, if they are able to do this not only with pigs but with livestock like cattle and reduce the gases they produce, it could lead to a big revolution in cleaning up the worlds atmosphere. "[25]

Wow! You've gone over the edge this time! You're stretching it now! You really think that by genetically modifying the insides of pigs that you're actually going to get rid of the red tide algae in the oceans across the world and somehow save the planet? Are you serious? I smell another bill of goods coming our way, how about you? Yeah, and by the way, I'm sure messing with the internal organs of pigs won't have any harmful internal side effects on you and me when we eat them? Yeah, right. First, it's rats, now it's gas.

But it gets even worse than that. We all know that pigs have worms inside of them, to the point where we're constantly warned that we better cook that pork thoroughly, right? Well, believe it or not, scientists have genetically engineered pigs to produce omega-3 fatty acids, you know, for our so-called "health." The problem is, they did it through the "expression of a roundworm gene!" That's right! First its rats, then its gas, now it's putting even more worms in the pigs! Can you just leave the pigs alone! You're messing up my bacon!

Unfortunately, they won't leave them alone. They've also found yet another way to make even more money off of genetically modifying pigs. You see, if you don't want to have to eat them on your plate, then hey, maybe you can make them your pet. But wait a second. Who wants a big ol' giant pig romping around the house, right? Well, hey worry no more! Thanks, once again to China, we now have Micropigs.

Buzz60 Reports: *"Scientists in China are selling these mini designer pigs as pets for $1,600.00 a pop. That's a lot of cash to swoon over some swine.*

Hi everybody, I'm Sean Dowling from Buzz60. According to Nature.com Chinese Genome Institute, BGI, began breeding micro pigs to study diseases. But now they are going to sell them as pets for $1,600.00 and give in to the micro pig craze. Miley Cyrus has one. They are even internet famous, Hamlet the micro pig has millions of YouTube viewers and thousands of social media followers and BGI is trying to cash in on the trend. To make the micro pig scientists started with the already small breed called Bama. These small pigs weigh between 70 to 100 lbs. Researchers clone pigs from altered Bama fetal cells and shut down the growth hormone receptor gene, resulting in stunted growth. Researchers haven't observed any health problems with the gene edited pig so far and they are working on being able to customize the pigs coat and color pattern."[26]

Color pattern? What's next? You going to make glow in the dark pigs? Funny you should ask.

Vimeo/UHMed Reports: *"Scientists in China tweaked some pig embryos so when the piglets were born, they would glow green. Using a technique developed by specialists at the University of Hawaii, each was injected with jellyfish DNA with the intention of rendering the little pigs fluorescent. The experiment was a success and now the babies have a greenish glow when placed under a black light. Adding to the success of the experiment, is that the life span of the animals was not compromised, and each is expected to live out a full life. Previously the method has only been tested on smaller specimens like rabbits."*[27]

Oh, so you've been doing this to rabbits too! Wow! First it was glow in the dark fish, then it was glow in the dark dogs, then it was glow in the dark cats, and now its glow in the dark pigs and apparently rabbits. Is there any pet safe from these people? Unfortunately, no. Let's moooove on to the next livestock category.

COWS: In case you haven't seen a pattern here yet with these scientists modifying our livestock, let me point it out to you. First, they make them more muscular to try to get more meat on them. Then they try to modify them to supposedly make them super healthy. And so, can anyone guess what they're doing to cows? That's right! All the above! Starting with huge massive meaty cows. Here's a breed called Belgian Blue Bulls. Arnold Schwarzenegger eat your heart out!

Bills Channel Reports*: "Hey guys, Bill here, I ran into the most amazing cows the other day. They are like these muscle-bound cows straight out of the gym. They are called Belgian Blue Bulls. Weighing in at over 1,000 lbs. these giants are the result of 100 years of natural breeding. For cattlemen it is pretty obvious. This species provides more meat to sell per cow. They also claim they eat less food. So lower food costs. For the beef consumers like you and me, the American Belgian Blue Bull Breeders Association claims it's a higher quality meat.*

The American Blues are supposed to be double muscled, low fat and their meat is a lot lower in cholesterol as other breeds and even some poultry. As far as taste goes, I really can't tell you since I've never had any. "[28]

But don't worry. I'm sure it's good for you. Anyone starting to see a pattern here? And speaking of which, it's not just making giant muscle cows to have more meat like the other livestock we ingest. It's also genetically modifying the cows so that their products will supposedly be even "healthier" for us. In fact, they've created a whole new Eugenics mooovement for cows to be the best "super cow" they can. And boy, they are raking in the bucks for these!

VICE News Reports: *"Farmers are raising super cows that sell for six figures. In Ann Arbor, Michigan an auction is about to begin."*

A bid taker tells the person on the phone, *"If you wanna bid it all, I'm fine with that too."*

The bidding begins. Daniel Brandt, Pedigree Expert says, *"It's lot number one, it's history making lot, 2900 GTBI, 1000 in that merit, it's never been sold before.*

The auctioneer says, *"Wow, here we go. We ought to be around $200,000.00."*

VICE: *"In a private suite overlooking the largest football stadium in the country, dairy farmers are casually dropping tens of thousands of dollars on cows they have only seen in a brochure."*

Dave Rama, Auctioneer: *"Think about it, don't think too long, but we gotta move. I'm asking $155,000 for a quarter of a million dollar heifer. $155,000 will get you in."*

VICE: *"These are some of the most genetically elite cows in the country. They have perfect udders, pristine lineages, and really high genetic scores. Almost half of the cows for sale today were raised by the auction's host, Jerry Jorgensen, a 29-yr. old farmer from Michigan."*

Dave Rama: *"$230,000, $235,000, what kind of cigars do you smoke? We're going to move. Sold, for $230,000.00.*

VICE: *"Nothing about 4ᵗʰ generation farmer Jerry screams 'I raise super cows.' But he's basically been raising genetically elite cows since he was a teenager. Back then it was just a side hustle on his father's farm. Now he handles the family's entire breeding program."*

VICE: *"These are healthy looking cows to you?"*

Jerry Jorgensen: *"Yes, those that are up and alert and ears up."*

VICE: *"How much have you grown the business?"*
Jerry Jorgensen: *"The genetic program has gone from having 3 to 5 calves born a year to a thousand."*

VICE: *"Selective breeding used to be much more romantic. Farmers would put two of their favorite cows in a pen together and hope for the best. Today, thanks to the advances in DNA testing, breeding cows is more like drafting Fantasy Football players. With a few hairs and about $50.00 you can get a Genome Total Performance Index or GTPI number for each cow, which includes all kinds of crucial stats like how much milk it will produce, how much fat will be in that milk, and how long and fertile its life will be. Get a high score and you could make the Holsteins Association list on this month's top new dairy cows."*

Jerry Jorgensen: *"So every animal here has its own profile. Any cow here I can look her up and say, here's what she is, here's the likelihood of her being able to make an elite animal."*[29]

You know, like an elite human from the Eugenics program, only this is for cows. But as you can see, this industry is huge money! Nearly a quarter of a million dollars for one cow...wow! But it's not just selective breeding using the latest DNA genome tools to speed up the process. It's literally genetically modifying the cows to supposedly make them "better" and more "tender" for us. Starting with this cow from Brazil.

Jason Bellini, WSJ Reports: *"Meet Ginzelle, a two-month-old Angus calf that could signal the dawn of a new era. Gene edited animals designed by humans for human consumption." "First in the world."*

Jason Bellini, WSJ Reports: *"The company that made her says she is born with traits spliced into her DNA that should allow a cold weather cow to thrive here in the Brazilian tropics. You are about to see why, if indeed it works and why our world is about to change. And why the economic incentives driving gene edited technology are so powerful."*

Driving Upstream ... Gene Editing ... The Golden Calf

WSJ Reports: *"With 200,000,000 people, Brazil is a vast country with a vast appetite for beef. That's because the US is the top producer of Angus meat. Most of Brazil's meat come from Zebu."*

Jason Bellini WSJ Sr. Correspondent: *"Do you think the regulators here are open to gene edited meat?"*

Fernando Flores, Assistant Director of Research: *"I think so, yes, the agricultural sector is very open and keen to new technology."*

Jason Bellini: *"Fernando Flores is one of the lead scientists at the Brazilian government's agricultural research entity. He shows us why Brazil wants to up its game. On the global market a pound of UD Beef is valued at around 50% more than a pound of Brazilian beef."*

Fernando Flores: *"The Zebu is less tender, it's leaner, not much fat, less marbling."*

Jason Bellini: *"So it's tougher."*

Fernando Flores*: "It's tougher, less tender, to be politically correct, you say it's less tender."*

Jason Bellini: *"Flores tells me that among Brazilian's demand for higher priced Angus Beef is rising. Ranchers would like to raise more Angus, but here is the problem. In the summer heat, Angus just don't feel like eating. They don't put on weight; they don't get beefy.*

Tad Sonstegard, Chief Scientific Officer, Recombinetics*: "If the temperature gets above 90 degrees they suffer."*

Jason Bellini: *"Tad Sonstegard, thinks he has found the solution. A few years back he discovered the gene for heat tolerance in the Senepol breed. It thrives in hotter climates. He believes it is possible to give Angus the same heat resistant trait known as 'slick' using the process called gene editing. Back in Minnesota, scientists at Recombinetics took cells from a red Angus and used a gene editing technology called 'Talan' to modify their DNA.*

They deleted a single base pair from its chromosome sequence to make the angus 'slick' replicating the mutation found in Senepol found in the heat resistant breed. After growing a colony of 20,000 of these gene edited cells, the batch was frozen and flown down to Brazil. Here on the ranch an American scientist, Mark Mosarati worked the magic that resulted in Genzille. It involved cloning. He took the DNA from the gene edited cells and inserted them into eggs.

A few steps from the lab, those that grew into embryos were inserted into recipient cows. Nine months later it was time for delivery. In July Genzille entered this world via cesarean section and a few firm tugs. She gets cleaned up and soon Genzille is romping around, getting to know her neighbors. Genzille was born alongside a sister. She died after about a week. Mosarati said it was due to birth defects resulting from the cloning process, not the gene editing."[30]

Oh no, of course not! What could go wrong with this technology? Actually, a lot, and we'll get to that in a little bit. But be that as it may, they're not only genetically altering cows to make them "heat tolerant," they're also genetically altering them to make them "hornless" using the same technology.

Alison Van Enennaam, Phd. Cooperative Extension Specialist Animal Biotechnology and Genomisc, UC Davis: *"If you look at our dairy cows and our beef cows, there is a lot of differences between them. The dairy cows were bred to be very optimal for dairy production and as it happens that brought along the horned breed or type, in other words, dairy cows grow horns.*

If we look at our beef animals they are bred for optimal beef production and as it happens, Angus, for example, is a breed that doesn't have horns and we don't really want horns in dairy production systems because the animals hurt each other with the horns, they can hurt the human workers. To protect Holstein cows, veterinarians perform an uncomfortable procedure to remove horns, known as disbudding.

Dr. Terry Lehenbauer, DVM UC Davis Veterinary Medicine Teaching and Research Center, UC Davis: *"It's a widely accepted husbandry practice that we dehorn cattle, both for the safety of the cattle, as well as for the safety of the people that take care of the cattle and work with them."*

Using precision breeding, scientists have developed a pain-free alternative to disbudding.

Alison Van Enennaam: *"We work in collaboration with a company called Recombinetics who had a vision to try to use precision braiding or genome editing to introduce genetics from Angus cattle to the Holstein dairy breed to produce dairy cattle that don't grow horns. We haven't altered anything about all the genetics that make them great milk producers. All their Holstein genetics are still in place. What we basically have done is a very precision technique of introducing just one trait that we want, which are polled or hornless and we haven't altered the rest of the genetics."[31]*

Or, so you hope. But hey, nothing to fear because nothing ever goes wrong with this genetic altering technology. Actually, let me give you just a few examples to the contrary. Starting with cows that have been genetically modified to produce human milk. Yeah, I wish I was making this up.

Sky News Reports*: "Humans have been drinking it for millennia, wholesome, healthy, full cream milk. But this dairy in Beijing isn't quite what it seems. These cows have all been genetically modified and this is human breast milk. The Chinese scientist responsible successfully inserted the human breast milk gene into a cow embryo and then implanted it into a surrogate.*

The result is a transgenic herd of 300 with milk that the scientists claim is healthier than the bovine variety. The human breast milk produced by the cow is anti-bacterial and helps boost the immune system. With government approval it could be on supermarket shelves within 3 years. You may find the idea hard to swallow but these dairy workers disagree. They say it is stronger and sweeter than cows' milk. It's a world first in a country that is leading the stampede to embrace genetically modified food. The scientists who created this herd have also produced animals that are resistant to mad cow disease as well as beef cattle that are genetically modified for more nutritious needs.

Critics say the risks of trans genetic food are not yet fully understood. But while the West worries about the dangers and morality of genetic modification, China says those scruples are misplaced. 'There are one and a half billion people in the world that don't have enough to eat. It's our duty to develop science and technology and not to hold it back. We need to feed people first before we consider ideals and convictions.' China is pushing the boundaries of genetic modification seemingly unperturbed of any ethical concerns.''[32]

In other words, they're doing this whether anybody thinks this is a bad idea or not. Who cares about the consequences, let's just push ahead. I'm sure it will work out. Really? And the Chinese are not the only ones with this dangerous attitude. Shortly after this human breast milk was made in cows, researchers from New Zealand also developed a genetically engineered cow that produced allergy-free milk. Well gee, that's great huh? I mean, what a breakthrough! What's next? A genetically modified cow that makes chocolate milk?

But do you really think you're not going to run into problems with all this? I mean, first of all, you're mixing actual human genes with animal genes, and somehow you think this won't create problems down the road? Or you really think it won't have horrible irreversible side effects?

And lest we forget, God "already" forbade this type of hybridization for a very good reason. He knows what He's doing, but we won't listen to Him, will we? No! We're repeating the same ol' mistake made in Noah's Day and it's a sign that Jesus is getting ready to come back and judge the planet again!

And keep in mind, I haven't even got to the Human/Animal Hybrid section yet. It gets even worse than what we've seen so far. But speaking of worse things, the horrible side effects of this genetic altering of cows is already starting to come out. Here's what this article shares.

"Gene-edited cattle have a major screw-up in their DNA.

They were the poster animals for the gene-editing revolution, appearing in story after story. By adding just a few letters of DNA to the genomes of dairy cattle, a US startup company has devised a way to make sure the animals never grew troublesome horns.

To Recombinetics – the St. Paul, Minnesota gene-editing company that made the hornless cattle – the animals were messengers of a new era of better, faster, molecular farming.

Except it wasn't.

Food and Drug Administration scientists who had a closer look at the genome sequence of one of the edited animals, have discovered its genome contains a stretch of bacterial DNA including a gene conferring antibiotic resistance.

The 'unintended' addition of DNA from a different species occurred during the gene-editing process itself, the government says. It went undetected by the company even as it touted the animals as 100% bovine and assailed the FDA for saying the animals needed to be regulated at all.

'It was not something expected, and we didn't look for it' says Tad Sontesgard, CEO of Acceligen, a subsidiary of Recombinetics that owns the animals. He says a more complete check 'should have been done.'

The blunder is a setback for Recombinetics, whose pioneering prototypes of gene-edited animals include heat-resistant cattle as well as pigs that never hit puberty. It's also a strike against efforts to make such gene editing a routine practice in animal reproduction.

All along, Recombinetics had noisily objected to oversight by the FDA, which categorizes gene-edited animals as new drugs that need extensive testing and approval. It even lobbied the Trump Administration to wrest oversight away from the health agency, saying it was holding back a barnyard revolution.

But gene editing isn't yet as predictable or reliable as promoters say. Instead, the procedure, meant to make pinpoint changes to DNA, can introduce significant unexpected changes without anyone noticing.

'As genome-editing technology evolves, so does our understanding of the unintended alterations it produces,' wrote the FDA scientists, led by Alexis Norris and Heather Lombardi, in a paper they released in July. They think gene-editing errors 'are under reported' and a 'blind spot' for scientists.

Eat the animals.

The University of California, Davis, veterinary scientist Alison Van Eenennaam, opened a file on the animals with the FDA last year, she says, to trade information with the agency.

According to Sontesgard, Van Eenennaam then chose to test the FDA's thinking by asking whether some of the surplus gene-edited animals taking up space at the Davis facility could go to a slaughterhouse, where they'd be made into steaks and hamburger.

Sontesgard thinks the animals are 'safe to eat with or without the plasmid.' Van Eenennaam had financial factors in mind. It costs 60 cents a pound to incinerate experimental animals, which weigh about a ton, which she considers a large expense for her university program. Better to sell them as hamburger.

The risk of haphazard engineering isn't just to barnyard animals. Genome-editing treatments to cure rare diseases are being tested on people and it is possible that patients will end up with unplanned genetic mutations.

Unintended consequences are a particular concern in connection with attempts to modify human children before birth with gene editing – as occurred for the first time in China last year.

Independent scientists still haven't had a chance to confirm whether the Chinese children – twin girls – also have unintended mistakes in their DNA.

This year the World Health Organization said any further attempts to make gene-edited people would be 'irresponsible' in part because of technical uncertainty."

In other words, we really don't know what we're doing here, let alone the long-term ramifications, maybe we should halt this. Or the Crone translation, "As God said, 'Thou shalt not!'" But we don't listen, to our own detriment, and we keep messing with the animal kingdom, including the next category.

BIRDS: Well, if you're going to mess up the food we eat from livestock including pigs and cows, I guess there's another one they need to tweak in order to be consistent. And that of course is birds, specifically chickens or even turkeys. But hey, they wouldn't mess with those, would they? Unfortunately, they already have! In fact, a quick look at the birds we ate in the past reveals that they have been slowly but surely modified into the meaty giants of today.

"People do not have a good track record with animals. The relationship animals have with humans results more often than not the exploitation of an animal for economic interest. More efficient breeding, housing, and slaughtering methods has resulted in the overall reduced welfare for many of these domesticated animals.

Animals that have been genetically chosen has resulted in making them so physically different from their ancestors that they have difficulty in the most basic of movements. Globally over 50 billion broiler chickens are bred for meat and often so obese that they can barely walk and suffer from crippling leg disorders.

When you buy chickens, you can find hot burns which are found on the upper joints of chickens which result from chickens sitting around in their own excrements for long durations. These chickens grow fast and this rapid growth rate results is due to facts know as nutrition and husbandry, however, between 50 and 60 percent of this growth is attributed to genetic selection. As a result, chickens have a decreased heart and lung size relative to the rest of their body causing cardiovascular problems and skeletal defects causing walking difficulties.

In fact, by the age of 6 weeks 90% of broiler chickens are so obese that they can no longer walk and many crippled chickens on factory farms die when they can no longer reach the water modules. Breeding programs have also resulted in chickens converting food into meat more efficiently resulting in a lower metabolic rate and lower oxygen consumption which in turn makes them more liable to heart failure and ascites.

Although genetic selection aims for an increased welfare of the animal and these commercial traits this balancing act is skewed heavily towards creating chickens to meet demands on commercial production. "33

In other words, we're modifying them to make them super meaty with big giant muscles, just like the hogs and cows. And they're not just making them freakishly big, but they are even genetically modifying them to work around the problem they created. You see, as you saw, they are raising these chickens in mass quantities and with so many birds in one place, literally thousands and thousands of them, that creates a lot of heat. Well, that heat that's generated from all these birds being housed in such manner in one spot can kill the livestock. And you can't have that. So, what's their solution? Better housing? Spread out the birds? No! Let's genetically modify them even more, yet this time we will make them be born without feathers! That'll keep them cool! I wish I was making this up.

"Featherless fowl play. At first you might not recognize these odd-looking critters as chickens. They were genetically engineered to be featherless, and were created at a laboratory in Telaviv, Israel. Aside from frightening you, the appearance of these naked cluckers do serve a valid purpose. According to experts, these featherless birds are more energy efficient. That is, their chances of surviving in warmer habitats are greater than they would normally be. That would make fiscal sense, because less money would have to be spent on cooling systems. But animal rights activists say the fowl's featherless condition makes them more vulnerable to parasites and sun burn."[34]

Boy, it's like you exchange one problem for another that YOU created. And didn't they already try this with the cows in Brazil? They were modified as well, the supposedly better deal with heat, but how did that work out? Not very well as we saw. In fact, it messed them up and created dangerous side effects, didn't it? And yet here they are, now with birds, modifying them as well for the very same reason. Yet they don't think there's going to be any serious consequences let alone horrible side effects, including our consumption of this meat. When will we ever learn?

But it gets even worse than that. Another problem they created with raising these birds in these conditions is diseases. And when those diseases spread, millions of them die at a whack and you can't have that. In fact, here's a report showing a recent outbreak of the Avian Bird Flu and its devastating effects.

Q-TV Reports: *"It's the worst outbreak of Avian Flu to ever hit the U.S., with more than 33 million birds now affected across 16 states. Including Iowa, which by far has been hit the hardest."*

Bill Northey: *"We haven't seen anything like this, certainly on the poultry side."*

Q-TV: *"Bill Northey, Iowa's Secretary of Agriculture. With more than 25 million egg laying hens set to be destroyed he says one in every 3 eggs produced in the state is now offline, many from facilities that supplied major food companies."*

Bill Northey: *"Over half the business of egg processors is done in Iowa, so certainly we're likely to see that ingredient market where eggs are an ingredient be even greater impacted than probably the shell egg market."*

Q-TV: *"The egg market breaks down into two categories, shell eggs that consumers buy at the store and breaker eggs processed and used by food manufacturers. While the price of a dozen Midwest large shell eggs has increased by 30% over the past 3 weeks, commodity analysist firm Erna Berry says it's the breaker market that is really feeling the pinch. With liquid whole egg prices up 77% as companies like Post Holdings which owns Michael Foods experience steep interruptions to their supply chain, the ripple effects are still to come for food companies that make everything from fast food breakfast sandwiches to mayonnaise. It's a situation industry consultant Joe Kern says may only get worse with so many facilities offline indefinitely."*

Joe Kern: *"Once we eradicate the disease from a physical site, when is it clean enough to safely repopulate? That is one very key component that myself as well as others in the industry are monitoring and keeping an eye on."*

Q-TV: *"And the cases keep coming. In Iowa, farmers are sending their sick birds here to Iowa State University Veterinary Medical Center where preliminary bird flu tests are conducted. Scientists are working around the clock to get results within hours."*

Scientist: *"Our normal laboratory operation is Monday through Friday but right now we are working 24 hours, 7 days a week."*[35]

Sounds to me like you've got an epidemic on your hands that's spiraling out of control! You're losing millions of birds not to mention their potential eggs! What will you do? How will you fix this? What's your solution? Better housing? Spread out the birds? Stop raising them in such unhealthy conditions? No! Let's genetically modify them AGAIN so they can no longer transmit the Avian Bird Flu. Really? Will that really work? And I quote directly from just one article:

"Attempts to produce genetically modified birds began before 1980. Chickens have been genetically modified for a variety of purposes. This includes studying embryo development and preventing the transmission of diseases.

One potential use of GM birds could be to reduce the spread of avian disease. Researchers at Roslin Institute have produced a strain of GM chickens (Gallus gallus domesticus) that does not transmit avian flu to other birds; however, these birds are still susceptible to contracting it."

Okay now, let me get this straight. Granted, I might not be the sharpest knife in the drawer, but I think even I can figure this one out. You genetically modified the chickens to eradicate the bird flu problem, but when all was said and done, they can still get the bird flu. You call that a success? I call that a big failure.

And speaking of failures, they're going even further with this genetic modification of birds in an even more detrimental direction. You see, another one of the big problems with the poultry industry and the concerns that people have with them, is not only the diseases and conditions these birds are subjected to, but also the drugs these livestock are injected with. And they inject massive amounts of drugs into these birds to hopefully counteract these diseases and growth-related issues they themselves created. Well, believe it or not, now they are even genetically modifying these same birds to actually "produce" drugs for our "supposed" benefit! I know, sounds like a major drug problem to me.

WBZ4 News Reports: *"Tonight a new and unusual way to make medicine. Researchers in Scotland say they have found a way to have* *chickens lay eggs filled with medicine. A method that could make some drugs much more affordable. Dr. Malaka Marshall has the story."*

Dr. Marshall: *"These chickens are far from ordinary. They are laying eggs containing cancer killing drugs. Scientists at the University of Edenborough have genetically modified birds who contain human protein in their eggs that boost the immune system."*

Dr. Lissa Herron, Roslin Technologies: *"In the past making these trans genetic animals has been very inefficient, expensive, and difficult and what we have done is found a method that makes it a lot faster and a lot more efficient."*

Dr. Marshall: *"Scientist say the egg white contains the treasure. Large quantities of medically important proteins which they can purify and package as medicines to treat arthritis and some cancers."*

Dr. Helen Sang: *"If you want to have more eggs then you just need more birds and that is why we have in this pen a cockerel and he can produce an awful lot of children in a short amount of time."*

Dr. Marshall: *"Eggs are already used for growing viruses used in vaccine such as the flu shot. Scientists say that making medicine using eggs is up to 100 times cheaper than producing it in a factory. Currently they can extract one dose of a drug from 3 eggs, and hens can lay up to 300 eggs a year. Researchers believe that they can breed enough chicks to produce medicine for patients commercially."*[36]

Wow! What could go wrong with that? You guys have such a great track record. Actually, only everything can go wrong with this, as these articles share:

"The floodgates are open for more genetically modified animals – possibly even humans.

Last week saw the approval of another genetically modified animal – this time a chicken genetically altered to produce a drug in its eggs. The drug is designed to replace a faulty enzyme in people with a rare genetic condition that prevents the body from breaking down fatty molecules in cells.

It is the third so-called 'farmaceutical' approved in the U.S. market. Last year the FDA also approved a drug for treating hereditary angioedema that is produced by transgenic (GE) rabbits.

Not for eating.

Unlike the genetically engineered salmon that was approved by the FDA last month, the transgenic chickens that are not intended to enter the food supply because every cell in the modified chicken contains altered DNA.

The FDA says that the chickens are not likely to accidentally enter the food supply or adversely affect the environment because they are raised in indoor facilities. (Yeah, we all know how that's going.)

William Muir, a geneticist at Purdue University in West Lafayette, Indiana, praised the FDA's decision to approve the transgenic chickens. 'The floodgates are opening,' he says, 'and I can't wait to see what comes next.'"

"We can. There is much talk of creating so-called designer babies, whose parents would be able to select the genetic characteristics that their child develops (being tall, intelligent, etc.)

Scientists are also working on performing DNA transplants into human embryos to eliminate genetic diseases. A baby born this way would have genetic material from three different people and pass on its genetic makeup to future generations.

Scientists are learning, however, that changing even one gene can result in harmful DNA mutations that reverberate throughout the entire DNA structure.

This is the stuff of dystopian science fiction stories, and we may be approaching such a world faster than we think."

In other words, the Science Fiction Movie nightmares of Frankenstein, X-Men to Marvel movies are about to become our present-day reality! Welcome to a world full of mutants, both animals and man! At this rate, how long will it be before there are any true animals or even true humans left? We'll get to that in our Human/Animal Hybrid section.

But speaking of stories, we all probably grew up singing the nursery rhyme, "Mary had a little lamb, its' fleece was white as snow." Remember that? Well, unfortunately in today's scientific genetic altering community, the song needs to be updated to, "Its' fleece had started to glow." And that's seen when we take a look at our next livestock category.

LAMBS & GOATS: Now I hear that a lot of people like lamb or mutton around the world, I personally don't care for it. It's definitely not my meat of choice. And believe it or not, many cultures in various regions actually enjoy eating even goat meat. That would be a strike two for me. But the point is this, lambs and goats are another one of our staple livestock foods from around the world, and so what do you think the genetic altering community is going to do with these? Leave them alone? Hands off? Don't touch? I wish. Sadly, even lambs and goats have become a part of their wild experimentations.

Tech Insider Reports: *"What you are seeing is not science fiction. It's a lamb fetus. In place of the mother is this artificial womb. The experiment is from Children's Hospital of Philadelphia. This is just a first step. Ultimately, scientists hope to help premature human babies. Each year, 30,000 Americans are born at 26 weeks or younger. The second they take that first breath of air their lungs stop developing. As a result, many preemies suffer long-term health problems.*

But what if they could finish developing after birth? That's what scientists did with 8 lamb fetuses. The lambs were born prematurely and placed in here. The tube acts like an umbilical cord, feeding oxygen to the lamb. Over the next 4 weeks they grew wool coats, gained weight and opened their eyes. Autopsies later showed that their organs also developed properly. Scientists estimate 3-5 more years before human tests."[37]

Okay, it's bad enough that you're growing lambs in an artificial womb, but did you catch that last part? Here soon, you're expecting to do that with who? Humans. I mean, gee whiz, what's next? You're going to start growing humans in artificial wombs like a crop, or like livestock? I didn't say that, this article did.

"An artificial womb successfully grew baby sheep – and humans could be next.

Inside what looks like oversized ziplock bags strewn with tubes of blood and fluid, eight fetal lambs continued to develop – much like they would have inside their mothers.

Over four weeks, their lungs and brains grew, they sprouted wool, opened their eyes, wriggled around, and learned to swallow, according to a new study that takes the first step toward an artificial womb. It's appealing to imagine a world where artificial wombs grow babies, eliminating the health risk of pregnancy. 'It's complete science fiction to think that you can take an embryo and get it through the early developmental process and put it on our machine without the mother being the critical element there.'"

But they've done it, starting with lambs, and humans are next. They go on to call this artificial womb a "Bio Bag." That doesn't sound very romantic. And to think we haven't even gotten to the Human Enhancement section with the actual cloning going on. You won't believe what's being done to humans! Growing them like a crop or a livestock is not that far off! Much closer than you think!

But be that as it may, growing lambs in artificial wombs is kind of freaky, I'll give you that. But that's not genetically altering them and messing with their genome like the other animals. Well hey, worry no more and wait no more. They're already doing that too, starting with the mixing of lamb DNA with Jellyfish DNA.

"A lamb, called 'Rubis' was born to a sheep that had its DNA modified. Researchers from the National Institute for Agricultural Research (INRA) used a jellyfish gene that produces a green fluorescent protein to make the research animal's skin transparent. This allowed researchers to see and study heart transplants."

Oh, so apparently you got tired of squinting at those tiny see-through mice you created for the very same supposed purpose, so you did it on something even bigger like a lamb. But hey, don't worry, these experiments always work out great and there's no risk to you and I. Yeah, right! Watch this. All it takes is one disgruntled employee and we're toast!

Google Reports: *"Officials at the National Institute of Agricultural Research in France are currently investigating a major breach. A genetically modified research lamb bred to have the DNA of a jellyfish was sold to a slaughterhouse amongst a group of normal unchanged livestock. It was then sold to a buyer in the Paris Metropolitan region in October of 2014 and is thought to have been consumed.*

Authorities of the research institute have released a statement assuring the public that neither humans nor the environment would be adversely affected by the animal's release. The lamb named Ruby was born into a program where the DNA of sheep was engineered with Jellyfish green fluorescent protein. The incident is believed to have been a malicious and deliberate act from tensions among the staff."[38]

So much for being secure! How foolish can we be? Even though France in this case has banned genetically modified foods, these experiments still find a way to make it on to our plate. As one writer stated:

"A lamb that was genetically modified to contain a fluorescent jellyfish protein somehow ended up on someone's dinner plate. The French authorities have launched an investigation to find out how the 'jellyfish-lamb' was sold as meat. I wonder if it tasted baaaaad?

The sale of any genetically modified food products for humans was made illegal in France in the 2000's after large-scale protests. There is a significant opposition to GM research in France, who demanded the EU allow individual countries to block the use of the 19 authorized GM crops.

This affair seems unbelievable and threatens to do harm to an institute that is renowned for its seriousness. But it also shows, if the facts prove correct, that the best-controlled institution cannot ward against individual waywardness."

In other words, no matter how much they say, "This is safe, we're on top of our procedures, these experiments are totally secure," they're still going to leak out into the world one way or another.

But speaking of baaaaad ideas, that was just lambs. Believe it or not, the same genetic modifications are being done to goats as well. Again, they just can't seem to leave well enough alone, certainly not our food supply. But wait until you see what they're doing with goats. You thought putting jellyfish DNA in a lamb was pretty wild? Of all things they're cramming into the genetic makeup of goats, it's this!

Miles O'Brien: *"This is a story about silk and milk. The silk is from Golden Orb weave spiders."*

Heather Rothfuss: *"Here you go pumpkin. They are incredibly inquisitive. They're a lot of fun."*

Miles O'Brien: *"The milk from specially bred goats. Good luck trying to connect those dots. So, what's the thread?"*

Randy Lewis, University of Wyoming Molecular Biologist: *"There is a lot of spider silk fibers because they are stronger than almost any other man-made fiber and they are also elastic."*

Miles O'Brien: *"Because it is stronger ounce per ounce than other materials, there are many possible medical uses, from artificial ligaments to sutures for surgery."*

Randy Lewis: *"So the question is, how do you produce large amounts of material?"*

Miles O'Brien: *"Spider farms don't work. They tend to kill each other, so molecular biologist Randy Lewis figured out how to put the spider's silk making genes into goats."*

Randy Lewis: *"What we did was put that gene into some goats in the situation where they would only make the protein in their milk and when the goats have kids and when they start lactating we collect that milk and we can purify that protein in a much, much higher quantity."*

Miles O'Brien: **"**Feeding and milking goats and wrangling spiders are sometimes part of the job."*

Randy Lewis: *"So, we collect the milk out here and we take it back to the lab for processing."*

Heather Rothfuss: *"The silk we are particularly curious about is angling, that is the outside of the web, it is the strongest part of the structure."*

Miles O'Brien: *"Chemical Engineer Heather Rothfuss, separates the silk protein from the milk. No arachnophobia for her, in fact she's actually warmed up to working with spiders."*

Randy Lewis: *"I'm on a roll now. It's collecting okay."*

Miles O'Brien: *"Just 4 drops of protein processed from the milk can be spun into 4 yards of silk."*

Randy Lewis: *"There will be a lot of applications, eye surgery, plastic surgery, neurosurgery."*

Miles O'Brien: *"The lab is also introducing genes into alfalfa plants. So how do people react to this tangled web of a tale?"*

Randy Lewis: *"They have to understand that you just cannot farm spiders, so you have to come up with a way to make the material."*

Miles O'Brien: *"No kidding, with help from the Natural Science Foundation, Lewis studies spider silk at the University of Wyoming and so far, Lewis says, he has seen no difference in the health or appearance of the transgenic goats."[39]*

Oh yeah, no problems whatsoever! They just crawl up the walls now and make their own webs and drop on top of people when they pass by. That's all! No big deal! Can you believe this? And did you see that they're doing this with plants as well? There's nothing safe or sacred with these guys is there? This is crazy folks!

But remember, we've seen their track record. They've got this all under control, it'll never make its way on to our forks! Yeah right! How's this for a future dinner conversation? "Hey, pass the spider alfalfa honey with the spider goat meat. Hold on. I got a web caught in my throat! Hey, did you hear that the kids got jumped again by a spider goat on their way home from school? We really should get them some spider-goat spray from that bug guy that comes around." And lest you think I'm totally joking; these kinds of genetic combos are already being "approved" for human consumption.

"Transgenic drug gets green light from the United States. The US Food and Drug Administration (FDA) has issued its first approval of a drug produced by a genetically engineered animal.

The drug, marketed as ATryn, is the human blood protein antithrombin and will be used to treat various blood-clotting disorders. It is produced in the milk of transgenic goats engineered by GTC Biotherapeutics, a company based in Framingham, Massachusetts.

The goat gene sequence has been modified, using fresh umbilical cords taken from kids, in order to code for the human enzyme lysozyme. Researchers wanted to alter the milk produced by the goats, to contain lysozyme in order to fight off bacteria causing diarrhea in humans.

The FDA's decision, released on 6 February, had been delayed while the agency worked out how to regulate products made from genetically engineered animals.

It finally issued industry guidelines on 15 January this year, and it was widely expected that approval of ATryn, which had already been given the green light by a scientific advisory committee, would soon follow. The drug was approved in Europe in June 2006.

The US Food and Drug Administration (FDA) has also approved a chicken that has been genetically engineered to produce a drug in its eggs.

And last year, the FDA authorized a drug for treating hereditary angioedema that is produced by transgenic rabbits."

In other words, these genetically modified animals are going to enter humans one way or another, be it on the end of a fork or in the form of a so-called medicine. But don't worry. I'm sure it's safe! And you wonder why Jesus is coming back to shut all this down!

SEA LIFE & AMPHIBIANS: But speaking of ending up on your fork, as we already saw a couple times before, fish, or specifically salmon were the very first transgenic animal to win U.S. approval for food. So once again, the track record is perfect. The genetic altering community can't leave any of our food supply or livestock alone. Hogs, cows, birds, lambs and goats, and the final thing that the bulk of our world ingests, that of seafood. Let's start off with Sea Cucumbers.

Business Insider: *"Cucumbers usually cost about $3 a kilo, but sea cucumbers can set you back over $3,000 per kilo. In fact, they are so valuable people will risk their lives to get hold of one. They might not look it, but sea cucumbers are pretty special creatures, just as this guy, Steve Purcell, one of the world's foremost experts on sea cucumbers."*

Steve Purcell: Southern Cross University Maine Ecologist: *"They're quite strange animals. They don't have any limbs, they don't have any eyes, but they have a mouth and they have an anus and a whole bunch of organs in between."*

Business Insider: *"These other worldly animals have been prized as a delicacy in Asia for centuries. Where the wealthiest class would eat these as a nutritious high protein treat. But it wasn't until the 1980's that demand exploded.*

A growing middle class in China meant more people could afford the luxury. Today they are typically dried and packaged in ornate boxes and then given as gifts and served on special occasion. So, the fancier and more unusual looking the better and more expensive."

Steve Purcell: *"The spikier the animals, the higher the price."*

Business Insider: *"And of the 1,250 different species of sea cucumber in the world the Japanese Sea Cucumber takes the cake."*

Steve Purcell: *"Imagine some sort of mystical dragon slug with all these sorts of spikes coming out of it."*

Business Insider: *"At up to $3,500 a kilo it's the most expensive sea cucumber on the market. Compared to other varieties, like the Golden Sandfish, ($850) Dragonfish, ($130) and the Curry Fish, ($430). And* *even if you order a common species on Amazon you could still pay over $170 for a plate.*

Besides presentation, cucumber connoisseurs also value the thick chewy bodies. And to a lesser extent, taste. But the experience of eating them is only part of their appeal. It turns out sea cucumbers contain high levels of a chemical called Fucosylated Glycosaminoglycan in their skin which people across Asia have been using to treat joint problems like arthritis for centuries. And more recently in Europe people are using it to treat certain cancers and to reduce blood clots.

The Sea Cucumber craze now comes from all sides. You have the original Asian delicacy demand that started in the 1980's and the new interest from western pharmaceutical companies. In response, nations have clamored to harvest their local species. From Morocco to the United States to New Guinea, everyone wants in on the sea cucumber trade."

Steve Purcell: *"It's just spread like a contagion from one country to another."*

Business Insider*: "For example, from 1996 to 2011 the number of countries exporting sea cucumbers, exploded from 35 to 83. But unfortunately, sea cucumbers couldn't handle the stream. In Yucatan Mexico, for example, divers saw a 95% drop in their harvest just between 2012 and 2014, and that is a problem for everyone. For one because the more sea cucumbers are harvested, the rarer and more expensive they become and as the demand continues to increase the problem is only getting worse."[40]*

Oh no! What will you do! How will we "fix" this sea cucumber supply problem? Our world is headed for a turmoil! Uh, can you say, "Genetic Modification" to the rescue? Believe it or not, one of the most desired of all sea cucumbers is the albino sea cucumber. They are not only extremely rare, but obviously who wants to wait around forever for one of those to pop up on the scene randomly, especially now when the overall supply of sea cucumbers is on the decline? Well, this is why a team of geneticists in China have decided to take the matter into their own hands.

"Albino Sea Cucumbers, a Delicacy, Could Become a Lot Less Rare.

Sea cucumbers, slug-like creatures that hug the seafloor, have long been a prized delicacy at Chinese banquets, the mark of a special occasion. And no variety of sea cucumber is more valued, or costlier, than the exceedingly rare albino. Just a few years ago, five white sea cucumbers sold at auction in the city of Jinan for 160,000 renminbi, or nearly $26,000 at today's exchange rate.

Now, Chinese scientists say they have cracked the genetic code of the albino sea cucumber, opening the door to its mass production.

According to the report by the Institute of Oceanology, Chinese Academy of Sciences, in Qingdao, researchers who have been studying the genetic makeup of sea cucumbers have identified the gene responsible for albinism and have begun producing genetically modified albinos. This year alone, it says, the scientists, led by Dr. Yang Hongsheng, have succeeded in breeding 150 million white sea cucumbers suitable for aquaculture.

With the prospect of large-scale production, can shoppers expect some day to find packages of inexpensive white sea cucumbers next to the frozen shrimp and scallops in their local supermarkets?"

Sounds like it's already here to me! But speaking of appearing right along with other seafood in the supermarket, genetically modified sea cucumbers are the tip of the iceberg of sea life that is currently being genetically altered. Another favorite seafood of people around the world enjoy is lobster or shellfish. But hey, surely, they wouldn't mess around with those, would they? Well, you might want to check out this article.

"More meat and fish from genetically engineered animals could be coming to your dinner plate. The Food and Drug Administration issued a

bombshell announcement, for the first time approving genetically engineered salmon. The fish, produced by AquaBounty, have been genetically engineered to grow to market size in just 18 months, rather than the customary three years.

The FDA issued voluntary labeling guidance but so far, the agency is not requiring fish vendors to inform shoppers if their salmon is a GMO variety.

What's next? GMO bacon? Maybe. The FDA reports that pigs are being bred so that their meat will have increased levels of omega-3 fatty acids.

GMO lobster? It could happen. Food scientists have successfully transplanted genes into crayfish. According to the National Oceanic and Atmospheric Administration, this technique 'could be applied someday to shrimp and other crustaceans such as crabs and lobster to improve characteristics like color, taste, growth rate, size, and disease resistance, for aquaculture.

Paradoxically, as genetic engineering technology spreads, lawmakers are working hard to limit consumer's rights to know what's in their food. A bill we call the DARK Act, introduced by Sen. Pat Roberts (R-Kan.), would make GMO labeling strictly voluntary for companies and would prevent states from imposing any labeling requirements. It could even make it harder for companies to voluntarily disclose GMOs.

What's more, the DARK Act would move GMO labeling jurisdiction from the FDA to the U.S. Department of Agriculture. If the DARK Act passes, GMO bacon and GMO lobster could show up on your dinner plate, and no one will have to tell you about it."

Well gee, that's a shocker! Anybody starting to see a pattern here? But you might be thinking, "Well hey, I'm not really into shellfish at all, let alone all those other wild fancy expensive seafood delicacies. I'm just a good ol' fashioned red-blooded fish eating American. Give me a fish from a lake or a pond and I'm happy. You can keep all that other weird sea creature stuff." Well, that's the problem as we saw before. Even traditional fish are being modified and oftentimes you won't even know, including the so-called Super Salmon! Let's take a look at that again.

"Not unlike the spider silk goat, super salmon, also known as the Aqua Advantage Salmon were bred with a specific purpose. These Salmon were not only bred to be huge; they were bred to get to that size in half the time a natural salmon would do it. This of course would speed up the time that the salmon would be ready to go to market to be sold all around the world.

This is being made possible by injecting the fish with a growth hormone, illegal for humans playing sports but not for fish going to market. Now these salmon are regulated by breeding them in areas that don't mingle with natural salmon. These have not been released into the wild because even if a few of these super salmon ever got into the waters it have devastating effects. The super salmon would probably completely destroy the regular ones. Beating them at everything and causing massive harm to their population numbers."[41]

But hey, don't worry. These guys can be trusted. And as we saw, they never make mistakes, they always keep things secure, and they never have disgruntled employees looking for a way to get back at their employers. Yeah right! It's just a matter of time before one of these gets out and as you saw, the effects will be deadly, devastating, and irreversible! But they're doing this with even more fish than that. Watch this.

"AquaBounty Technologies have produced a salmon that can mature in half the time as wild salmon. The fish is an Atlantic salmon with a Chinook salmon (Oncorhynchus tshawytscha) gene inserted. This allows the fish to produce growth hormones all year round compared to the wild-type fish that produces the hormone for only part of the year.

The fish also has a second gene inserted from the eel-like ocean pout that acts like an 'on' switch for the hormone. Pout also have antifreeze proteins in their blood, which allow the GM salmon to survive near-freezing waters and continue their development.

In November 2015, the FDA of the USA approved the AquAdvantage salmon for commercial production, sale and consumption, the first non-plant GMO food to be commercialized.

The FDA has indicated these salmon will not even need to carry a label identifying them as genetically modified – so you may have no idea what you are eating
.

GM fish have been developed with promoters driving an over-production of 'all fish' growth hormone for use in the aquaculture industry to increase the speed of development and potentially reduce fishing pressure on wild stocks. This has resulted in dramatic growth enhancement in several species, including salmon, trout and tilapia."

In other words, it started with salmon, but it's not stopping there. It's moving to the other fish we eat as well. In fact, just about any kind of sea life you can think of is currently under some sort of modification, including amphibians.

"Genetically modified fish are used for scientific research, as pets and as a food source. The GloFish is a brand of genetically modified fluorescent zebrafish with bright red, green, and orange fluorescent color. It was originally developed by one of the groups to detect pollution, but is now part of the ornamental fish trade, becoming the first genetically modified animal to become publicly available as a pet when it was introduced for sale in 2003.

Aquaculture is a growing industry, currently providing over half the consumed fish worldwide. Through genetic engineering it is possible to increase growth rates, reduce food intake, remove allergenic properties, increase cold tolerance and provide disease resistance.

Other organisms that have been genetically modified include snails, geckos, turtles, crayfish, oysters, shrimp, clams, abalone and sponges.

Flatworms have the ability to regenerate themselves from a single cell. Until 2017 there was no effective way to transform them, which hampered research. By using microinjection and radiation, scientists have now created the first genetically modified flatworms.

The bristle worm, a marine annelid, has been modified. It is of interest due to its reproductive cycle being synchronized with lunar phases and regeneration capacity.

Cnidaria such as Hydra and the sea anemone Nematostella vectensis are attractive model organisms to study immunity and certain developmental processes.

Genetically modified frogs, in particular Xenopus laevis and Xenopus tropicalis, are used in development biology. GM frogs can also be used as pollution sensors, especially for endocrine disrupting chemicals. There are proposals to use genetic engineering to control cane toads in Australia."

Really? Genetically modified frogs? Is there nothing sacred with these guys? Oh, but it gets worse than that. Not only are "they" doing it, but now even the so-called "Average Joe" can do it. Believe it or not, you can get your very own DNA modification kit to modify your very own frog and see what you come up with!

Josiah Zayner, CEO, The Odin: *"We are going to learn how to genetically modify frogs. Turn them into little fighting Ninja Turtles. No, they're not turtles. At the Odin we are a genetic engineering educational company. So, we sell kits and supplies and teach classes that teach people with no experience in science, how to do genetic engineering in their own home.*

We are going to inject some of them with some gene therapy and others of them we are just going to leave. Then we are going to see if they build up muscle and grow up bigger and stronger.

The first thing we have to do is we want to anesthetize the frog and what happens is they don't feel any pain. We are going to wait a couple minutes and then after a couple minutes we will rinse them off in some non-chlorinated water. The gene we are going to inject today is a gene call Fluvastatin. Now what Fluvastatin does is that it down regulates this gene called Miostatin which inhabits muscle growth.

If we're making muscles all the time, we'd burn so many calories that our bodies would have a hard time existing. But when you give a gene therapy, that makes that gene not work so well. You grow muscles because these gene therapies are temporary. You see the maximum expression of the gene that we put in there, 24-48 hours after it is injected. In the experiment you inject the frogs once a week. Then see how the changes in muscle growth are compared to the frogs we did not inject. We hope you do not create zombies."[42]

Yeah, real funny! Can you believe this? This is a nightmare waiting to happen, with irreversible consequences! I mean, you open up this technology to the average Joe and it's going to get really wild! What's next? You're going to start mixing aquatic creatures with other creatures just to see what you come up with? Unfortunately, the scientific community isn't waiting for the average Joe to come up with that idea themselves, they're already doing it.

"Turtle Ducks, one of the most unlikely hybrids we have encountered, is the offspring of a turtle and a duck. The animals do share a common ancestor because such breeds couldn't be bred. Some researchers in 2013 found a way around that. The creature's embryos were mixed first by taking duck cells and implanting them into turtle embryos. A second experiment reversed that procedure with turtle cells implanted into duck embryos and all the creatures survived. One question remained though, why would such a hybrid even be necessary?[43]

Yeah, I would agree, that's a commonsense question. Because the next thing you know, you keep this kind of behavior up, you're going to end up with a world full of <u>these</u> things running around.

"A clip from the Teenage Mutant Ninja Turtle show a view of the skyline. A train is coming into the station. Suddenly there is gunfire and people are running all around. Then you hear the words, 'Let's rock and roll.' The reporter sees some large strange creatures coming in to fight. She climbs to the top of a building to take pictures of them and slips. As she is falling a hand grabs her and brings her back to the top of the building where she is safe. This creature that just saved her is green and it resembles a turtle with a mask on. He tells her 'Do not tell anyone about this! If you do, we will find you!' Then she looks up and another one is coming at her, 'Yes we will find you!' She looked back at the first one and he says, 'That came across super creepy, we will find you though.' Then she faints.

They have come to save the world from the giant steel monster that is destroying the city. The father Ninja says, 'I have trained you your whole life to protect this city. You are ready to exploit this threat.'

The evil villain tells the monster, 'We are taking your armor to the next level.' There is an explosion and the metal monster rises. He has swords coming out of both of his arms. The war has begun. The rat leader says, 'You are stronger together than he can ever be.' They join together and one says, 'Let's go get my father.' Now they mean business. Together they are going to save the father. The reporter is trying to explain who is out there fighting to save the city. 'No, they are turtles!' Another officer worker asks, 'Is there anything else we should know about them?' She replies, 'They are ninjas.'"[44]

Now as wild as that movie, let alone cartoon seemed to be back in the day, based upon what we've seen so far in this book, and all the different genetic mixing of different animals and sometimes even mixing these with people, a mutant ninja turtle doesn't seem as farfetched anymore, does it? Again, we haven't even gotten to the Super Soldier section yet. Wait until you see that.

Oh and by the way, for the sake of time, I'm not only skipping over a ton of other material I could share on the genetic modification of the animal kingdom, but I'm really not diving into the plant kingdom like I could, which is another huge area they're getting into. Yes, we did talk about some of the genetic modified crops out there like corn and tomatoes, etc. But they really want to mess up the plant kingdom as a whole on the same level as their doing with the animal kingdom, including things like trees! Starting with glow in the dark trees!

Did You Know: *"MIT researchers have made an important breakthrough in their quest to make plants that glow in the dark a reality. What they call plant nano bionics. The engineers implanted nano particles into the leaves of a watercress plant that caused the plant to give off a dim glow for three and a half hours. Their next goal is to create plants bright enough to illuminate a workspace, but if successful, the technology could also transform trees into self-powered streetlights, the scientists claim.*

The team's ultimate goal is to engineer plants to replace many of the functions currently performed by electrical devices and appliances. The vision is to make a plant that will function as a desk lamp, a lamp you won't have to plug in. The light is ultimately powered by the energy metabolism of the plant itself, said Michael Strano, professor of chemical engineering at MIT and the senior author of a recently released study on plant's nano bionics. The researcher's previous endeavors include designing plants that can detect explosives and report that information to a smart device as well as plants that can monitor drought conditions.

They decided that lighting, which accounts for about 20% of worldwide energy consumption, was a sensible subsequent objective as bioluminescent plants would significantly cut back on CO_2 emissions.

Plants can self-repair. They have their own energy and they are already adapted to the outdoor environment Strano told MIT news. We think this is an idea whose time has come. It is a perfect problem for plant nano bionics. The main component of the MIT team's luminous plants is

Luciferase, the class of oxidative enzymes that give fireflies their signature glow.

Luciferase converts a molecule called Luciferin to Oxy Luciferin causing it to emit light. A molecule called Coenzyme A supports the process by removing the by-product that can hinder Luciferase activity. The MIT team package these components into a separate nanoparticle carrier made from materials that the US Food and Drug Administration classifies as generally regarded as safe.

These carriers help each component arrive in the right part of the plant as well as prevent them from reaching concentrations that could harm the plants. Early efforts resulted in plants that could glow up to 45 minutes, but subsequent tweaks increased the glow time to 3 ½ hours. The light generated by one 10-centimeter water cress seedling is currently about 1000th of the amount needed to read but the researchers believe that they can boost the light output and duration significantly by optimizing the concentration and release rates of the enzymes. They hope to eventually expand this technology to find a way to paint or spray the nano particles on the plant leaves enabling them to convert trees into light sources.

Our target is to perform one treatment when the plant is a seedling or a mature plant and have it last for the lifetime of the plant, Strano said. Our work very seriously opens up the doorway to streetlamps that are nothing but treated trees and into direct lighting in and around homes. Interestingly the researchers can turn off the lights in the plants as well by adding a Luciferase inhibiter enabling them to ultimately produce plants that shut off their lights in response to environmental conditions such as sunlight."[46]

Oh yeah, because you can't waste the plant light energy coming from plants now. But can you believe this? Glow in the dark plants? Glow in the dark trees? Did these guys not have enough glow sticks growing up? Did their Mom withhold them from them or something? They always want to make things glow! Glow in the dark fish, glow in the dark cats, glow in the dark pigs and now glow in the dark trees! Are you kidding me? This is starting to look like a scene from this movie.

"A clip from the movie Avatar shows an Avatar man chasing an Avatar woman he has just met in the forest. It is so beautiful with the plants and trees glowing.

He is calling to her, "If I'm like a child then maybe you should teach me." He almost catches her, and she turns around and says, "Sky people cannot learn what they do not see." But he doesn't give up. "Then teach me how to see." But her reply is, "No one can teach you how to see."

He almost falls off the limb but proceeds after her. "But can't we talk? Where did you learn how to speak English?" Again, he almost falls but she grabs him by the arm. She says, "You are like a baby." Then seriously he says, "I need your help." But her reply is, "You should not be here!" He says, "Okay, take me with you." But again, she says, "No! Go back!" Again, he says, "No!" And she says, "Go back!"

Then suddenly they look up and what looks like little glowing spiders with many legs start falling down upon them. He starts to swat them away, but she says, "No!" As they slowly start to land on his arm she is in awe. They are covering his body. "What are they?" He asks. She answers, "Seeds to the secret tree, very pure spirits." She stares in amazement. They have all landed on him and he is glowing. Then they all drift away in unison."

Yeah bud! Stop smacking on our glow in the dark plants! They're sacred, don't you know? Yeah, there's your glow in the dark forest coming to a planet near you, only the planet's called planet earth, not some make believe science fiction movie planet.

Oh, by the way, wasn't the premise of that movie also about how there were not only a bunch of weird hybrid looking creatures all over that planet as well as people who had a mind transference into another body to navigate around on that planet? Yeah, believe it or not, that's exactly what today's Modern Transhumanist Movement is working towards, right now as we speak. But we'll get to that at the end of the next volume. In the meantime, it sure seems Hollywood, once again, is preparing us for some freaky future that the elite really is building for us!

But let's back up a little bit there. Did you catch the one part previously that these scientists can not only create these glow in the dark plants in the seedling stage, but even spray and change already mature developed plants, including trees, with this genetic concoction? Just like the animals, there is no plant that is safe from these guys!

But it gets worse! They not only want to make plants and trees glow, they want to change their whole genome, just like with animals, and might I add, with some pretty devastating effects.

"Brazil considers transgenic trees. Genetically modified eucalyptus could be a global test case. On September 4, a public hearing will consider bringing an even more vigorous recruit into the ranks: genetically engineered eucalyptus that produces around 20% more wood than conventional trees and is ready for harvest in five and a half years instead of seven. Brazilian regulators are evaluating the trees for commercial release; a decision could come as early as the end of this year.

The trees were developed by FuturaGene, a biotechnology firm in Rehovot, Israel, that was spun out of the Hebrew University in Jerusalem in 1993. The company found that certain proteins accelerate plant growth by facilitating cell-wall expansion. FuturaGene inserted into eucalyptus a gene that encodes one such protein from thale cress (Arabidopsis thaliana), a common laboratory plant. In 2010, the firm was bought by Suzano Pulp and Paper of São Paulo, Brazil, one of the world's largest producers of eucalyptus pulp.

FuturaGene's chief executive Stanley Hirsch is quick to point out the environmental benefits of his company's creation. The tree's speedy growth boosts absorption of carbon dioxide from the air by about 12%, he says, aiding in the fight to reduce greenhouse-gas emissions. The genetically modified trees may also require less land to produce the same amount of wood, reducing the conversion of natural forest into plantations.

Genetically engineered trees do pose some biosafety issues that do not apply to agricultural crops such as maize (corn) or soya, notes forest geneticist Steven Strauss of Oregon State University in Corvallis. They remain in the environment for years, increasing their potential impact on the plants, animals and soil around them. And trees tend to disperse pollen further than crops nearer the ground do, raising concerns about gene flow to native relatives. We also wonder what this will do to the composition of honey made by bees that visit the trees.

While FuturaGene tests the waters in Brazil, a U.S. company awaits a regulatory decision regarding its genetically engineered, freeze-tolerant eucalyptus. In 2008, ArborGen of Ridgeville, South Carolina, petitioned the U.S. Department of Agriculture to allow commercialization of the trees in the southeastern United States. Delays of this length are not uncommon in the U.S. regulatory system, says ArborGen's director of regulatory affairs Leslie Pearson.

Researchers, businesses and activists are watching closely. Eucalyptus (Eucalyptus spp.) – native to Australia – is grown on about 20 million hectares throughout the tropics and subtropics, and approval of the genetically engineered trees in Brazil could encourage their adoption elsewhere. 'It would have ripple effects worldwide,' says Zander Myburg, who studies the genetics of forest trees at the University of Pretoria in South Africa."

Yeah, I would say so. It would not only create massive trees with the potential to spread its genetic modifications to other trees, but it could mess up the bee population even more than what it already is, maybe even alter the honey they produce that we consume, and it would even have an actual impact on the amount of carbon dioxide the plants/tress absorb from the atmosphere. Yeah, sure! What could go wrong with that scenario! Are you serious?

I think we can all agree on the fact that this genetic modification behavior of plants and animals is not only crazy, but it's flat out dangerous. And that's precisely what these researchers are warning about!

"Developments in biotechnology over the past 25 years have allowed scientists to engineer genetically modified (GM) animals for use in various areas of agriculture and medicine. Some animals with an anticipated use in food production are close to reaching the grocery shelf – at least, they will be soon available for marketing.

GM livestock include many different kinds of animals and species modified with the intention of improving economically important traits such as growth-rate, quality of meat, milk composition, disease resistance and survival. Pigs have been engineered to grow faster and to produce more meat with less feed; the composition of pork has also been improved for healthier human consumption. Scientists have paid particular attention to pig health, raising piglet survival rates, reducing the risks of infectious disease, and fortifying the porcine immune system.

Sheep have been modified to improve wool production and immunity, and to reduce the risk of mortality following infections by bacteria and lethal viruses.

Growth-rate in chickens has been increased with only limited success, because conventional selection has already improved this trait close to its biological limit.

Udder health and survival are the most important traits improved by transgenic technology in cattle. GM cows with resistance to BSE have been bred.

Similar traits are targeted in fish, dominated by salmon, carp and tilapia species, where the focus is on meat production, meat quality, and disease resistance.

Not only is the number of GM farm animals and fish developed in laboratories increasing, but the genetic engineering of food animals entails certain risks.

It is possible, for example, that the expression of novel proteins could cause allergic reactions in susceptible people. The likelihood that a foreign protein is allergenic depends on the particular gene product, the food in which it appears, and the individuals who consume it.

As part of the regulatory process, it is therefore essential to test that meat, milk, or other food products derived from transgenic farm animals are not substantially different from those produced by standard methods.

There are also concerns that the mass-breeding and potential escape of transgenic animals could pose long-term risks to the environment.

Another problem is a lack of transparency. Although researchers appear to be looking into many different aspects of transgenic livestock, biotech companies are not required to disclose these activities. All that is known about such research and development activities comes from published academic papers and what companies have chosen voluntarily to disclose."

In other words, it's a closed loop system without any real accountability and therefore we'll never know what long-term or irreversible side effects this is having upon the plant and animal kingdoms, let alone what all this is this doing to the people who ingest these modified organisms. It's not looking good.

World News Reports: *"There has been a lot of outcry as the FDA just approved the genetically modified animal for human consumption for the first time. Sure, tweak 80% of U.S. food but keep your test tubes off our salmon. Genetically modified organisms incite heat from both sides of the debate. Many believe genetically modified organisms are more efficient than crossbreeding plants from many generations and crossing their* *fingers. While detractors believe that we shouldn't genetically modify the food we eat and should keep it natural.*

I use finger quotes not to make fun but because what natural means in context is confusing for many if not most people, even the FDA gets confused about it. Now joining the list of tomatoes, potatoes, soy or tofu, rice, cotton, corn, canola oil, squash, alfalfa or mosquitoes is genetically modified salmon. According to AquaAdvantage, the company that modified the fish, the salmon contains genes that contain Chinook Salmon and an eel like species which means it will grow all year and at a faster rate than natural salmon. And now they have been approved for human consumption.

So, they are going to swim their way on to our store shelves and on top of our bagels. This has unsurprisingly caused a huge outcry from anti-GMO activists. People are still nervous, and I get why. You are messing with my food, man. Most genetically modified grains sold in the U.S. are used for animal feed. Although, according to consumer reports pretty much every food sample that they tested contained GMO except those that explicitly said otherwise and that included breakfast cereals, baby formula, veggie burgers and popular chip brands. According to the FDA, this salmon, dubbed a Frankenfish by activist groups, is safe to eat. It will allegedly cause no threat to the environment.

The FDA approval requires the salmon to live only in fish farms but even if one did escape somehow, 95% of the fish are sterile. Cross your fingers that any escapees aren't one of the 5%. We already have genetically modified plants growing in nature all over the US that have escaped from farms and no one knows what is going to happen with them. This isn't the only GMO animal in the research and approval pipeline. A line of goats was created whose milk can prevent deadly diarrhea in children. The company is marketing it to the government of Brazil where children still die from diarrhea.

A species of chicken was modified that suppresses the replication of bird flu virus and pigs are also being bred that are resistant to swine flu. All this sounds pretty good, but it seems to me that people get increasingly uncomfortable as the animals come closer to their tables. In a partnership between Harvard Medical University of Missouri and the University of Pittsburg, a genetically modified pig was created which produces higher Omega 3 fatty acids. Omega 3's are essential for health but aren't synthesized by mammals naturally, instead they are found in microorganisms, like algae, plankton and worms.

Fish get their Omega 3's from algae as well. By modifying a worm enzyme for a pig species, this pig is now a source for Omega 3's. There are plants to modify cattle to stop them from growing sharp horns, which can be dangerous for farm hands or other cows but also plans to mix various traits from different cow species to produce more milk or more beef, or whatever is required. Medically modified meat is here. "[45]

Not coming, it's here. And did you notice all the other Genetically Modified foods he mentioned we are already consuming as well? Not just meat, or corn or tomatoes, but breakfast cereals, baby formula, veggie burgers, popular chip brands. In fact, he even stated, and I quote "Pretty much every human food sample they (the Consumer Reports) tested contained GMO's." Did you know that? I didn't know that. And we're supposed to trust these guys? You didn't tell me that genetically modified foods were already in just about everything I eat, yet I'm supposed to trust them in the event some horrible freaky irreversible accident occurs? No worries, you'll be sure to let us know. Yeah, right!

But be that as it may, put all this together, and it sure makes you wonder again if this is in fact the reason why Russia was building that massive DNA facility.

Jasmine Baily: *"Researchers at Moscow State University have quite the task on their hands. One that many are comparing to the Biblical story of Noah's Ark. The University plans to collect DNA material from every living thing on earth. That includes plants, animals on land and water."*

Fox 5 Reports: *"Moscow State University got a $194,000,000 grant to freeze and store genetic codes. Now, also cellular materials that could eventually be used to clone extinct species."*

RT Reports: *"One researcher from Moscow State explained a little more about the project's implication, telling RT, 'It will enable us to cryogenically freeze and store various cellular materials which can then reproduce. It will also contain information systems. Not everything needs to be kept in a Petri dish."*

Jasmine Baily: *"Now there really will be an ARK of sorts. A gigantic 166 square mile facility where all the genetic material will be stored. The project is expected to be completed sometime in 2018 and will be kept on one of the University's central campuses. Russia is not the first to complete a feat of this nature. British scientists are working on a similar project called 'Frozen Ark.' That project 'is a strategy to conserve the genetic resources of the world's endangered species.' It is the animal equivalent of the 'Millennium Seed Bank' created by Kew Gardens to conserve the seeds of the world's plants.'*

The biggest difference between the two, Britain is focusing on endangered species while Russia collects material from all species. As far as Russia's Noah's Ark there are big expectations as the grant given to MSU is believed to be Russia's single largest science grant."[47]

Wow! Somebody's serious about this. But is this starting to make more sense to you? It is to me. Of all things to be throwing this kind of money at, the largest you've ever done, it's to hurry up and build a DNA database of "all living things" stored in some giant secured facility. Gee, I wonder why? And notice it wasn't just the Russians, other countries are doing the same thing. It's almost like somebody realizes that we're playing with fire here with all this genetic modification and we better have a backup handy just in case. Not only the "master seeds" of every plant, but now even the "master DNA" of every living thing on the planet. I wonder if this was what the people of Noah's day were doing?

But remember, this is still only "part" of what the scientific community is doing to alter the animal kingdom. We still have two more unfortunate behaviors to go. "Cloning" the animal kingdom and "Resurrecting" if you will, the animal kingdom. Let's now take a look at the "cloning" of the animal kingdom.

CLONING ANIMALS: We've already seen several examples of cloning going on in the animal kingdom today. It sure didn't end with Dolly the Sheep as we saw before. Rather, it's actually much more advanced and widespread than people realize and of course we're being told it's perfectly safe and harmless.

"Meet Debbie, Denise, Diana and Daisy. They are identical, in fact they are clones. They are the exact same as the most famous sheep in the world, Dolly. The four are also celebrating turning the grand old age of 9, the equivalent of being in their late 70's in human years. Along with 9 other cloned sheep they have proved that cloned animals can live normal lives."

Prof. Sandra Corr: University of Nottingham: *"You cannot see any difference at all between these or any other sheep in any field and we actually struggled to tell them apart."*

"Unlike their predecessor, they have spent most of their lives outside. For security reasons, Dolly had to spend most of her life indoors. She was born in 1996. She was the very first mammal to be cloned. She died at just 6 years old after developing osteoarthritis and a lung infection. It raised concern that cloned animals may age more quickly.

The clones are made by taking the sheep's egg and replacing it with the DNA of a dead sheep and then zap it with electricity to make it grow. Farm animals can only be cloned for research purposes in the UK, but the cloning of livestock does happen in the U.S. When Dolly was born 20 years ago, many people feared the technology would be used to clone humans."

David Gardner: University of Nottingham: *"The public opinion toward cloning was one of misunderstanding and not really sure of where it might go. I think now we know that it's been interesting, it's been used to some extent elsewhere in the world, but people can rest assured we aren't going to be cloning humans."[48]*

Yeah real funny. And if you believe that, I've got some swamp land to sell you in the middle of the desert here in Las Vegas. But did you catch that one part where it said cloning of "livestock" is "already" happening in the U.S.? And it's much more prolific than you might think. In fact, cloning of animals in the U.S. has been going on for a long, long, time now.

Nina Mak: American Anti-Vivisection Society: *"The media covers pet cloning, it's often fluff pieces, it's warm fuzzy pieces of, 'Oh look how cute these animals are, isn't it cool that we can do this.' But there is very little coverage, if any, of what it really meant to clone that animal. And what it took."*

The Clone Farm

Dr. Duane Kraemer: Transfer Scientist, Texas A&M: *"My name is Duane Kraemer and I have been working in the area of embryo transfer, cloning and genetic engineering. My dream was to become a farmer and I went to the University intending to get just what I needed to come back, but I got bit by the research department. My father was very disappointed that I didn't come back to the farm. My mother said that she knew I would find something better. I didn't mean it was better, just different. Cloning, as it is most customarily practiced at present involves transfer of nuclei from cells and transferring those cells into eggs where the nucleus has been removed and then the nucleus from the animal to be cloned is put into its place. If it's a mammal those new embryos, then have to be transferred into recipient females for them to carry them on to term. Usually those recipient animals nurse them and raise them as well.*

This is the first of the deer to be cloned. This is Dewey, the students named him after me. I think it is because I insisted that he be allowed to be born natural birth and he survived. I think that earned me that privilege, I guess. Some people just don't like anything that is unnatural. I think they can abide by that but most of the things they do are unnatural. I think it has something to do with the Hollywood version to some extent of cloning. It pretty much made it a monster.

I hope there will be continued research to make it more dependable. At present about 25% of offspring have some type of abnormality. They are developmental abnormalities, they are not mutations, they don't get passed on to the next generation, but they need special care.

These are microscopes that are used to find the eggs. We have to get the egg out of ovaries. It is simple after you learn how to do it. There is just many, many details that have to be followed. If you do one thing wrong, then the chain is broken, and you get nothing.

Our team is working on genetic engineering of livestock to produce animals that are resistant to disease. This is a cloned bull that is resistant to brucellosis which is a disease that causes abortion in cattle and fever in humans. The original bull was naturally resistant to it. The cells that were used for cloning him had been stored for 15 years. His name is Bruce after Brucellosis.

The process of selective breeding to produce superior individuals has been going on for many years, even using natural breeding. And then embryo transfer and artificial insemination made that process more efficient. You can get more offspring from the genetically modified animal if they are superior, but they can't reproduce themselves, then the technique such as cloning can produce offspring."

Lab assistant: *"I worried when Ceci was expecting. I thought what if she is born with two children without ears and one without a tail. I'm going to have to say, 'Oh boy, this isn't good.' But she came through for us. Ceci came through. Ceci is a good kitty."*

Nina Mak: *"The truth is that cloning is highly experimental and very problematic and most of the time it doesn't work. There are only a few clones that have been born successfully and others that, a good percentage, actually end up dying within the first six months because they have some sort of complication, health abnormality, physical deformity, something like that. They talk about using a very large number of animals to even try to produce one clone."*

Duane Kraemer: *"Anything we do could be used incorrectly and wrongly and most things are by somebody, somewhere, at some time."*

President George Bush: *"Chinese scientists have derived stem cells from cloned embryos that were created by combining human DNA and rabbit eggs. Others have announced plans to produce cloned children despite the fact that laboratory cloning of animals have led to spontaneous abortions and terrible, terrible abnormalities. Human cloning is deeply troubling to me and to most Americans."*

Duane Kraemer: *"Anyone who could effectively culture and preserve cells from animals would be able to do so with humans as well."[49]*

But don't worry, that'll never happen! Yeah, right! But did you see they not only already cloned cats, but cows and deer and who knows what else? Did any of you guys know about this? I didn't. I think we were left with the faulty impression that cloning of animal's kind of died out with (no pun intended) Dolly the sheep. That's not true! Not only do we not hear much about it, but it's obviously very much in high gear! And that's just one U.S. facility. What about all the other facilities around the world doing the same thing? In fact, here's a current list of the different animals that have already been cloned around the world, even after Dolly!

- Camels
- Carp
- Cats
- Cattle
- Coyotes

- Deer
- Dogs
- Frogs
- Fruit flies
- Gaurs
- Goats
- Horses
- House mice
- Monkeys
- Mouflon
- Mules
- Pigs
- Pyrenean ibex
- Rabbits
- Brown rats
- Sheep
- Arctic wolves

Yeah, like we need more of those creatures. But be that as it may, it sure sounds to me like Dolly the Sheep was the tip of the iceberg! And here we thought nothing was going on when in reality they're cloning all kinds of things all over the place!

And keep in mind, this is just what's being done and admitted to in public. What else are they doing behind the scenes in facilities we don't know of and we're never being told about from around the world? You know they exist.

But let's back it up a little bit. Previously, they freely admitted that cloning is not a perfect science, at all. There's all kinds of complications and abnormalities that occur when you clone things and most of the time the organisms die shortly thereafter due to the complications of the cloning attempts. Yet, the cloning of animals is going public right now as a so-called "safe procedure" in two different areas that I want to deal with. First, with the cloning of your pet. Second, in the cloning of your meat. Uh oh, that doesn't sound good! You're right.

But let's first take a look at cloning your pet. How many of you remember that scene from the Science fiction movie, again with Arnold Schwarzenegger, he seems to be the choice for this kind of stuff, but it was the scene in the movie called "The Sixth Day," about not only cloning animals, but even humans.

Repet Commercial: *The husband/father is at work when his wife comes on his computer. He says, "What's up Honey? You look upset." She is so distressed and responds to his question. "Oh, Adam, I just talked to the Vet and he found ... they had to put Oliver to sleep." "What? He wasn't even that sick," he asks. She answers, "Oh, I know, but apparently he had some kind of highly infectious canine virus or something and they had to put him down." Suddenly, he says, "He was licking Clara's face this morning." She says, "Don't worry I asked the doctor the same thing and the virus is harmless to humans, so she's fine." He says, "This is going to break her heart, you know that."*

She replies, "No, it won't. I want you to go down to Repet and get Oliver replaced." He replies, "I'm not going to do that. Oliver can live on in our memories." But she doesn't agree. "She is only 8. She won't understand that, Honey." But he comes back with, "It's the natural process of life. You're born, you live and then you die. You should really appreciate that Honey." But she keeps trying to convince him, "Will you do it Honey?" "No!" She says, "Thank you, thank you," and hangs up.

Now he is walking in the mall, looking for the store with the name Repet written on the window. He sees it and starts to walk through the door, but he is stopped by two guys who say, "Save your soul, don't go in there, don't go in there, atheist!"

Inside there is a TV screen turned on with a guy telling each individual going in that they can have their pet replaced in just a few short hours. "How can we do it? It all begins with the growing with blanks, animal drones stripped of all animal characteristics DNA in an embryonic tank at the repro factory."

Salesman: *"Welcome to Repet, where love means no surprises. Your pet doesn't want to break your heart and thanks to Repet it doesn't have to. We can clone your pet in just a few short hours. How can we do it? It all begins with the growing of blanks, animal drones stripped of animal characteristics DNA in an embryonic tank at the repro factory. In stage two your pet's DNA is extracted from a lock of fur or drop of blood and then infused on a cellular level into the blank.*

In the final stage using Repet's patented cerebral and recording process, all your pet's thoughts, memories, and instincts are painlessly transplanted via the optic nerve. It's important to have your pets sync recorded on a regular basis and we will do this free at any Repet store. But if you have lost a pet that hasn't been syncrecorded, in most cases we can still take the postmortem syncrecording within 12 hours of your pets' demise. Your cloned pet is exactly the same as he was before right down to the DNA, with all training and memories intact. You and your child will never know the difference.

But cloning is just the beginning of the story here at Repet. We also offer many genetic engineering options to make your experience with your pet even better than before. Are you allergic to your cat? We can make your Repet hypoallergenic. So, you wish your dog was smaller or larger? We can do that too. Let's say you just redecorated your home; we can coordinate your pet's colors to your decorating scheme. Does your otherwise perfect pet have one or two behavior flaws? Does your cat scratch the furniture? Does your dog dig up the back yard? We can eliminate these behaviors for a slight additional cost.

Both the cloning and the genetic engineering are backed by the same simple pledge, zero defects, guaranteed. If you have any questions or you wish to hear about today's special offer, one of our knowledgeable sales staff will be more than glad to help. Once again, welcome to Repet. Where love means no surprises."

As the husband/father listens to what the salesman just said on the TV, a salesman comes up to him and says, "Still can't make up your mind? You lost a dog, right?" He answers, "Yes, my daughter's." The salesman says, "How heartbreaking. What did you say his name was again.?" "Oliver," he replies. The salesman continues, "Oliver is in luck, we have a special this week, 20% off. When did Oliver die?" "Sometime this morning," he answers.

The salesman says, "That is perfect, we can still have a postmortem syncrecording, but you have to act fast because you only have a 12-hour window." "I have a problem with this whole idea," the father says. "Suppose the clone has no soul, are they dangerous?" The salesman was ready for that question. "Cloned pets are every bit as safe as a real pet plus they are insured." Again, the dad asks, "If it is so safe why is it against the law to clone human beings?"[50]

Yeah, that's a great question. Yet, what most people don't realize is that there are many states even here in America that "do not" ban human cloning, let alone animal cloning. States such as:

- **Alabama**. There are currently no laws in Alabama that prohibit human cloning, whether for biomedical research or to produce children.

- **Alaska**. There are currently no laws in Alaska that prohibit human cloning, whether for biomedical research or to produce children.

- **California**. Cloning-to-produce-children is illegal in California, while cloning-for-biomedical-research is protected under the state's constitution and is funded by a state agency.

- **Delaware**. There are currently no laws in Delaware that prohibit human cloning, whether for biomedical research or to produce children.

- **Florida**. There are currently no laws in Florida that prohibit human cloning, whether for biomedical research or to produce children.

- **Georgia**. There are currently no laws in Georgia that prohibit human cloning, whether for biomedical research or to produce children.

- **Hawaii**. There are currently no laws in Hawaii that prohibit human cloning, whether for biomedical research or to produce children.

- **Idaho**. Idaho state law currently does not include any statutes prohibiting either cloning-for-biomedical-research or cloning-to-produce-children.

- **Illinois**. It is legal to conduct cloning-for-biomedical-research in Illinois but cloning-to-produce-children is outlawed in the state.

- **Indiana**. Indiana law does not directly prohibit human cloning either for the purposes of biomedical research or to produce children.

- **Iowa**. Iowa prohibits cloning-to-produce-children but permits cloning-for-biomedical-research.

- **Kansas**. There are currently no laws in Kansas that prohibit human cloning, whether for biomedical research or to produce children.

- **Kentucky**. There are currently no laws in Kentucky that prohibit human cloning, whether for biomedical research or to produce children.

- **Louisiana**. There are currently no laws in Louisiana that directly prohibit human cloning, whether for biomedical research or to produce children.

- **Maine**. There are currently no laws in Maine that prohibit human cloning, whether for biomedical research or to produce children.

- **Maryland**. Maryland prohibits cloning-to-produce-children while permitting cloning-for-biomedical-research.

- **Massachusetts**. Massachusetts prohibits cloning-to-produce-children while permitting cloning-for-biomedical-research.

- **Mississippi**. There are currently no laws in Mississippi that prohibit human cloning, whether for biomedical research or to produce children.

- **Missouri**. Missouri prohibits cloning-to-produce-children but permits cloning-for-biomedical-research.

- **Montana**. Montana prohibits cloning-to-produce-children but permits cloning-for-biomedical-research.
- **Nebraska**. Nebraska has no laws directly prohibiting either cloning-for-biomedical-research or cloning-to-produce-children.

- **Nevada**. There are currently no laws in Nevada that prohibit human cloning, whether for biomedical research or to produce children.

- **New Hampshire**. There are currently no laws in New Hampshire that prohibit human cloning, whether for biomedical research or to produce children.

- **New Jersey**. New Jersey permits cloning-for-biomedical-research and prohibits cloning-to-produce-children.

- **New Mexico**. There are currently no laws in New Mexico that prohibit human cloning, whether for biomedical research or to produce children.

- **New York**. New York law does not directly prohibit cloning-to-produce-children or cloning-for-biomedical research.

- **North Carolina**. There are currently no laws in North Carolina that prohibit human cloning, whether for biomedical research or to produce children.

- **Ohio**. There are currently no laws in Ohio that prohibit human cloning, whether for biomedical research or to produce children.

- **Oregon**. There are currently no laws in Oregon that prohibit human cloning, whether for biomedical research or to produce children.

- **Pennsylvania**. There are currently no laws in Pennsylvania that directly prohibit cloning, whether for biomedical research or to produce children.

- **Rhode Island**. Rhode Island permits cloning-for-biomedical-research while prohibiting cloning-to-produce-children.

- **South Carolina**. There are currently no laws in South Carolina that prohibit human cloning, whether for biomedical research or to produce children.

- **Tennessee**. There are currently no laws in Tennessee that prohibit human cloning, whether for biomedical research or to produce children.

- **Texas**. There are currently no laws in Texas that prohibit human cloning, whether for biomedical research or to produce children.

- **Utah**. There are currently no laws in Utah that prohibit human cloning, whether for biomedical research or to produce children.

- **Vermont**. There are currently no laws in Vermont that prohibit human cloning, whether for biomedical research or to produce children.

- **Washington**. There are currently no laws in Washington that prohibit human cloning, whether for biomedical research or to produce children.

- **West Virginia**. There are currently no laws in West Virginia that prohibit human cloning, whether for biomedical research or to produce children.

- **Wisconsin**. There are currently no laws in Wisconsin that prohibit human cloning, whether for biomedical research or to produce children.

- **Wyoming**. There are currently no laws in Wyoming that prohibit human cloning, whether for biomedical research or to produce children.

- **Territories, Protectorates, and the District of Columbia**. Neither in the U.S. territories and protectorates nor in the District of Columbia are there currently any laws that prohibit human cloning, whether for biomedical research or to produce children.

So, it sure looks to me like the gates are wide open for not just animal cloning, but even human cloning, even here in America! And that's just America. What about all the other countries around the world? You know their laws are probably a lot worse than ours!

But my immediate point is this. The "Sixth Day" Science Fiction Movie scenario, which by the way was made almost 20 years ago, is "already" becoming our modern-day reality! Haven't you been paying attention to the news? All kinds of people are cloning their pets just like in that Repet Commercial!

Junichi Fukuda: *"He is very happy; he really loves his puppy. She is really cute, her gestures or expressions – she is just so cute."*

Tech Insider Reports: *"This googley eyed 5-month-old pug is named Momotan. And for now, she is living amongst dozens of other newborn puppies. But these aren't your standard run of the mill puppies. They don't know it but Momotan and each of her puppy companions are clones."*

Junichi Fukuda: *"I am calling her Momoko now, but I am thinking of changing her name. I am thinking that her name should be Momotan, not Momoko."*

Tech Insider Reports: *"For 16 years Mr. Fukuda was the proud owner of another pug named Momoko. The two were inseparable."*

Junichi Fukuda: *"I divorced my wife when Momoko was six-years-old and it was just me and Momoko after that."*

Tech Insider Reports: *"When Momoko recently died Mr. Fukuda wanted to bring her back. He returned to a company named Sooam to recreate her."*

David Kim, Sooam Researcher: *"Currently we have cloned over 600 dogs of various different breeds and there are no particular limitations to the different breeds."*

Tech Insider Reports: *"Sooam claims they can clone any dog no matter the age, the size or the breed. We recently visited South Korea to see for ourselves. First for you to even consider getting your dog cloned you need $100,000, also the dog you want to clone needs to be alive or dead for fewer than 5 days. If you want to clone your dead dog, you have to first wrap the entire body with wet bathing towels and then keep it cool by placing it in a refrigerator. You can't freeze it. This all might seem a bit odd but Sooam needs live skin cells in order to clone your dog. This process prevents the skin on your dead dog from drying out or freezing and it gives Sooam the highest chance of finding preserved skin cells. Next you need to take your dog to the vet and get a biopsy sample. Using a tool called a biopsy punch your vet will cut out an 8-millimeter-wide sample of flesh from the abdominal area of the dog.*

If your dog is alive, just one sample is enough. But if the dog is dead you will have to provide Sooam with as many samples as possible to increase the chances of finding live skin cells. You then pack the samples with ice packs in a Styrofoam box to keep it chilled and expedite it to Sooam, which you can do using simple shipping services, like FedEx. Once the sample has passed through Korean customs which could take an additional 2 or 3 days, Sooam can finally get to work on cloning your dog.

First the sample is sterilized and cut into smaller pieces. Then it is treated with a reagent and chemically disassociated, meaning the cells are separated from the tissue. The sample is then placed in a centrifuge which allows the scientists to collect the cells and transfer them into a growth medium. One to two weeks later Sooam has the cells necessary for the cloning process. Sooam then goes to a laboratory animal provider where they rent two dogs, an egg donor and a surrogate mother.

Starting with the egg donor doctors take the dog into an operating room where they sedate her, place her on an operating table, slice her open, pull out her ovaries and collect her eggs."

Dr. Woo-Suk Hwang, Sooam Founder: *"We have six from left ovary and six from right."*

Tech Insider Reports: *"Once the eggs are collected a scientist places them under a microscope and uses an instrument to extract the nucleus."*

Dr. Woo-Suk Hwang: *"You see the shiny part; this is where the material is."*

Tech Insider Reports: *"Sooam is removing the DNA from the eggs."*

Dr. Woo-Suk Hwang: *"As you can see, we can verify that all the material has been taken out."*

Tech Insider Reports: *"And by removing the DNA, Sooam is creating genetically empty eggs, meaning the breed of the egg donor dog won't matter since none of its DNA will be passed on to the cloned puppy. From here a Sooam scientist injects the cells taken from the biopsy sample from the original dog into the empty eggs. Under normal circumstances sperm is a necessary component for reproduction but in this cloning process sperm is replaced by two things, the cell from the original dog and a series of short electrical shocks from a machine called the electro cell manipulator. The electrical currents from this machine activate and fuse together the membranes of the egg and cell creating a fertilized embryo.*

After just one minute, Sooam has a whole batch of cloned dog embryos to work with. Next Sooam moves on to the second rental dog, the surrogate mother. Back in the operating room the doctors sedate the surrogate. Place her on the operating table, slice her open pull out her ovaries and uterus and inject up to 15 cloned embryos into her uterus. Thirty days later, Sooam is able to verify the surrogate's pregnancy, which they say has about a 40% success rate. If the procedure fails, they will examine what went wrong and repeat the process using a different surrogate mother. When a successful pregnancy is confirmed it takes another 30 days for the surrogate mother to give birth. During this time Sooam will closely monitor the surrogate and check on the condition of her fetus.

When the cloned puppy is finally born, Sooam will take care of the clone until the customer is able to bring their new pet home. The facility at Sooam can house up to 50 dogs at a time. Customers can either make the trip to Seoul to pick up their cloned pup or arrange to have a Sooam employee deliver their new pet directly to them. They will have to wait until their quarantine period is up which varies from country to country. Now with the high cost of the procedure and invasive surgery is performed on the rental dogs, it is easy to see why dog cloning is controversial. But for Mr. Fukuda there is no hesitation in his decision to bring back his dog."

Mr. Fukuda: *"To me, spending $100,000 for a dog that has a similar color as Momoko, smells like Momoko, and feels like Momoko when I touch her, I never thought it would be too much as $100,000 for such a dog whose attributes are the same as Momoko."*

Tech Insider Reports: *"Of course while the current puppy might look exactly like the original dog, it's personality will be shaped by the environment it's raised in. In other words, a cloned puppy might not behave like the original dog."[51]*

Yeah especially if you don't even use the sperm to regenerate and instead just shoot a bolt of electricity through it to make it come alive. Gee, those scenarios always work out!

"In a clip from the old Frankenstein movie you see the monster laying on the table and Dr. Frankenstein working at his controls. Igor is watching Dr. Frankenstein's every move. He also has spectators watching to see

how this is going to be pulled off. A storm is brewing and there is lightning flashing. Suddenly the lightning strikes the antenna and a jolt strikes the monster. They rush to uncover him, and Dr. Frankenstein is watching his hand as it slowly starts to move. He tells the spectators, "It's moving! It's alive, it's alive, it's alive, it's alive!!!"[52]

Yeah, it's alive alright, Mr. Frankenstein. But it didn't work out too well, did it pal? Not at all. But hey, don't worry, shocking our cloned pets with electricity as well will be just fine! Sure thing, what could go wrong!

But you might be thinking, "Well hey, this is just stuff that people in South Korea are doing. Offering Pet Cloning services. People aren't going to pay for their pets to be cloned here in the West...are they?" Well, you might want to pay attention to the news. We actually already are doing it. In fact, all kinds of celebrities are lining up to have their pets cloned.

The Doctors Report: *"Many may find it lighthearted, but others find it very controversial as well. Barbara Streisand revealed in an interview with Variety that her two new puppies are actually clones of her dog Samantha who passed away in 2017. Before Samantha passed, Barbara had the cells taken from the dog's mouth and stomach for replicating purposes. Streisand said they had different personalities, 'I'm waiting for them to get older so I can see if they have Samantha's brown eyes and seriousness.' The dog's names are Miss Violet and Miss Scarlet."*

"It's a little creepy, I think," says one of the co-hosts. "As a parent I was just sitting here thinking. There is a process you go through with your kids when their pet dies. Teaching them about death and cherishing relationships and memories and moving on. I don't know, what do we teach our kids? Well, if Miss Piggy dies, if Fido dies, let's just make another one."

Doctor: *"Well she's right, she can afford it, it's her decision and it's her thing."*

Second co-host: *"Is this legal? Are there any ramifications of this potentially?"*

Doctor: *"It deals with really tough ethical issues. If you can clone a dog, that means you can clone a human being. I wouldn't be surprised if next season we are on this stage and we are talking about someone that wants to clone their loved one."*

Second Co-host: *"Instead of being frozen just clone them and just bring them back right now."*

Co-Host: *"Is it the good people that get cloned, just the rich people?"*

Doctor: *"Ethically, I would be challenged, I am just going to shut it down. That is when I am officially going out in the woods somewhere, find me a cabin, with my two dogs and we will just do our thing."*

Co-Host: *"And when they die, just let them be dead, Right?"*[53]

But that's the problem. They think they're God and they won't let the dead, be dead. But notice how the conversation always seems to start off with cloning animals and even pets, but then what does it quickly pivot to? Cloning of humans every single time! Why? Because you know that's what's coming next! They're just working the bugs out with animals and pets. And it's not just Barbara Streisand here in the West who can afford 100 grand to clone her pet. It's all kinds of people doing this.

"Billionaire Barry Diller and Diane von Furstenberg clone their beloved Jack Russell terrier, Shannon, into two new pups.

Sources say Diller, the chairman of IAC, became so attached to Shannon that he got the pampered pooch's DNA cloned by a specialist company, which created a pair of puppies who are almost exact replicas.

Streisand has spoken at length about cloning her late dog Samantha, who passed away in 2017. The singer penned an op-ed for the New York

Times in which she explained why she made the decision. After being 'very impressed' with her friend's cloned dog, a doctor took cells from her ailing dog Sammie's cheek and stomach before she passed away.

Eventually, Streisand turned to a Texas pet cloning company ViaGen Pets. ViaGen offers a cloning service for dogs, cats and even horses and has been operating for over 15 years. The company's president, Blake Russell, owns a stallion cloned from the DNA of a racehorse champion.

Simon Cowell also confirmed that he was interested in cloning his Yorkshire terriers Squiddly, Diddly and Freddy. Speaking last year to The Sun, Cowell said, 'I am 100 per cent cloning the dogs, all of them. We've thoroughly looked into it; got all the details and I can prove to you I'm going to clone them. There is documentation.'

'I am doing it because I cannot bear the thought of them not being around,' he continued. 'I might actually do it sooner rather than later, which will mean we have six dogs running around. It doesn't hurt them. It's like a swab, a DNA thing. I cannot imagine Squiddly, Diddly and Freddy not being around, so this is the solution.'

Pet cloning isn't without its controversies, however. One of the earliest achievements in cloning came when a dog clone named Snuppy was created in 2005 by a South Korean firm and was dubbed Time's Invention of the Year.

According to Vanity Fair, it was a long arduous process to get Snuppy there as it took 'more than 100 borrowed wombs, and more than 1,000 embryos.'"

But be that as it may, cloning your pet is catching on all over the world.

"Despite the $100,000 price tag, requests for the service have poured in from around the world, Wang said – around half from North America.

Walls around the five-story Sooam Biotech center are adorned with dozens of photos of cloned dogs and their smiling owners – tagged with their national flags including the US, Mexico, Dubai, Russia, Japan, China and Germany.

In fact, some have sought clones of other pets like cats, snakes and even chinchillas."

Sounds like they're about ready to clone anything! But you might be thinking, "Well, that's still way too high of a price for me. I'm not a billionaire or some rich Hollywood mogul. I'll never be able to clone my pet at that price." Well hey, worry no more. The price just keeps coming down for the average Joe. Watch this.

ITV Reports: *"Can I ask you, are you happy with the results? Because there will be a lot of people saying Frankenstein creatures and whatever. How happy are you with what you have got?"*

Guest: *"Really, really happy. Really, really, pleased. They are beautiful."*

ITV Reports: *"But are they like Dillan? Dillan was your beloved boxer that died last year and the idea of going overseas to keep his memory but are they actually similar to him in any way. Are their personalities...?"*

Guest: *"Yes, they are really similar, they look just like him, but these guys are a bit skinnier, I'm trying to fatten them up a bit. The markings are a little bit different, because the markings always vary, but otherwise they are both very similar to Dillan."*

ITV Reports: *"As this treatment becomes cheaper, you guys originally spent a lot of money but as the price of this falls you can see so many other people doing it, couldn't you?"*

Guest: *"Definitely, yes."*

Dr. Drew reports: *"Lisa Polanski, clinical psychologist, is back with me and one of the pet lovers you just saw, Danielle Tarantolla, whose dog Trouble was everything to her, we heard her talking about it there, her cloned pet there, Double Trouble is here tonight. Alright Danielle, just how big a presence in your life was Trouble.*

Danielle: *"Oh very, very, very big. He was with me through most of my adult life, from about 18 to 36, which basically it was a very important time in your life."*

Dr. Drew: *"So is Double Trouble significantly different or very close?"*

Danielle: *"Well, so far, Double Trouble is exactly like the original Trouble was since the day I got him, when I took him out of his little doggie carrying case and I put him on the floor and I was watching him, how he would act and interact with me. He was bouncing around like Trouble used to do then he started laying down with his legs extended in the back and his front paws extended like a seal. Then he started laying underneath my bed. Trouble used to do that, he loved it, he lays on pillows like Trouble used to do. He really, really has the same personality."[54]*

Yeah, for now, or as you said, "So far." Maybe next week he'll grow a third eye and bite your leg off...I don't know! But seriously this is not without problems as we've been seeing. Yet, the price keeps coming down and people keep jumping on the bandwagon to clone their pets. In fact, some of the current rates are $35,000 to clone a cat, $50,000 for a dog and $85,000 for a horse. It's becoming more and more feasible for people to partake in this. I mean, at this rate, there's going to be a chain of Repet's on every corner or in the Mall just like in the movie! I just hope it doesn't turn out like "this" movie.

"A clip from the movie 'Pet Semetary' has a little girl walking through the woods. When she got home, she is sitting on the bed talking to her parents. Her mom is telling her dad that 'while walking through the woods today Ellie discovered a charming little landmark'. While she was walking in the

woods, she came across a sign posted on a tree that says Pet Sematary. She walked past it and came to a graveyard.

He tells her, "I used to bury our pets, to remember them. It may seem scary but it's not, it's perfectly natural. Just like dying is natural."

The old man brings the little girl back to this spot and says, "The whole town has been using this place for generations. Folks make a kind of ritual out of it." As one procession is walking to the graveyard one kid turns around and he has on a mask. Gradually you see they all have on masks. It looks like a satanic ritual of going to the graveyard.

"It's not some campfire story, I saw them on the trees out there." The dad tells the old man. He shows him some pictures in a book of what they look like. The old man says, "It's a warning! The local tribes carved them before they fled. They feared that place. There is something out there."

They proceed to go out there to take a look. They are hearing sounds that are not natural. The trees are cracking, those woods belong to something else. Something. Something that dates way back.

Later in the day when they are back home the dad and the little girl are looking down the road and there is a cat walking towards them. The dad says, "That cat was dead!" The old man says, "It brings things back." As the little girl runs to get the cat, she doesn't see it, but a semi-truck is coming down the highway at a very high speed. It is too late; the truck can't stop. The little girl is dead. But at the funeral the old man is looking at the father and says, "I know what you're thinking of doing, but they don't come back the same."

He buries his daughter in the graveyard and leaves to go back home. When he gets there, he is looking at her room. Tears running down his cheeks. Suddenly from behind him he hears his daughter voice, "Daddy." His wife comes in a little bit after that and sees that her husband is acting strange. She says, "What's going on?" Then she turns and sees her daughter standing in the hallway. She backs up against the wall, but the girl walks towards her. He says, "Hug your daughter."

He knows he has done something horrible and doesn't know if it can be fixed. He goes to the old man and the old man says, "I should have never shown you that place. Your child is not the only things that will come back."

Now strange creatures are coming to his house. One tells him, "The barrier has been broken." He tells the old man that they have a second chance. But the creatures are all over his house. His wife is scared to death. They are coming through the windows, they are under the bed, climbing up the stairs. But the old man tells him, "Sometimes dead is better."[55]

Yeah, real funny. Probably shouldn't have gone down that route buddy. Sometimes "dead is better" is right! They don't come back the same! And that's not just true for a scary pet cemetery movie plot, but for this cloning technology! As we've already seen admitted several times before, cloning animals is not a perfect science and it's fraught with all kinds of problems.

"Dolly, the first mammal to be successfully cloned, stunned the world when she was born in 1996, but her subsequent ill health, premature ageing and death at the age of six and a half raised doubts about the safety of the process that created her.

Dolly was the only lamb to survive to adulthood from 277 attempts by Professor Sir Ian Wilmut at the Roslin institute in Edinburgh.

Professor Kevin Sinclair said: "One of the concerns in the early days was that cloned offspring were ageing prematurely and Dolly was diagnosed with osteoarthritis at the age of around five, so clearly this was a relevant area to investigate."

"If you love animals, don't clone your pet. Just because Barbara Streisand did it with her dog doesn't make it right.

Shelling out $25,000 to get your cat cloned or $50,000 to duplicate your dog might sound tempting if you've got the cash and can't imagine life without your furry best friend. But there's a dark side to pet cloning and customers can't even be sure they get a clone that looks the same as their original pet, much less acts like it.

There are two companies right now that you can pay to clone your pet. Other services you see online might facilitate the process, but they are basically subcontractors for either ViaGen (based in Texas) or Sooam Biotech (in South Korea). Sooam actually licenses the technology from Start Licensing, a subsidiary of ViaGen, which owns the cloning patent.

More often than not, multiple animals are needed to achieve one successful live birth (or alternately, you could end up with more than one kitten/puppy). The host animals are bred to be especially docile, so they don't cause trouble for the scientists and lab techs. It's a creepier, more scientific puppy mill.

We're also not entirely sure how animals are being treated in the laboratory. It takes many surrogates to create one clone – so what happens to the rest, especially if they can't be re-inseminated right away? What happens to puppies or kittens born too soon or with deformities that makes them 'damaged goods' that can't be given to the customer?

To top it all off, we don't even know how long cloned pets will live. Older DNA can develop all sorts of problems that may shorten an animal's life. Imagine paying $50,000 for just a few years with a pet that is only kind of like your original.

Despite these issues, there are currently no regulations in place anywhere to deal with this technology or even ensure that it's being done as

*humanely as possible; and there's been very little public debate as the
technology has further developed.*

*And while it may not move you to consider the plight of cats and dogs in
pet cloning, the technology does bring us closer to normalizing not just
cloning but genomic manipulation for other species as well, including
humans."*

There it is again. You start with animals, then it moves on to
humans very quickly. Sounds to me like we're being prepared for some
weird freaky future nightmare way of life. Maybe even something like
what was going on in Noah's day. Hmmm. Makes you wonder, doesn't it?

But remember, that's only half the problems of the cloning of
animals. It's not just the issue of cloning your pet, as we saw, it's also the
issue of the cloning of your meat. Now they want you to ingest this stuff.
And I'm sure there's no problems with that. Yeah right! Remember, the
swampland? But let's take a look at what's going on currently with the
cloning of our meat, whether you realized it or not.

"The Dolly legacy: Are you eating cloned meat?

*Two decades after Scotland's Dolly the sheep became the first cloned
mammal, consumers may well wonder whether they are drinking milk or
eating meat from cookie-cutter cows or their offspring.*

The simple answer: 'probably.'

*The fact is, there is no way to know for sure, say the experts, even in
Europe, which has come closer to banning livestock cloning than
anywhere else in the world.*

*'Without knowing it, Europeans are probably eating meat from the
descendants of clones that cannot be traced,' said Pauline Constant,
spokeswoman for the European Office of Consumer Associations, based in
Brussels.*

'The most dramatic impact of the cloning of Dolly has been on animal cloning in the United States,' said Aaron Levine, an expert in bioethics and cloning at Georgia Tech.

In 2008, the US Food and Drug Administration concluded that 'food from cattle, swine and goat clones is as safe to eat as food from any other cattle, swine or goat.'

Not even scientists can distinguish a healthy clone from a conventionally bred animal, the regulatory agency said.

There are no requirements to label meat or milk from a cloned animal or its offspring, whether sold domestically or abroad.

Among the leaders in commercial livestock cloning in the US are Cyagra, based in Elizabethtown, Pennsylvania, and ViaGen, in Austin, Texas. At least one company, ViaGen, also provides services for copying cherished cats and dogs.

Argentina, Brazil, Canada, and Australia are among the other countries which clone livestock.

Then there's the Boyalife Group's new cloning factory near the northern coastal city of Tianjin in China. It is aiming for an annual output of 100,000 cows this year, scaling up to a million by 2020.

Boyalife has said it is working with South Korean partner Sooam and the Chinese Academy of Sciences to improve primate cloning technology, to create better test animals for human disease research.

And in December, Boyalife's lead scientist and chief executive Xu Xiaochun, said he would not shy away from cloning humans if regulations allowed it."

Boy, how many times have we seen this pattern? First it begins with animals, genetic manipulations and even cloning, including our livestock whether we realized it or not, then it moves on to our pets, and then wonder of wonders, guess who's next? It always seems to go right back to humans. Cloning humans really are what's coming next.

But did you see that not only are they really "already" cloning our livestock around the world, but it's getting geared up on a massive scale. One million cows cloned by 2020. And that's just one animal and one cloning company in China. What about the rest of the world? What other livestock are they doing this to? And why are we not being told about this? In fact, most people don't even realize that the FDA here in America already approved cloned meat for consumption in the U.S. as far back as 2008.

Dr. Randall Lutter, FDA: *"After years of detailed study and analysis, the Food and Drug Administration has concluded that meat and milk from clones of cattle, swine, and goats and the offspring of clones of any species traditionally consumed as food are as safe to eat as food from conventionally bred animals."*

Dr. Stephen Sundlof, FDA: *"We understand that members of the public may have strong opinions about animal cloning for agricultural purposes. The FDA mandate is to make science-based decisions based on data, and the American public counts on that.*

We take our commitment to ensure food safety very seriously and will not stop our review of animal cloning with the release of these documents. In fact, we will continue to monitor this technology and if we see anything that causes us to have concerns about the safety of the food from these animals, we will take the appropriate action."[56]

In other words, if we got it wrong and something horrible happens to everything and everyone, we'll be the first ones to let you know we were wrong and made a horrible mistake. Really? First of all, you don't require labeling, so we don't even know if we're eating this stuff or not. That doesn't sound like transparency to me! Secondly, your track record is to whitewash and cover things up when things go wrong. In fact, there's already signs that they're already being sneaky about this cloned meat.

ABC News Reports: *"The Food Standard Agency in the UK is investigating how the offspring of a cloned cow entered the food chain. Authorities say that the meat from two bulls was sold despite the rules to keep it out of consumers mouths."*

Alma Almabarichie: *"This farm in the northeast of Scotland is one of the biggest dairy producers in the UK. It's now under investigation as authorities trying to understand how one hundred offspring from a cloned cow were allowed to be bred here for human consumption."*

Steven Innes, Farmer: *"In 2008 we bought two bulls privately which were the offspring of a cloned cow. We investigated to see if it was legal and understood there was no issue."*

Alma Almabarichie: *"Iced embryos from a cloned cow in the US were imported to Britain. Farmers are paying tens of thousands of dollars for exact replicas of animals known to provide high milk and beef yields. Scientists say food from cloned animals is safe but in the wake of so-called mad cow disease and hoof and mouth scares in Britain, consumers are weary."*

Consumer: *"I just think that everything that we eat or that we consume should all be natural."*

Consumer #2: *"These things coming into the food chain, untested, without any rigorous examination of side effects, I'm very concerned about that."*

Alma Almabarichie: *"Confusion around food safety laws means it's virtually impossible for authorities to say how many cloned animals have entered the UK and exactly where their food products are being sold."*[57]

In other words, so much for transparency! And I'm supposed to trust these guys? That was a news clip from 2010. So right after the FDA approves cloned meat for consumption in the U.S., 2008, with promises of tight security and total transparency, it immediately hops the pond to Great Britain and they immediately began to be sneaky about it there too! And as we saw in the previous article, cloned meat is being ratcheted up on a massive scale whether we want it to or not.

Chris Chappell, China Uncensored: *"China will do anything to meet market demand. Including Attack of the Clones. If you are like me, you want answers to the questions that matter most."*
From an old commercial, "Where's the Beef?"

Chris Chappell: *"Where's the beef, indeed. If you answered on a farm, that's so cute. No, the beef is in China, where the world's largest animal cloning facility is under construction. Chinese genetic company, Boyalife Group, wants to be the first to take animal cloning to an industrial scale. Boyalife's $31 Million cloning plant will go into production in 2016. It will start by producing 100,000 cloned cows per year eventually reaching 1 million cows. Holy Cow! Their goal is to provide 5% of the beef eaten in China. You know the meat that is not wrapped and falsely labeled as lamb. Yum, my mouth is already watering. So how does this cloning work?"*

A clip from Jurassic Park: "A DNA strand like me is a blueprint for building a living thing."

Chris Chappell: *"Actually in that case it worked more like this...."*

A clip from Jurassic Park: "The dinosaur is chasing the jeep down the road."

Chris Chappell: *"But here is a better explanation."*

John Nelson, GE Principal Scientist Diagnostics and Life Sciences: *"Cloning is where you take all the genetic contents from one cell and move them somewhere else and reproduce them."*

Chris Chappell: *"Helping Boyalife is a joint venture partner. South Korean company Sooam Biotech. It's run by a man once known as the king of cloning until he was fired from the Sooam Research University for research fraud and gross ethical lapses in the way he obtained human eggs for his experiments. This new Chinese cloning plant is in good hands. As for practical concerns like, how will they manage to feed so many cattle and what will the environmental impact be, that was somehow left out of the Boyalife press release. Also left out of the press release, all the ethical concerns.*

Cloned animal meat is a hugely controversial topic in many countries. That topic Boyalife dismissed with a single vague sentence, 'edging the controversial science closer to mainstream acceptance.' In Europe it is illegal to sell cloned meat. Parliament voted to ban it because of human health and animal welfare concerns. Which is why people freaked out when a lamb crossed with a jellyfish was sold for meat in Paris. What's the big deal, it's like lamb with mint jelly, but all in one?

Now the long-term health effects with eating cloned meat are unknown, though there is some evidence that cloned animals may die earlier. In the U.S. the FDA says cloning can improve the quality of animals and approved cloned meat for human consumption. No special labeling is required. So, are you already eating cloned meat if you are living in the U.S.? Well, since no special labeling is required for cloned meat, how would you know?"[58]

Yeah, and remember, this is coming from the guys who promised to be totally transparent and let us know if anything ever went wrong. I don't think so. But as you saw, odds are, we are "already" eating cloned meat unawares, and it's being ratcheted up on a massive production scale. All this while there's been no long-term studies on adverse health effects, not only to animals but to us as humans. And they even admit there could very well be some health concerns for humans who eat this stuff. Well gee, again, how about at least give us a choice? Why do you always have to hide behind no labeling? What do you know that we don't know?

But hey, speaking of "choices," if you thought eating cloned meat was bad enough. Believe it or not, it gets even worse. Now they're talking about skipping the whole traditional cloning process and going straight to what's called "lab grown" meat. You won't believe what's coming next.

Buzz Feed Reports: *"If it doesn't have a face, if it never had a face, would you eat it?"*

"My name is Sarah and I am a video producer here at Buzz Feed and I just found out about lab grown meat. So, if you are like me, you're thinking, wait, what is that? What is it called? Is it like real meat? Quick explainer. Lab grown meat is actual meat, but they didn't slaughter the animal to get it."

Person questioning this: *"Is it a cloned meat? It's originally from, like an animal so they have to get something from the animal that they grow."*

Sarah: *"Stem cells are taken from an animal and then they are grown in a culture. The cells multiply until they become muscle tissue."*

2nd Person: *"This looks like somebody is getting pregnant."*

Sarah: *"That muscle tissue is what forms meat. Some of this sounds really cool and sci-fi right, but what are the benefits of lab grown meat? According to the UN, meat consumption is expected to rise as much as 73% by 2050."*

3rd Person: *"Do we have like a huge global food problem and if it helps solve that then awesome."*

Lab grown meat taste test: *"There is quite some flavor with the browning, and I know there is no fat in it so I didn't really know how juicy it would be."*

Sarah: *"Lab grown meat lacks the fat from traditional livestock, so unless you are super into lean meat, the taste may not be your thing."*

Taste Test: *"There is some intense taste, it's close to meat, it's not that juicy."*

Sarah: *"But for the meat eaters there are some concerns."*

4th Person: *"I would be down as long as they could prove it's not a carcinogen. Thirty years from now people aren't growing arms out of their heads, or something."[59]*

Yeah, but don't worry, that will never happen. But as you can see, as wild as it is, "lab grown" meant is the latest concoction they have made out of our food supply. Skip the whole traditional cloning process and just "grow meat" in the lab. Hey, what could go wrong with that? Well, first of all you admitted that it's not even "real" meat at all. There's not any fat in it. So, how's that "just like the real deal?"

Secondly, even though the makers of this keep pounding away at the propaganda machine that it's "just like real meat" over and over again, they even admit that are constantly tweaking it in the laboratory with other ingredients that are not meat.

Narrator: *"In San Francisco, in Silicon Valley, there is a race going on. Some of the biggest players are investing in the search to make commercially viable clean meat. That is meat that is grown in a bioreactor rather than on an animal, that is in every other way identical."*

Narrator: *"Clean meat is real meat that is grown from animal cells rather than from animal slaughter. So right now we have the capacity to take a sesame seed sized biopsy from an animal and inside of that tiny biopsy there are millions of cells and when you put those cells inside of a cultivator and make them think they are still inside of the animals body they do what they do best which is grow into mexal. So, this isn't an alternative to me, it isn't a substitute to me, it is real meat simply without the need to raise and slaughter animals."*

Narrator: *"This is one of about half a dozen companies in the race to develop clean meat. They are called JUST. They invited me in to see how they are doing although there were parts of their operation I wasn't allowed to film. One of the big challenges is finding the right liquid in which to grow the meat. It's this that provides the rapidly dividing cells with all the nutrients that they need. That is what researcher, Parendi Birdie, is working on. Up until now the only reliable growth medium has been something called fecal bovine serum. It's harvested from unborn calves and is both ethically and economically a known starter for commercial clean meat production."*

Parendi Birdie: *"So we are working on a lot of different experiments to find ways to eliminate that serum. So, to do that we are harnessing the technology from our discovery platform to find different proteins that come from plants that can replace the protein that are in that serum that comes from animals.*

And I think here at JUST we are very well positioned to do that because we have years of experience in understanding, analyzing proteins from plants because at the end of the day animals eat plants. Cows for example eat grass. So, the proteins are similar enough, we just need to figure out the best ones that our cells are happiest with and grow naturally."

Narrator: *"In the basement of JUST is a huge plant library. Hundreds of samples, ready for testing to find the ones with the right nutrients in which meat can grow. One thing the researchers haven't yet solved is how to replicate the structure and texture of animal grown meat, how to make a steak rather than just a pound of meat. It's difficult and we're not there yet."*

Promotional video from JUST Inc.: *"I'm going to make the best chicken nuggets, ever. A man is putting one in his mouth. It says that the name of that nugget was 'Ian'. He and several of his friends are sitting at a picnic table in the back yard enjoying the delicious chicken nuggets."*

Narrator: *"JUST has made a clean meat product. Chicken nuggets made from cells taken from a chicken very much still alive. They promise commercial sales will begin in a small way by the end of the year. We are all going to have to get used to familiar, yet strange foods in the coming year. Clean meat industry is aware it has to tread carefully. Headlines about unnatural Frankenstein food could turn the public against it."*[60]

And you can't have that, so let's just tell the public over and over and over again this is "real meat" that's just grown in the lab, YET it contains no fat whatsoever like "real meat" does, and you're growing it in various plant based solutions that you're still experimenting with, and when all is said and done you can't even get it to come out looking like a proper piece of meat, like a steak or something, it's a pile of mush. Sorry, that's not meat! But don't worry, it's all safe and you can trust us. Sure thing. What's next, you're going to sell me some swampland too?

But if you thought that was bad, you still haven't seen anything yet. It's bad enough that you are cloning our meat and not even telling us and now you're growing it in the lab and saying it's meat when it's not. Well, I kid you not, these same folks who are saying we need to do this to our meat supply in order to supposedly save ourselves and the whole planet, are now saying, "While we're at it, why don't we just consider eating "human meat" as well. That'll save some animals." Excuse me? That's called cannibalism.

Fox News Reports: *"A Stockholm professor reportedly believes eating human meat might be able to help save the human race. Economics professor and researcher Magnus Soderlund says the human meat could be derived from dead bodies. He said taboos against cannibalism could change if people were 'awakened to the idea' and simply tried human flesh. The 'Sweeney Todd' idea of human meat pies doesn't come without risks or social taboos for that matter. Some tribes practiced eating their dead which led to kuru, a disease known as laughing death. The disease is caused by an infectious protein found in contaminated human brain tissue.*[61]

Wow! What kind of a sick world are we turning into? Good thing nobody's falling for this stuff. Yeah, right! The same people who are pumping out the propaganda that climate change is about to destroy the planet any day now and we need to make these albeit shocking yet drastic changes to our food supply in order to save ourselves, have also created a whole new generation of young people who are brainwashed into going along with it, including cannibalism.

One lady speaks: *C-Span Reports from a Town Hall Meeting in Corona New York Queens Public Library: "We aren't going to be here for much longer because of the climate crises. We only have a few months left. I like that you support the 'Green Deal' but getting rid of fossil fuel is not going to solve the problem fast enough. A Swedish Professor is saying that we can eat dead people, but that is not fast enough. So, I think your next campaign slogan has to be this. We must start eating babies.*

We don't have enough time, there is too much CO2, all of you, you are a pollutant. Too much CO2, we have to start now, please. You are so great, (speaking to OAC) I am so happy that you are really supporting the New Green Deal but it's not enough. You know, even if we would bomb Russia, we still have too many people, too much pollution, so we have to get rid of the babies. That's a big problem, to stop having babies, it's not enough, we need to eat the babies. This is very serious."[62]

Yeah this is very serious! Can you believe this? First, it's cloned meat, then lab grown meat, then human meat, and now we need to eat the babies in order to keep the planet from blowing up! Are you kidding me? I mean, you keep this up, the next thing you know this science fiction movie of the past is about to become our modern-day reality.

Movie Clip from Soylent. *'What is the secret of Soylent Green?*

"New York City in the year 2022, nothing runs any more, nothing works, but the people are the same. The people will do anything to get what they need. What they need most is Soylent Green. 'The supply of Soylent Green has been exhausted,' it is announced by a policeman. 'Return to your

homes.' The crowd is going crazy. They are pushing through the barriers and knocking down the police.

Detective Sargent Thorne (Charleton Heston), he has a two-year backlog of unsolved murders. Now he is on a case that must be solved. Saul Roth (Edward G. Robinson) is Thornes private library. A living book in a world without books."

Thorne: "Hey Saul, have some pencils, courtesy of your next assignment."

William R. Simonson, (Joseph Cotton) he was the first to know the secret of Soylent Green.

"They told me that they were sorry but that you had become unreliable." As he took a tire iron and killed him in his living room.

Saul Roth was the next to know. "How did we come to this?" he asks. And he chose to die rather reveal the secret of Soylent Green.

As Sargent Thorne is hitting a guy (Chuck Connors) he is trying to find out why this guy has set up Simonson. But he says, "I didn't." Then he goes to a girl named Cheryl (Leigh Taylor Young), officially she is part of the furniture, she comes with the apartment. He checks her hands. She belongs to the tenant. Thorne asks her, "How many times have you been in trouble with the police, Cheryl?" "Never" is her reply.

Captain Hatcher, at first, he wanted this case solved. "Simonson, what do you say?" Thorne replies, "It was an assassination." Now he just wants it closed. "Who bought you?" Captain Hatcher replies, "They just want this case closed! Closed permanently! Now you sign this!" But Thorne answers with, "You sign it!!!"

It goes back to the government and the leader is told that Thorne refuses to close the Simonson case. The leader says, "Just do what you have to do."

Back at Cheryl's apartment Thorne is asking her, "Where did you go with Simonson?" She answers, "He took me to church." "Church?" The scene then goes to the church and you see the character played by Chuck Connors saying, "Bless me Father, for I have sinned. It's been 6 months since my last confession." Then he sticks a gun to the priest's head and pulls the trigger.

Thorne is on a garbage truck that leads to a factory where they make Soylent Green. He looks up at the top of the conveyor belt and sees what looks like bodies under white sheets coming down, one by one. But then someone comes up behind him and he falls down to the lower level.

They all fight for survival and try to solve the most bazaar riddle ever to face mankind. The search for the secret of Soylent Green. You will find out why Soylent Green means life, you will find out why Soylent Green means death. Thorne yells to the people, "We've got to stop them, please!"[63]

Well, if you saw the movie, the secret of Soylent Green was that it was human meat. Keep in mind, that movie was made in 1973 and it depicted a horrible futuristic society of 2022 that actually ate human flesh in order to survive unbeknownst to the people. And "today" we have people who are now saying we need to eat human flesh including babies "out in the open" in order to survive. Talk about hitting the nail on the head. That movie was almost prophetic.

And speaking of the prophetic, when you put all this together, is it really a wonder why God is getting ready to come back and judge this planet again? Are you kidding me? All this wickedness? He's got to put a stop to it! It's common sense!

But remember, that's still not all of what they're doing to modify the animal kingdom. We have one more to go. First it was "Modifying" the animal kingdom, then as we just saw it was "Cloning" the animal kingdom. Now we will see that that they are even trying to "Resurrect" if you will the animal kingdom. That's right folks! Jurassic Park eat your heart out! It's almost looks like Hollywood is preparing us for some freaky future, like depicted here.

Clip from Jurassic Park..._Hammond (played by Richard Attenborough) has pulled Grant (Sam Neill and Ellie (Laura Dern) out of the field to tell them, "I own an island off the coast of Costa Rica and I spent the last 5 years setting up a kind of biological reserve." Grant asks, "What kind of park is this?" Soon they find themselves flying to this island to find out what Jurassic Park is all about._

When there they meet up with Malcolm (Jeff Goldblum) and Gennaro (Martin Ferrero). Hammond shows them all around the laboratory and explains, "We have made living biological attractions more astounding and will capture the imagination of the entire planet." They go to the next stage of the journey and get in a jeep to see what has been living on this island. They are amazed that full-grown dinosaurs are walking around in herds.

Hammond says, "There is no doubt our attraction will drive kids out of their minds." Gennaro is in awe of this place. He says, "We are going to make a fortune with this place." Suddenly Hammons grandkids come running through the front door. "Grandpa." They yell, so happy to be there.

They hold the new babies in their hands right after they hatch, they help a sick dinosaur, they walk with the dinosaurs. This is all unbelievable. But then Grant gets concerned, "What species is this?" he asks. The scientist replies, "It's a velociraptor." The light has gone on and he realizes how dangerous this is. Hammond assures him all is well and takes them back out to the jeeps. He says, "The park is going to open with the basic tour that you are about to take. But Malcolm asks, "Don't you see the danger here, the genetic powers are the most awesome forces that the planet has ever seen, and you wield it like a kid that found his dad's gun."

Ellie says, "These are aggressives that have no idea of what century they are in and they will defend themselves." Meanwhile, Nedry (Wayne

Knight) is making plans to sell off some of the embryos secretly, but in order to do that he has to turn off the electricity for a few minutes so he can get them out of the container. Unfortunately, he is running late and is anxious to get back to his buyer and he doesn't turn the electricity back on. All he can think about is getting out of there and getting rich. Grant is very concerned. "Two species separated indefinitely and then suddenly thrown back into the mix together. We don't have the slightest idea what to expect." So, while they are driving in the jeep which is controlled by electricity, it suddenly stops. They are stuck. "What did I touch?" Grant asks. Malcolm answers, "You didn't touch anything, we just stopped." While they are sitting there waiting for things to be turned back on, they look at a glass of water that is sitting on the dash. The water is moving. Malcolm asks, "Did anyone feel that?" Back at headquarters they are trying to figure out what happened and are trying to get things working again. But since the electrical fences aren't working the dinosaurs are free to roam. Arnold (Samuel L. Jackson) says he can't get Jurassic Park back online.

The fences are torn down, the dinosaurs are loose. A jeep is missing with Grant and the kids. Muldoon (Bob Peck) and Ellie are on foot trying to find out what happened to Grant and the kids. Unknown to Ellie the jeep was pushed over the edge of the bridge and has been caught in a tree. Grant and one of the kids managed to get on the ground but the boy is still in the car. It slides down a few branches and then stops. The boy tries to get out, but it slides again. They know it's not going to stay in the tree for very long and Grant is trying to instruct the boy the best way to get out of there. But the branch gives way and the jeep comes crashing to the ground. As it falls on its nose they can't see where the boy is. It falls flat and he comes climbing out the side, unhurt. Now they have to walk on foot back to the main compound.

Ellie and Muldoon are trying to get everything turned back on and finally succeed. They believe they are safe now. They meet up with Grant and the kids. But while the kids are trying to eat some of the food that was laid out for the celebration a shadow shows up on the wall and it is a raptor. But they travel in pairs. The kids run into the kitchen for safety.

Meanwhile, Nedry has run into trouble. He ran off the road due to the rain and mud, he is stuck, so he wraps a chain around a tree to pull himself out of the mess and he drops the can of embryos. He tries to go after the can but slips and slides down the hill losing his glasses. Now he can't see. He manages to get back into his truck only to be sitting next to a dinosaur.

The whole place is a mess. Ellie says, "The only thing that matters now is the people we love." Malcolm has managed to hurt his leg while trying to get away and Hammond is trying to bandage it, talking to him like this is not as serious as it looks. This has just caused some delay. But Malcolm tells him that in Pirates of the Caribbean when the ride breaks down the pirates don't eat the tourists.[64]

Wow! Remember that movie when it first came out? It seemed so futuristic, didn't it? Wild and crazy! Well, I'm here to tell you, that movie is about to become our modern-day reality. In fact, as you'll see in a moment, it's already begun. But hey, I'm sure it won't have any of the horrible side effects and deadly ramifications like the move predicted. Yeah, right! Once again, how much swampland would you like to buy?

But let's take a look at the actual "resurrecting" of the animal kingdom that is currently underway and believe it or not, as you're about to see, is the next logical outcome of all this cloning of animals and pets as these scientists freely admit.

Smithsonian Channel Reports: *"Seoul South Korea, the Sooam Labs await the arrival of samples from Siberia."*

Researcher: *"Our colleagues are doing their best to transport the samples to us as quickly as possible."*

Narrator: *"In the meantime they focus on the cloning of farm animals and not without controversy, pet dogs, for a price of $100,000 per clone."*

Researcher: *"The process that we are doing is basically copying the genetics of the original so that we can give birth to a clone that has the same genetic makeup."*

Narrator: *"They plan to clone the mammoth using the same process they use for cloning dogs. To clone this Beagle, they simply use a skin cell. It's painless and easy to remove and its nucleus contains the DNA necessary to create a clone. They even add a genetic marker to help identify any clones that are born. They need to put the cell into an empty egg."*

Researcher: *"So this is the step where we extract eggs out of the egg donor."*

Narrator: *"In a harmless procedure eggs are removed from a sedated mongrel dog."*

Researcher: *"We are going to flush the medium through the aqueduct and the eggs go out the other way. Our researchers are working with the liquid we just extracted from the domestic dog and she is working with a very small pet. She can pick up the eggs along all the debris."*

Narrator: *"Next the nucleus of the dog egg is identified under ultraviolet light and removed."*

Researcher: *"The nucleus is glowing blue; we just take out the nucleus and then replace it with a whole cell."*

Narrator: *"The Beagle skin cell is then inserted in the dog egg."*

Researcher: *"They are removing the maternal side of the gene and then replacing it with the full genome from the skin cell."*

Narrator: *"The egg is given an electric shock. This kick starts cell division and it turns into an embryo, which is inserted into the surrogate mother. Two months later cloned puppies are born. These two pups are the exact copies of the original Beagle except for the proof that they are* *clones, their fluorescent toenails, a result of the marker they added to the cell earlier."*

Researcher: *"As you can see on the paws their nails are glowing green right now. It's a visual marker that these are indeed clones."*

Narrator: *"But using these techniques to create a mammoth embryo and then implanting it into a womb of an Asian elephant will be highly controversial. Many scientists have concerns about the ethics of the project."*

Dr. Tori Herridge, Natural History Museum, London: *"What are their intentions, what are they going to do if they are successful and create a mammoth? Who is responsible for the mammoth that is produced? Is it them, is it the wide world, do we get a say in them doing it in the first place?"*[65]

My guess would be no! As we've seen with the track record with these guys, they're going to move ahead with this venture and do whatever they want regardless. Remember, there is virtually no oversight on this field of science.

But as you can see, this is apparently the next logical step. They can't leave anything alone. First clone animals, i.e. livestock, then pets, then animals that went extinct long ago, like the wooly mammoth. As if we don't have enough current specimens to work with, you actually go back in time and get those that died out long ago. Yet you don't know hardly anything about them, what diseases they had, characteristics, deformities, oddities in their genetic structure, etc., but here you are "resurrecting" them again back on planet earth. Gee what could go wrong with that! I'm sure nothing horrible will be loosed upon us.

Or maybe, we should take a deep breath and realize that there's just certain things that are better left alone, or as in the previous nightmare movie stated, "better left dead." How do you know there's certain things about their genetic structure that we don't want to unleash on the planet again? All you know is it was dead, and maybe it died out for a good reason. Have you really thought this through? I kind of doubt it.

But be that as it may, they charge ahead again. In fact, they're already doing it.

Newsy, Megan Judy Reports: *"The wooly mammoth has been extinct for some four thousand years, but now researchers are attempting to bring it back to life. A team at Harvard University has successfully inserted wooly mammoth DNA into the genetic code of an elephant. The project was led by Harvard's Genetics Professor George Church. He told the Sunday Times, 'We prioritized genes associated with cold resistance including hairiness, ear size, subcutaneous fat and especially, hemoglobin. Church has spoken about this type of genetic splicing in elephants before."*

George Church: *"We would propose to make a hybrid elephant that has the best features of modern elephants and the best features of the mammoth."*

Megan Judy: *"The Asian elephant is the closest relative to mammoths although the size of the mammoth was similar to that of the size of the African Elephant. Church's project is not without its critics though. Some scientists are against using elephants to potentially bring back the wooly mammoths. Professor Alex Greenwood told the Telegraph, 'Why bring back another elephantid from extinction when we cannot even keep the ones that are not extinct around? What is the message? We can be as irresponsible with the environment as we want. Then we'll just clone things back?'"*[66]

Well yeah, that seems to be the mindset with this behavior. Just play around and mix and match things and if it creates something freaky or something goes wrong, oh well, science to the rescue. What could go wrong?

But speaking of science, they were using the term of "de-extinction." That's what they are calling this kind of endeavor. We can clone things back into existence, i.e. de-extinct them and believe it or not, the wooly mammoth is just the beginning. Here's what a team of scientists are doing right now in Russia.

AP News Reports: *"Scientists in Russia hope they can clone an extinct cave lion. They want to use DNA from an Ice Age cub found in Russia. There may be some chances to get some good samples from the cave lion remains. If we get good samples, then we will do our best to try to restore the cave lion. I believe these samples are unique in the world and I hope to get some better samples. I strongly believe that these samples are unique therefore I want to get some more and better samples from the cave lion."*[67]

So first it's the Wooly Mammoth, now it's an extinct cave lion. What's next? Well, funny you should ask. This is all just the tip of the iceberg of extinct animals they want to bring back. There are tons of them that these same scientists want to "resurrect" from de-extinction real soon.

Narrator: *"Resurrecting extinct animals is no longer a fantasy but is it a good idea? From the Woolly Mammoth to the Sabre Tooth Tiger. Here are eight animals that scientists are trying to bring back from extinction.*

Number 8: Sabre Tooth Cats. *There are many animals from the ice age that scientists are talking about bringing back. But easily more surprisingly is their suggestion they have is the Sabre Tooth Cat. These massive cats were the ancestors of many of the big cats in the world today with the exception that they had fangs that our cats could only dream of and they were much more vicious. Just it's fangs alone were nearly a foot long and it would use them with such deadly precision that prey rarely got away.*

But their fangs weren't all they had to offer. They were fast, so much so that they would not only catch up to their prey, but they would pounce on them with impeccable speed to tackle them to the ground and go in for the kill. They would eat large elephants, rhinos, and other huge herbivores.

However, due to fossils found in the La Brea tarpits in Los Angeles, there is potential DNA that could be used to bring them back.

Just because we can doesn't mean that we should. These big cats could be extremely dangerous if released into the wild. And would we be able to protect them from poachers? Habitat loss is also a huge problem that hasn't gone away. Many argue that the extinction should be the conservation strategy for animals that we have now, not for animals that have been gone for thousands of years.

Number 7: Baiji River Dolphin. *Also known as the Yangtze River Dolphin, this dolphin is listed as critically in danger, but most scientists agree that it is already extinct. This dolphin actually died out pretty recently. So, scientists feel they can bring them back or at least try to. The last documented sighting was in 2002, although every so often someone claims to have seen one jumping out of the river. Because river dolphins are restricted to certain rivers, they are extremely vulnerable, and the Baiji Dolphin was severely affected by human activity.*

Fishing, hydroelectricity, poaching and habitat loss were just too much for this creature. Dolphins were often hunted to make gloves and other clothing and got stuck in fishing nets and drowned. All that being said, the reasons scientists have hope is because of the recent loss of this species. There might be fresh DNA that might be used to genetically engineer a river dolphin. I'm sure you have seen Jurassic Park or Jurassic World by now, taking an extinct species genome and bringing it back to life is known as de-extinction and we are closer to doing this that you might think.

Number 6: The Woolly Rhinoceros. *Some very well-preserved specimens have been found in the ice. Scientists have decided to take advantage of this opportunity and bring back megafauna from the ice age, including the Woolly Rhinoceros. In Siberia in 2015 a baby Woolly Rhinoceros was found completely frozen in ice. The Rhino was found by a hunter named Sasha and so the baby was named after him. Paleontologist* *were thrilled that they could maybe harvest some undamaged DNA from the tissue.*

After some research it was discovered that the baby Rhino was only 3 to 4 years old when it died. It became frozen in the river fully preserved. Though scientists have known for years that the Woolly Rhinoceros once existed, including having fossils, no one had ever found a complete specimen until Sasha showed up. All that being said, even with Sasha's perfectly preserved body it won't be easy to bring this Rhino back to life. According to one scientist to birth such an ancient animal it would take a suitable mother, which in this case would likely be the Sumatran Rhino which is slightly problematic because that particular species of Rhino is endangered. Still the potential is there, and scientists are trying to make the most of the opportunity granted to them.

Number 5: Passenger Pigeons. *The Passenger Pigeon may be one of the truly tragic extinction stories as the Passenger Pigeon was once one of the dominate bird species in the United States. According to the Smithsonian there was once around 5 billion of these birds in the United States before settlers came. Once the settlers arrived, they started to destroy their habitat and hunt them for food and sport.*

Even though they had their uses including being messenger birds, technology advanced past them and then it actually consumed them. As these pigeons were hunted down by the millions as time went on, and then shipped all over the country for various purposes, eventually this trend led to the bird being declared extinct in 1914 with the very last one in captivity dying at the Cincinnati zoo.

However, despite the bird being dead for over 100 years at this point, a group of scientists are trying to bring it back. The project itself is being called 'The Great Passenger Pigeon Comeback' and it has been going on now for about 6 years. Scientists have been manipulating the DNA of other birds to de-breed them and give modern birds the traits of Passenger Pigeons. They are at a disadvantage because unlike other animal revival projects, they can't accept the DNA from the fossils or remains found at museums. *They truly have to try and reverse engineer the DNA of this bird which is not an easy feat. They don't know when or if they will be able to do it, but they are trying and will keep trying until the Passenger Pigeon lives again.*

No 4: Tasmanian Tiger. *Also known as the Thylacine or the Tasmanian Wolf, this animal was the largest carnivorous marsupial to live in modern times. This creature was the apex predator of its ecosystem on the island off of Australia. It would hunt all kinds of animals with lethal intent which actually led to its downfall. The settlers of Australia didn't like that this animal was eating their livestock so they would actually put bounties on its head and many, many people were happy to take that up. These Tasmanian Tigers could grow up to six feet long and would raise their young in a pouch.*

They were known for eating the organs of animals such as the eyes and intestines. The years of hunting added up and in 1936 they were declared extinct. Even though there have been reports over the decades since saying they are still alive. Even if there are a few left it doesn't mean that they aren't basically extinct. A few specimens aren't enough to keep a species going. Regardless of this, a group of scientists are actually working together to bring the Thylacine back to life. And ironically, it's Australian scientists who are trying to do it.

They have a secret weapon of sorts that they are hoping will help their crusade. They actually have a baby Thylacine preserved in alcohol since 1866. They intend to use this pup to help build their DNA map for the Thylacine and then once they can make an egg for it, they are hoping to us the Tasmanian Devil mother. While bringing this animal back may not be the best idea, animal parks and zoos are willing to pay whatever it takes to be the first to get their hands on one of these animals brought back to life.

Number 3: The Moa. *The Moa were flightless birds that lived in New Zealand. They went extinct about 700 years ago and now scientists are very close to bringing them back. They were very tall birds, reaching 12* *feet tall at times and could weigh over a ton. However, with the arrival of humans in the 13th century, they were hunted to extinction.*

Now researchers at Harvard University have assembled a nearly complete genome of the extinct moa thanks to a single toe bone from a moa at the Royal Ontario Museum in Toronto. They have used a new form of DNA sequencing that could revolutionize the field of recovering ancient DNA. It's not quite clear if giant birds are the best candidates for revival, but these experiments are a game changer.

Number 2: The Woolly Mammoth. *The Woolly Mammoth has been documented and studied immensely ever since the first bones were found by modern scientists. And so, it should come as no big surprise that there are many scientists trying to bring back this massive creature. The Woolly Mammoth roamed across Europe, Asia, Africa and North America during the last ice age and went extinct between 10,000 to 4,000 years ago.*

Many samples have been found frozen in ice, with well-preserved DNA. You'd think that it would be easy to get an intact genome from a Woolly Mammoth, however viable mammoth DNA has been very difficult to get. Harvard scientists are developing a mammoth/elephant hybrid (a mamophant) and are hoping to have an embryo in the next 2 years. There are many reasons why scientists want to bring them back, and one of them is simply because of our fascination with them. They are closely related to today's Asian elephants but were covered with thick brown hair to keep them warm.

They were around 13 feet (4 meters) tall and could weighed around 6 tons. Their tusks could get up to five feet long! But just as important as that is that there is an ecological reason to bring them back. Scientists feel that it could restore balance to the Siberian ecosystem and the Woolly Mammoth Revival project is trying to make this idea a reality.

As with all of these animals there is an ethical debate. And what about habitat loss and hunting? There aren't many places where you can reintroduce large animals without any problems and who is going to protect them? Many scientists argue that we should use this technology to save animals that are disappearing now, before bringing animals back from the dead.

Number 1: The Dodo Bird. *The Dodo Bird has always stood out amongst extinct animals as the poster animal for human-induced extinction. So why do we care? This would be the best species for scientists to bring back! The last Dodo died out about 350 years ago and it had a reputation for being fat and stupid. But that's revised history talking, in truth, the Dodo were wiped out by numerous things, and their stupidity wasn't one of them. In fact, not unlike the Moa, settlers to their lands were the biggest fact in their death.*

These flightless birds weren't necessarily hunted to death, but sailors brought cats, and pigs, and rats to the Dodo's homeland. While this may not sound bad, these invasive species brought disease and ate the Dodo's eggs and hunted the same food that the Dodo would eat. When you add all these factors, and throw in the expansion of the human settlements, you get an extinct flightless bird.

However, many today are talking about trying to bring the legendary and infamous bird back to life. However, they have a massive hill to climb, because there is only one complete Dodo skeleton in the world, and it may not have what it takes to bring the species back. If it does though, this bird could get a second chance at life. And it would be one of the safest species to bring back since it could be released back to its native habitat in Mauritius in a protected area without any negative consequences. We hope!"[68]

Yeah, we "hope" is the key word there. Sounds like something a Dodo would say! And I state that because as you just saw, they admit this might not be the smartest thing to do. Release long extinct giant wild ferocious game back into the ecosystem? Saber-toothed tigers, Tasmanian tigers. Gee, what could go wrong with that? And that's still the tip of the iceberg. There's a ton more of extinct animals that they want to resurrect, and the list just seems to be getting longer and longer as the days go by.

And wonder of wonders, they are already showing signs in the scientific community to "deviate" from the norm when even trying to "resurrect" these long extinct animals. Watch what these Japanese scientists are combining with the Wooly Mammoth.

Mashable Reports: *"Scientists revive DNA from ancient Woolly Mammoth. The extinct beast's remains were found in Northern Asia in 2010. The breakthrough occurred at Japan's Kindai University. Scientists say DNA from Yuka's muscle sprang back to life after being injected into mice cells."*[69]

Oh yeah, inject Wooly Mammoth cells into a mouse. That's all we need, Mammoth Mice running around. What could go wrong with that scenario! Are you serious?

But hey, that's just the Jurassic Park scenario. At least we don't have to worry about them trying to pull off the Jurassic World scenario where they turned dinosaurs into horrific military killing machines. Unfortunately, there's already work being done in that direction, as this article reveals.

"You don't have to watch 'Jurassic World' to see bioengineered animal weapons. This summer's sci-fi blockbuster imagines a world where scientists genetically engineer animals for war. It's already here.

The latest installment, Jurassic World, revisits the series' core plot points: Dinosaurs, brought back into existence through science, wreak havoc in a jungle setting, leaving dead bodies and lessons about hubris in their wake.

As with the original, released in 1993, many have taken issue with the science of the movie. But there is one arena in which the film comes remarkably close to reality. As in Jurassic World, scientists in real life are already well on their way toward genetically modifying animals for military use.

In the real world, the film is not far off in its assumptions about the militarization of genetic science. As the limitations of robotics become increasingly apparent, the United States military – in a high-tech extension of a tradition that stretches from George Washington's cavalry to the dogs, dolphins, and rats of the modern battlefield – has already set off down the road toward genetically engineering animals for war.

In 2006, the Defense Advanced Research Projects Agency asked scientists 'to develop technology to create insect-cyborgs' capable of carrying surveillance equipment or weapons, journalist Emily Anthes wrote in her 2013 book, Frankenstein's Cat: Cuddling Up to Biotech's Brave New Beasts.

The agency quickly realized that tiny flying machines were impossible to build well – but that insects, already abundant in nature, were better than whatever humans might make.

So DARPA changed its approach: In the past decade, the agency has encouraged and funded research into methods that can let humans control insects and mammals through electronic impulses to the brain, and through genetic modifications to the nervous systems of insects to make them easier to manipulate, with surprising success.

Researchers are already able to hijack the brains of beetles and order them to stop, start, and turn, with more fine-tuned control in the works. Insects created by humans, loaded with spy technology and controlled by drone operators, are on the horizon.

Scientists in Korea over the past decade have used viruses to deliver payloads of jellyfish genes to felines, thereby creating glow-in-the-dark cats, Scientific American reported – much like the chameleon-born camouflage genes scientists give Indominus rex in Jurassic World.

'Future generations are going to grow up tinkering not with computers, but with life itself,' Anthes wrote. 'There is a growing community of 'biohackers,' science enthusiasts who are experimenting with genes,

brains, and bodies outside the confines of traditional laboratories, working on shoestring budgets in their garages and attics, or joining the community labs that are springing up around the globe.'

Given the possibilities, it's not hard to imagine private companies using these breakthroughs for their own dubious purposes – on an island off Costa Rica, say, far from government scrutiny.

Jurassic World may be off base about what reincarnated dinosaur species would look like, but its right about where biotech is going. We already live in a world of unfolding genetic engineering possibilities, and militarization – already underway – seems inevitable.

And science fiction has a long history of predicting (and influencing) the future of technology, from the tablet computers in 2001: A Space Odyssey to William Gibson's 'cyberspace' in Neuromancer and surveillance drones in Robert Sheckley's Watchbird."

In other words, this really could become our soon everyday reality.

A clip from Jurassic World: *A mother is telling her son that she is very proud of him for going on this trip. He is kind of unsure of the whole thing but shakes his head in agreement. She is trying to encourage him by telling him he is going to have so much fun. Jokingly she says, "Remember, if something chases you, RUN!" and she smiles.*

He gets on the ferry and they are off to the beautiful island for the adventure of a lifetime. He arrives at the park on a trolley and they come to the entrance. The giant doors open and above the doors is the sign telling him and his brother that they have arrived at 'Jurassic World.' It is the first day the park is opened and there are hundreds of people there. Excitement is in the air. The place is amazing.

After he gets settled in, he takes a jeep ride out on the plains where the dinosaurs are running free. Then on a canoe ride down the river. This couldn't be any more exciting than this. Dinosaurs are all over and they

*are real, not the fake ones you see back home. But what was the most
exciting was when they got into the plastic bubble built for two. He and his
brother are rolling right alongside of the dinosaurs. He could almost
reach out and touch them. He is so glad his mom got him to come on this
trip. It is so safe here. All his worries are gone. The next attraction they
are visiting is the water show.*

*Now that is really exciting. They held a large fish in the air and this huge
prehistoric monster jumps out of the water, opens its mouth with all these
huge teeth and grabs hold of the fish and takes it down. The boy got it all
on his cell phone to take home to show everyone. This whole place is
unbelievable.*

*On the other side of the park a helicopter lands on site. Someone is
coming to visit the park and just see how they have managed to put this all
together. The lady in charge is telling him how it all works as she is taking
him for a tour. She says, "We have learned more in the past decade, from
genetics, than a century of digging up bones. A whole new frontier has
opened up. We have our first genetically modified hybrid."*

*The visitor who just arrived on the scene asks her, "You just up and made
a new dinosaur? Probably not a good idea." He goes out to look at how
the dangerous dinosaurs are contained. Not really happy with what he
finds. One wall that is about 40 feet high has claw marks all over it.
Something is trying to get out! One worker asks, "Do you think it's trying
to get out?" He answers, "Depends on what kind of dinosaur they are
cooking up in that lab."*

*A worker's hard-hat with blood on it is found, with no body to be seen.
Evidence shows he may have been eaten. The character played by Chris
Pratt is telling her that she must evacuate the island. They proceed to go
investigate what he thinks is going on with the dinosaurs. They come upon
the bubble that has been destroyed and no occupants around. But they do
find a large tooth stuck in the metal.*

Now he finds out that this thing is a highly intelligent animal and kills anything that moves. This monster dinosaur has gotten loose and now the people are panicking. They have to get off this island immediately. The two boys are alone and don't know which way to run. The crowds are going in all different directions. They manage to find a place to hide but unfortunately it is the same place as Blue, one of the Raptors, and her nose is right in the little boy's face, growling and blowing hot air at him. What is he going to do now? He should have stayed home. [70]

Coming to a planet near you, only it's not make-believe, it's our reality today. Can you believe all this? They just can't seem to leave well enough alone. First you mix and match existing animals, then you do it with even extinct animals, and now you want to even weaponize them! I wonder if this was some of the crazy stuff going on back in Noah's Day. What did he have to put up with before he got into that ark? And why did God destroy the planet in the first place?

But speaking of crazy, with this wild track record, I mean, what's next…are you going to do this with humans? I didn't say that, they did!

Narrator: *"Definitely the most controversial, we have the Neanderthal. The idea of resurrecting this species evokes the most heated debate. The main reason is the logistics, since the closest surrogate species would have to be a human. So, while cloning them would be very enlightening, it could also be quite unethical. In any case, bringing the Neanderthal back would be the easiest task of them all. Scientists already have a map of its genome. It's not a question of whether or not we can, but if we should."*

Motherboard Reports: *"South Korea is one of the fastest growing economies in the world. It's also the global epicenter for cloning technology. Here scientists have perfected a Doctor Moreau method for cloning several species, including dogs. And one of their biggest goals is bringing back the prehistoric Woolly Mammoth from the flesh of the perfectly preserved specimens buried in Northern Siberia. At the same time tusk hunting Siberians looking for mammoth ivory support the Korean cloning project by discovering frozen mammoths in the quickly* *melting permafrost of the far north. This bizarre supply chain inspired us to travel to Seoul, Yakutsk and Moscow to learn about humanity's quest to both profit from and resurrect the legendary Woolly Mammoth.*

To start off our journey we hopped on a flight to Seoul, South Korea. Cloning is controversial everywhere in the world. 'The international community must act now to send a clear message that human cloning is an affront to human dignity. That cannot be tolerated. We're gonna be cloned just for the organs. You get old and then you grow a new guy out of yourself and just take your brain out, throw it into a new body."

Obama: *"And we will ensure that our government never opens the door to the use of cloning for human reproductions."*

Minister: *"Are we acting more like the creator than creatures? Are we trying to play the role of God on this?"*

Motherboard Reports: *"In South Korea the cloning of animals is not just accepted it's a business. At Sooam Biotech labs in Seoul, you can have your favorite pooch cloned for $100,000. The Lab is ground zero for cloning and is led by Dr. Hwang Woo-Suk, a South Korean scientist with an alleged shady past. He also partners with the Siberian lab that supplies him with frozen mammoth meat found in the Russian far north."*

Dr. Hwang Woo-Suk: *"My team already have tried to find the intact cell from frozen mammoth tissues from Siberia. The potential surrogate mother will be the Asian elephant. A very difficult process. I think we have to try."*

Dr. Jeong Yeon Woo: *"Cloning technology was first invented in 1950. Robert Briggs first introduced the idea. He used frog's eggs. He removed the nucleus of a frog's egg cell and added a blastocyst cell to reproduce. Everyone from that time period rejected the idea and called it nonsense. And exactly 50 years later, Dolly was cloned with a somatic cell."*

Motherboard Reporter: *"Why clone a mammoth?"*

Dr. Woo: *"Someone on this Earth will have to do it. And I think it's us. We have cloning technology, if we find the viable, live cell, I believe that we can do it. Don't you think it will be fun to find out what comes out?"*

Motherboard Reporter: *"In a few years this could be an Asian Elephant that is birthing this giant mammoth and we are all waiting with bated breath to see if the Asian elephant will accept the 30,000-year-old beast."* As he looks at a mother dog with a baby puppy. *"What would you say to people who would say Sooam is playing God.?"*

Dr. Woo: *"In the case of the Siberian mammoth, the Siberian climate kept it buried in a frozen state. Not to play God, but I believe we are obligated to bring it back, as humans."*

Motherboard Reporter: *"So how do we get from cloning dogs to an animal that has been extinct for over 4,000 years?"*

Researcher: *"This looks like wood chips, but this is the stuff that can be cloned and possibly bring back the mammoth from its extinction. So, in other words I am literally holding a plot line from Jurassic Park in my hands."*

Motherboard Reporter: *"Once they find that living cell the plan is to insert it into an egg of an Asian elephant, the nearest relative and have the AE give birth to a freaky cloned calf from the ice age. We sat down with another Sooam scientist to find out what exactly we can expect from cloning technology in the future."*

David Kim, Researcher: *"When we try to bring back the extinct species it also means that we will be able to help endangered species by using our cloning process to repopulate them and to help them reestablish into their environment."*

Motherboard Reporter: *"Why exactly do you want to bring the mammoth back?"*

David Kim, Researcher: *"Because it's available. We are starting with the mammoth, other big animals that have gone extinct, if we are able to find a sample, we would like to try cloning them."*

Motherboard Reporter: *"The mammoth is the one you have access to, maybe a hairy Rhino, what if you got a Neanderthal?"*

David Kim: *"Maybe there will be an interest. Because it's still considered human cloning, I'm not sure that it will be legally allowed."*

Motherboard Reporter: *"Would you clone yourself?"*

David Kim: *"I don't think we would be able to clone a complete human being."*

Motherboard Reporter: *"You don't think so?"*

David Kim: *"Like legally or ....?"*

Motherboard Reporter: *"Because, right now you clearly could. If you were allowed to. The gloves were off, cloning is the name of the game, you probably could do it."*

David Kim: *"Seriously, yes!"*[71]

Wow! Not maybe. Not might. But yes! Which means, you know what's coming next! Humans WILL be cloned, it's just a matter of time! Playing God is right!

And speaking of which, if in fact some of these extinct animals did die as a result of Noah's flood or the after effects of it, and there's good evidence for that, (for more information get our studies, "In the Days of Noah" and "The Truth about Dinosaurs") then this means that some of them very well could have existed in Noah's day when all this original hybridization was going on. And so stir all this together and here we have people today not only repeating the same hybridization mistake of Noah's day with animals, but you even have the audacity to bring back the very animals that were destroyed in Noah's Day, by God, and now you're showing signs of doing it to people! I mean, what's next? You going to call these hybrid people Nephilim? It's crazy isn't it?

And here's the point. If God didn't put up with it the first time, do you really think He's going to so this second time? Do you really think He's not going to put a stop to this? No wonder Jesus said, "As it was in the Days of Noah, so shall it be at the Coming of the Son of Man."

But all this leads us perfectly into our next section in Volume 2. It really is true folks, the next genetic modification that is being done, just like in Noah's Day, is now humans! Wait until you see how far they've already gone!

How to Receive Jesus Christ:

1. Admit your need (I am a sinner).

2. Be willing to turn from your sins (repent).

3. Believe that Jesus Christ died for you on the Cross and rose from the grave.

4. Through prayer, invite Jesus Christ to come in and control your life through the Holy Spirit. (Receive Him as Lord and Savior.)

What to pray:

Dear Lord Jesus,

I know that I am a sinner and need Your forgiveness. I believe that You died for my sins. I want to turn from my sins. I now invite You to come into my heart and life. I want to trust and follow You as Lord and Savior.

In Jesus' name. Amen.

Notes

Chapter 1 *The Sign of Hybrids*

1. *Article from The Institute for Ethics and Emerging Technologies*
   https://ieet.org/index.php/IEET2/more/pelletier20141217
2. *Freitas & Kurzweil Interview*
   https://www.youtube.com/watch?v=ie6w63-LJIg
3. *Nano Factory Demonstration*
   https://www.youtube.com/watch?v=vEYN18d7gHg
4. *Hollywood Preparing us for Hybrid Future*
5. *The Days of Noah*
   https://store.rightnow.org/Products/Downloadable_Video_Illustrations
   /1366/Noah_-
   _A_World_Full_of_Evil_with_Teaching_by_Chris_Seay
6. *The Flood of Noah Animation*
   https://answersingenesis.org/media/video/bible/flood-initiation/

Chapter 2 *The History of Hybrids*

1. *The Date of Noah's Flood Until the Time of the Writing of Leviticus*
   https://answersingenesis.org/the-flood/
   https://www.gty.org/library/questions/QA176/when-were-the-bible-
   books-written
2. *The Dangers of Mixing Genes*
   https://www.hope-of-israel.org/mixedclothing.html
   https://www.naturalnews.com/2019-09-18-gmo-mosquito-experiment-
   goes-horribly-wrong.html
3. *History of Genetic Engineering*

https://geneticliteracyproject.org/2017/07/18/biotechnology-timeline-humans-manipulating-genes-since-dawn-civilization/
https://www.synthego.com/learn/genome-engineering-history
https://en.wikipedia.org/wiki/History_of_genetic_engineering
https://en.wikipedia.org/wiki/Genetic_use_restriction_technology
https://easydna.com.au/knowledgebase/history-testing/
http://www.rcmp-grc.gc.ca/en/national-dna-data-bank-privacy-impact-assessment-abbreviated-executive-summary
https://www.23andme.com/
https://isogg.org/wiki/AncestryDNA
https://en.wikipedia.org/wiki/Svalbard_Global_Seed_Vault
http://www.foodcircles.missouri.edu/whstudy.pdf
https://gmo.geneticliteracyproject.org/FAQ/whats-controversy-gmos-terminator-seeds/
https://www.rt.com/news/217747-noah-ark-russia-biological/
4. *The Origin of Vaccines*
https://www.youtube.com/watch?v=E_PKQ_M7AtU
5. *The Hybrid Corn Miracle*
https://www.youtube.com/watch?v=fkkHvsYXens
6. *The Discovery of Penicillin*
https://www.youtube.com/watch?v=7qeZLLhx5kU
7. *The Discovery of the DNA Structure*
https://www.youtube.com/watch?v=V6bKn34nSbk
8. *Jonas Salk's Legacy*
https://www.youtube.com/watch?v=swPdkPmIEpk
9. *What is Gene Splicing*
https://www.youtube.com/watch?v=c2PDGcN0p18
https://www.youtube.com/watch?v=p_E4hVKer3s
10. *Stanley Cohen & Herbert Boyer*
https://www.youtube.com/watch?v=G3H-Uzts108
11. *Human Growth Hormone*
https://www.youtube.com/watch?v=8Yfic6UJev4
https://www.youtube.com/watch?v=uwWKGJbgais
https://www.youtube.com/watch?v=re3mk7JQvgQ
12. *Mouse Microinjection*
https://www.youtube.com/watch?v=r7cgNmQ1zfw

13. *Genentech Interview*
    https://www.youtube.com/watch?v=B5NjuzR5Kb4
14. *The First DNA Fingerprint*
    https://www.youtube.com/watch?v=Hzq7Tb10M1c
15. *How DNA Changed Forensics*
    https://www.youtube.com/watch?v=nPVkooi8m9I
16. *The First BT Corn*
    https://www.youtube.com/watch?v=ScJn01Jo-Hk
17. *Human Genome Project*
    https://www.youtube.com/watch?v=AhsIF-cmoQQ
18. *Global Seed Vault*
    https://www.youtube.com/watch?v=QHw4AxJX5Wo
    https://www.youtube.com/watch?v=B95Pem9XW7k
19. *Dolly the Sheep*
    https://www.youtube.com/watch?v=QO2yyS0CMQw
20. *What Use is a National DNA Database*
    https://www.youtube.com/watch?v=qIq6Czio7DU
21. *DNA Database Mandatory*
    https://www.youtube.com/watch?v=XIHdo0o-2Lo
22. *23 and Me Commercial*
    https://www.youtube.com/watch?v=C6O9xKdCl9U
23. *Craig Venter Synthetic Life*
    https://www.youtube.com/watch?v=aRzrYNVXF28
24. *Ancestry Commercial*
    https://www.youtube.com/watch?v=Fw7FhU-G1_Q
25. *What is CRISPR*
    https://www.youtube.com/watch?v=SyAo51IYgUw
26. *Womb Transplant*
    https://www.youtube.com/watch?v=qJR-247YYI4
27. *Gene Drives*
    https://wyss.harvard.edu/media-post/crispr-cas9-gene-drives/
28. *Russia World DNA Databank*
    https://www.youtube.com/watch?v=D_SYFv69ANk
29. *GMO Salmon*
    https://www.youtube.com/watch?v=PQSArjT8j9o
30. *Human Embryo Editing*

https://www.youtube.com/watch?v=NCPLM2IIJ28
31. *Human Organs in Pigs*
https://www.youtube.com/watch?v=Fc6sXG23kGo
32. *Brain Machine Interface*
https://www.youtube.com/watch?v=A4BR4Iqfy7w
33. *Genetic Engineering Change Everything Forever*
https://www.youtube.com/watch?v=jAhjPd4uNFY

Chapter 3   *The Dangers of Hybrids*

1. *General Information on Human Genome, CRISPR, Gene Drives, Dangers*
https://www.theguardian.com/science/occams-corner/2014/apr/25/epigenetics-beginners-guide-to-everything
https://www.wired.com/2015/07/crispr-dna-editing-2/
https://www.latimes.com/science/la-sci-gene-editing-embryo-20150503-story.html
https://www.huffpost.com/entry/crispr-opportunities-for_b_6295608
https://www.independent.co.uk/news/science/crispr-breakthrough-announced-in-technique-of-editing-dna-to-fight-off-deadly-illnesses-10420050.html
https://www.thedailybeast.com/new-dna-tech-creating-unicorns-and-curing-cancer-for-real
https://www.extremetech.com/extreme/196795-ingenious-molecular-mechanisms-in-the-age-of-transformable-dna
https://www.fastcompany.com/3061591/illumina-owns-the-dna-sequencing-market-now-its-building-an-app-store-too
https://www.theverge.com/2016/6/23/12005892/synthetic-human-genome-patent-hgp-ethics-controversy
https://time.com/4626571/crispr-gene-modification-evolution/
https://www.theguardian.com/science/occams-corner/2014/dec/11/epigenetics-xfiles
https://www.wired.com/2015/03/brave-new-world-dna-synthesis/

https://www.stltoday.com/news/science/tech/new-technology-at-wash-u-maps-human-genome-in-days/article_9ed22975-a385-5b53-897a-ff88cba2442b.html
https://www.bloombergquint.com/business/berkeley-fights-harvard-mit-over-profits-from-gene-editing-tech
https://www.shearsocialmedia.com/2017/09/orig3ns-ravens-dna-test-promotion-will-harm-nfl-fans-privacy-safety-security.html
https://newatlas.com/crispr-flower-change-color/51276/
https://www.sandiegouniontribune.com/business/biotech/sd-me-transplant-stemcells-20170421-
https://www.kurzweilai.net/how-to-program-dna-like-we-do-computers.html
http://www.pmlive.com/pharma_news/altering_genes_on_demand_60 7085
https://www.wired.com/story/crispr-tomato-mutant-future-of-food/
https://www.huffpost.com/entry/crispr-opportunities-for-_b_6295608?guccounter=1
https://www.bbc.com/news/health-36439260
https://www.newscientist.com/article/2117460-gene-silencing-spray-lets-us-modify-plants-without-changing-dna/
https://www.cnsnews.com/commentary/john-stonestreet/new-technology-may-allow-scientists-modify-human-genes-what-could
https://www.vanityfair.com/news/2018/11/is-gene-editing-more-dangerous-than-nuclear-weapons

2. *The Genetic Tool That Will Modify Humanity*
https://www.bloomberg.com/news/articles/2016-06-01/the-genetic-tool-that-will-modify-humanity
https://www.youtube.com/watch?v=UKbrwPL3wXE
3. *Zombie Apocalypse Plans*
https://www.youtube.com/watch?v=UGpLjJGsCtU
4. *Planet of the Apes Trailer*
https://www.youtube.com/watch?v=T3tidwW1gGM
5. *The Utopian Dream of CRISPR*
https://www.youtube.com/watch?v=Nhe6xYc6E9M
6. *CRISPR Not Controlled in China*
https://www.youtube.com/watch?v=Nhe6xYc6E9M

7. *Vaccines Laced With Cancer*
   https://www.youtube.com/watch?v=LxyZHuza4bA
8. *Gattaca Movie Trailer*
   https://www.youtube.com/watch?v=BpzVFdDeWyo
9. *The History of Eugenics*
   https://www.pbs.org/wgbh/americanexperience/films/eugenics-crusade/#part01
10. *Doudna Dreams of Hitler*
    https://www.youtube.com/watch?v=9nCHK97kwR4
11. *Gene Drives Have Irreversible Effects*
    https://www.bloomberg.com/news/articles/2016-06-01/the-genetic-tool-that-will-modify-humanity
    https://www.bbc.com/news/health-36439260
12. *The Future Consequences of Genetic Altering*
    https://www.youtube.com/watch?v=kkvslrfaCLY

Chapter 4 *Animal Enhancement*

1. *General Information on Various Animal Enhancements*
   https://www.foxnews.com/tech/scientists-create-worlds-first-mutant-ants-with-gene-editing-technology
   https://www.newscientist.com/article/mg22429972-300-first-digital-animal-will-be-perfect-copy-of-real-worm/
   https://www.businessinsider.in/Chinese-scientists-just-made-the-worlds-first-genetically-edited-super-muscly-dogs-and-they-named-one-Hercules/articleshow/49485192.cms
   https://www.cnn.com/2016/09/14/europe/mice-sperm-reproduction-eggs/index.html
   https://www.theguardian.com/science/2015/nov/23/anti-malarial-mosquitoes-created-using-controversial-genetic-technology
   https://www.inc.com/lisa-calhoun/meet-the-first-artificial-animal.html
   https://phys.org/news/2014-11-images-invisible-mouse.html
   https://healthimpactnews.com/2015/gmo-chicken-that-produces-drugs-in-eggs-approved/

https://www.independent.co.uk/news/science/mutant-extra-muscular-dogs-created-by-chinese-scientists-a6701156.html
https://www.newscientist.com/article/2117460-gene-silencing-spray-lets-us-modify-plants-without-changing-dna/
https://www.newscientist.com/article/mg22630243-300-worlds-first-biolimb-rat-forelimb-grown-in-the-lab/
https://ieet.org/index.php/IEET2/more/brin20140925
https://www.science20.com/brinstorming/intelligence_uplift_and_our_place_big_cosmos-94351
https://www.wired.com/2015/01/save-ecosystems-will-design-synthetic-creatures/
https://bgr.com/2015/10/20/china-dna-manipulation-stronger-dogs/
https://www.scmp.com/tech/science-research/article/1838655/chinese-scientists-edit-genes-produce-artificial-sperm-capable
https://animals.mom.me/difference-between-ligers-tigons-3506.html
https://www.livescience.com/15994-glow-dark-cats-aids-virus-research.html
https://www.sciencedirect.com/science/article/abs/pii/S1871141313000334?via%3Dihub
https://en.wikipedia.org/wiki/Genetically_modified_animal
https://www.businessinsider.com/chinese-genetically-engineered-mini-pigs-2015-9
https://en.wikipedia.org/wiki/Genetically_modified_insect
https://listverse.com/2016/06/20/10-implausible-technologies-from-fiction-that-are-on-their-way/
https://pagesix.com/2016/03/14/billionaire-barry-diller-clones-his-dog/
https://www.bbc.com/news/av/science-environment-35731722/can-scientists-clone-extinct-ice-age-cave-lion
https://www.foxnews.com/science/2014/11/17/can-long-extinct-woolly-mammoth-be-cloned/
https://www.livescience.com/48769-woolly-mammoth-cloning.html
https://www.standard.co.uk/insider/living/dog-cloning-why-stars-like-barbra-streisand-diane-von-furstenburg-and-simon-cowell-are-cloning-their-a4194311.html
https://www.telegraph.co.uk/news/2016/07/26/dolly-the-sheep-clones-ageing-normally/

https://phys.org/news/2016-07-fido-korea-dog-cloning-clinic.html
https://www.independent.co.uk/news/science/jurassic-park-in-real-life-the-race-to-modify-the-dna-of-endangered-animals-and-resurrect-extinct-10176678.html
https://www.aol.com/article/2015/03/23/scientists-successfully-add-woolly-mammoth-dna-into-elephant/21156457/#
https://www.nbcnews.com/news/world/scientists-want-bring-back-woolly-mammoths-why-n575581
https://www.yahoo.com/news/dolly-legacy-eating-cloned-meat-055536475.html?ref=gs
https://foreignpolicy.com/2015/06/15/you-dont-have-to-watch-jurassic-world-to-see-bioengineered-animal-weapons/
http://www.genewatch.org/sub-566989
https://www.technologyreview.com/s/614235/recombinetics-gene-edited-hornless-cattle-major-dna-screwup/
https://arstechnica.com/science/2019/09/part-cow-part-bacterium-biotech-company-makes-heifer-of-gene-editing-blunder/
https://www.livescience.com/32860-why-do-medical-researchers-use-mice.html
https://www.express.co.uk/news/world/828981/China-genetic-engineering-super-soldiers-dogs
https://www.newscientist.com/article/dn17003-fluorescent-puppy-is-worlds-first-transgenic-dog/
https://www.wired.com/2014/04/night-vision-contact-lenses/
https://www.popularmechanics.com/military/research/a23457329/augmented-super-soldiers-reversible/
https://modernfarmer.com/2013/08/the-rise-and-fall-of-the-great-american-hog/
https://www.healthline.com/health/heart-disease/good-fats-vs-bad-fats
https://www.newsweek.com/fat-meat-vegetables-science-discovery-research-burgers-are-healthy-586482
https://qz.com/1109868/scientists-in-china-used-crispr-to-genetically-modify-low-fat-pigs/
https://web.archive.org/web/20090816010157/http://pmbcii.psy.cmu.edu/evans/2006_Lia.pdf
https://www.nature.com/news/2009/090211/full/457775e.html

https://www.nature.com/news/us-government-approves-transgenic-chicken-1.18985

https://www.theverge.com/2017/4/25/15421734/artificial-womb-fetus-biobag-uterus-lamb-sheep-birth-premie-preterm-infant

https://www.iflscience.com/plants-and-animals/genetically-modified-lamb-jellyfish-protein-accidentally-sold-meat-paris/

https://geneticliteracyproject.org/2015/08/07/gmo-white-sea-cucumbers-could-make-costly-chinese-delicacy-affordable/

https://www.ewg.org/agmag/2016/03/gmo-lobster-gmo-bacon

https://fas.org/biosecurity/education/dualuse-agriculture/2.-agricultural-biotechnology/risks-associated-with-gm-farm-animals.html

https://en.wikipedia.org/wiki/List_of_animals_that_have_been_cloned

https://www.thenewatlantis.com/publications/appendix-state-laws-on-human-cloning

https://www.forbes.com/sites/jessicabaron/2018/12/24/if-you-love-animals-dont-clone-your-pet/#3a1dbc454c28

https://www.fda.gov/animal-veterinary/safety-health/animal-cloning

https://www.sciencealert.com/25-animals-that-scientists-are-planning-to-bring-back-from-extinction

2. *Making Malaria Resistant Mosquitoes*
   https://www.youtube.com/watch?v=AP2bVeK4vP8
3. *Silkworms Produce Spider Silk*
   https://www.youtube.com/watch?v=2tHqq-AaBYk
4. *Attack of the Ants*
   https://www.youtube.com/watch?v=dhRB6lihqq4
5. *Killer Bees*
   https://www.youtube.com/watch?v=aX3gkCjHhvM
6. *Making Mice Without an Egg*
   https://www.youtube.com/watch?v=D9XSwZCoeFc
7. *Mice Manipulation Gone Wrong*
   https://www.youtube.com/watch?v=ccObjX2yVQg
8. *See Through Mice*
   https://www.youtube.com/watch?v=GpspIoKjiAw
9. *The Invisible Man*
   https://www.youtube.com/watch?v=KXMOURHEMpY

10. *Mouse Plague*
https://www.youtube.com/watch?v=IOwinLWrEIw
11. *Rat Stingray*
https://www.youtube.com/watch?v=PTf2M5_NfiI
https://www.youtube.com/watch?v=-D_XrRo0h20
12. *Attack of the Leeches*
https://www.youtube.com/watch?v=dym92R3843E
13. *Rat Limbs*
https://www.youtube.com/watch?v=iB2Jc4iabSg
14. *Rat Man*
https://www.youtube.com/watch?v=8PWH745MMMY
15. *Glow in the Dark Dogs*
https://www.youtube.com/watch?v=X7JIkfSSm50
16. *Wendy the Muscle Dog*
https://www.youtube.com/watch?v=5ia5zdfoou0
17. *Making Muscly Dogs*
https://www.youtube.com/watch?v=0zOM9P7kHvY
18. *Incredible Hulk Trailer*
https://www.youtube.com/watch?v=PYVccTVP4mg
19. *China Modifying Humans*
https://www.youtube.com/watch?v=0zOM9P7kHvY
20. *Glow in the Dark Cats*
https://www.youtube.com/watch?v=AGQNztpOnDw
21. *The Liger*
https://www.youtube.com/watch?v=Z-wIbjodlAo
22. *The History of Pigs*
https://www.youtube.com/watch?v=FjvIoRbeYEk
23. *Cambodia Super Pigs*
https://www.youtube.com/watch?v=W1ChHcpWn9Y
24. *Low Fat Pigs*
https://www.youtube.com/watch?v=rv0rxgInmJ8
25. *Enviro Pigs*
https://www.youtube.com/watch?v=jIOt9SGFtjM
26. *Micro Pigs*
https://www.youtube.com/watch?v=XsyvpX0UGPg
27. *Glow in the Dark Pigs*

https://www.youtube.com/watch?v=EswypQRW0q4
28. *Making Super Cows*
https://www.youtube.com/watch?v=EKs_Rjhmlts
29. *Eugenics for Cows*
https://www.youtube.com/watch?v=GafZSH2GztQ
30. *Genetically Modified Cows*
https://www.youtube.com/watch?v=lvDYGSAMiWk
31. *Hornless Cows*
https://www.youtube.com/watch?v=-Qks_LMmodw
32. *Human Milk Cows*
https://www.youtube.com/watch?v=1vJGY8h2D2U
33. *Genetically Modified Chickens*
https://www.youtube.com/watch?v=AUec9t5JwQU
34. *Featherless Chickens*
https://www.youtube.com/watch?v=aX3gkCjHhvM
35. *Avian Bird Flu Problem*
https://www.youtube.com/watch?v=ZQ-QhfKOwQA
36. *Chickens That Produce Drugs*
https://www.youtube.com/watch?v=TOduua7jPKo
37. *Lamb in Artificial Womb*
https://www.youtube.com/watch?v=dt7twXzNEsQ
38. *Lamb & Jellyfish DNA*
https://www.dailymotion.com/video/x2vkdzc
39. *Goat & Spider DNA*
https://www.youtube.com/watch?v=leq1prezI6E
40. *Why Sea Cucumbers are So Expensive*
https://www.youtube.com/watch?v=sRH5KzNQxmc
41. *Super Modified Salmon*
https://www.youtube.com/watch?v=jIOt9SGFtjM
42. *Genetically Modified Frogs*
https://www.youtube.com/watch?v=0VAKdwUxETo
43. *Turtle Ducks*
https://www.youtube.com/watch?v=aX3gkCjHhvM
44. *Teenage Mutant Ninja Turtles Trailer*
https://www.youtube.com/watch?v=OdgNSJiWJTo
45. *The Dangers of Genetically Modified Foods*

https://www.youtube.com/watch?v=xTqmTx26DhE
46. *Glow in the Dark Trees*
https://www.youtube.com/watch?v=jU9ZVG2cJUU
47. *Russia Building DNA Databank*
https://www.dailymotion.com/video/x2dn0ev
48. *Dolly the Sheep Sisters*
https://www.youtube.com/watch?v=VzDcq-kxnfw
49. *Cloning in the U.S.*
https://www.youtube.com/watch?v=dV2OxSGhwjY
50. *Repet Commercial*
https://www.youtube.com/watch?v=DU0_JhQIbog
https://www.youtube.com/watch?v=CtoLvF_TlSA
51. *People Cloning Pets*
https://www.youtube.com/watch?v=DmHYUvmiXQI
52. *Frankenstein He's Alive*
https://www.youtube.com/watch?v=1qNeGSJaQ9Q
53. *Barbara Streisand Cloned Pets*
https://www.youtube.com/watch?v=curqgQ5ved4
54. *Price of Cloning Lowering*
https://www.youtube.com/watch?v=7jBa-WRQzzw
https://www.youtube.com/watch?v=HLkSPzS4tuU
55. *Pet Cemetery Trailer*
https://www.youtube.com/watch?v=zK0LNzU2TQI
56. *Cloned Meat Approved by FDA*
https://www.youtube.com/watch?v=VWdqDIH2Ys4
57. *Cloned Beef Sold Unawares*
https://www.youtube.com/watch?v=W2UJ936zBrE
58. *Cloned Meat Goes Massive in China*
https://www.youtube.com/watch?v=8xJzSe9Sdb0
59. *What is Lab Grown Meat*
https://www.youtube.com/watch?v=vgX9GTie0_0
60. *Is Lab Grown Meat Real Meat*
https://www.youtube.com/watch?v=kReHrebnzzc
61. *Swede Calls for Eating Human Flesh*
https://www.foxnews.com/world/swedish-scientist-eat-human-flesh-climate-change

62. *Girl Calls for Eating Babies*
https://www.youtube.com/watch?v=epwUTVUwB7A
63. *Soylent Green Movie Trailer*
https://www.youtube.com/watch?v=fTBSimtbX7w
64. *Jurassic Park Movie Trailer*
https://www.youtube.com/watch?v=lc0UehYemQA
65. *Cloning Leads to Resurrection*
https://www.youtube.com/watch?v=AVj3zR4wR20
66. *Making a Wooly Mammoth*
https://www.newsy.com/stories/scientists-add-woolly-mammoth-dna-to-elephant-cells/
67. *Making an Extinct Lion*
https://www.youtube.com/watch?v=GMGlRBP6jLM
68. *Making Other Extinct Animals*
https://www.youtube.com/watch?v=4JF3z84qo2U
69. *Making Mouse Mammoth*
https://www.youtube.com/watch?v=EoDNoRDg52o
70. *Jurassic World Movie Trailer*
https://www.youtube.com/watch?v=RFinNxS5KN4
71. *Making Mammoth Leads to Humans*
https://www.youtube.com/watch?v=cHZ5mJK4J5Q
https://www.youtube.com/watch?v=xmlpSOHc5A4